REPRESENTATIVE MEN

SEVEN LECTURES

BY

RALPH WALDO EMERSON

BOSTON AND NEW YORK
HOUGHTON, MIFFLIN AND COMPANY
The Riverside Press, Cambridge
1904

CONTENTS

LIST OF ILLUSTRATIONS

I

USES OF GREAT MEN

USES OF GREAT MEN

IT is natural to believe in great men. If the companions of our childhood should turn out to be heroes, and their condition regal it would not surprise us.' All mythology opens with demigods, and the circumstance is high and poetic; that is, their genius is paramount. In the legends of the Gautama, the first men ate the earth and found it deliciously sweet.

Nature seems to exist for the excellent. The world is upheld by the veracity of good men : they make the earth wholesome. They who lived with them found life glad and nutritious. Life is sweet and tolerable only in our belief in such society ; and, actually or ideally, we manage to live with superiors. We call our children and our lands by their names. Their names are wrought into the verbs of language, their works and effigies are in our houses, and every circumstance of the day recalls an anecdote of them.

The search after the great man is the dream of youth and the most serious occupation of manhood. We travel into foreign parts to find his works,—if possible, to get a glimpse of him. But we are put off with fortune instead. You

say, the English are practical; the Germans are
hospitable; in Valencia the climate is delicious;
and in the hills of the Sacramento there is gold
for the gathering. Yes, but I do not travel to
find comfortable, rich and hospitable people, or
clear sky, or ingots that cost too much. But if
there were any magnet that would point to the
countries and houses where are the persons who
are intrinsically rich and powerful, I would sell
all and buy it, and put myself on the road to-
day.[1]

The race goes with us on their credit. The
knowledge that in the city is a man who in-
vented the railroad, raises the credit of all the
citizens. But enormous populations, if they be
beggars, are disgusting, like moving cheese, like
hills of ants or of fleas, — the more, the worse.[2]

Our religion is the love and cherishing of
these patrons. The gods of fable are the shining
moments of great men.[3] We run all our vessels
into one mould. Our colossal theologies of Ju-
daism, Christism, Buddhism, Mahometism, are
the necessary and structural action of the human
mind. The student of history is like a man going into a warehouse to buy cloths or carpets.
He fancies he has a new article. If he go to the
factory, he shall find that his new stuff still re-

peats the scrolls and rosettes which are found on the interior walls of the pyramids of Thebes. Our theism is the purification of the human mind. Man can paint, or make, or think, nothing but man. He believes that the great material elements had their origin from his thought. And our philosophy finds one essence collected or distributed.

If now we proceed to inquire into the kinds of service we derive from others, let us be warned of the danger of modern studies, and begin low enough. We must not contend against love, or deny the substantial existence of other people.¹ I know not what would happen to us. We have social strengths. Our affection towards others creates a sort of vantage or purchase which nothing will supply. I can do that by another which I cannot do alone. I can say to you what I cannot first say to myself. Other men are lenses through which we read our own minds. Each man seeks those of different quality from his own, and such as are good of their kind ; that is, he seeks other men, and the *otherest*. The stronger the nature, the more it is reactive. Let us have the quality pure. A little genius let us leave alone. A main

difference betwixt men is, whether they attend
their own affair or not. Man is that noble endogenous plant which grows, like the palm, from
within outward. His own affair, though impossible to others, he can open with celerity and in
sport. It is easy to sugar to be sweet and to
nitre to be salt. We take a great deal of pains
to waylay and entrap that which of itself will fall
into our hands. I count him a great man who
inhabits a higher sphere of thought, into which
other men rise with labor and difficulty; he has
but to open his eyes to see things in a true light
and in large relations, whilst they must make
painful corrections and keep a vigilant eye on
many sources of error. His service to us is of
like sort. It costs a beautiful person no exertion
to paint her image on our eyes; yet how splendid is that benefit! It costs no more for a wise
soul to convey his quality to other men. And
every one can do his best thing easiest. " *Peu
de moyens, beaucoup d'effet.*" [He is great who is
what he is from nature, and who never reminds
us of others.]

But he must be related to us, and our life receive from him some promise of explanation. I
cannot tell what I would know; but I have observed there are persons who, in their character

and actions, answer questions which I have not skill to put. One man answers some question which none of his contemporaries put, and is isolated. The past and passing religions and philosophies answer some other question. Certain men affect us as rich possibilities, but helpless to themselves and to their times, — the sport perhaps of some instinct that rules in the air ; — they do not speak to our want.[1] But the great are near ; we know them at sight. They satisfy expectation and fall into place. What is good is effective, generative ; makes for itself room, food and allies. A sound apple produces seed, — a hybrid does not. Is a man in his place, he is constructive, fertile, magnetic, inundating armies with his purpose, which is thus executed. The river makes its own shores, and each legitimate idea makes its own channels and welcome, — harvests for food, institutions for expression, weapons to fight with and disciples to explain it. The true artist has the planet for his pedestal ; the adventurer, after years of strife, has nothing broader than his own shoes.

Our common discourse respects two kinds of use or service from superior men. Direct giving is agreeable to the early belief of men ; direct giving of material or metaphysical aid, as of

health, eternal youth, fine senses, arts of heal-
ing, magical power and prophecy. The boy
believes there is a teacher who can sell him wisdom. Churches believe in imputed merit. But,
in strictness, we are not much cognizant of direct
serving. Man is endogenous, and education is
his unfolding. The aid we have from others
is mechanical compared with the discoveries of
nature in us. What is thus learned is delightful in the doing, and the effect remains. Right
ethics are central and go from the soul outward.
Gift is contrary to the law of the universe. Serving others is serving us. I must absolve me to
myself. 'Mind thy affair,' says the spirit: —
'coxcomb, would you meddle with the skies,
or with other people?' Indirect service is left.'
Men have a pictorial or representative quality, and serve us in the intellect. Behmen ² and
Swedenborg saw that things were representative.
[Men are also representative; first, of things,
and secondly, of ideas.]

As plants convert the minerals into food for
animals, so each man converts some raw material in nature to human use. The inventors
of fire, electricity, magnetism, iron, lead, glass,
linen, silk, cotton; the makers of tools; the
inventor of decimal notation; the geometer;

the engineer; the musician, — severally make
an easy way for all, through unknown and impossible confusions. Each man is by secret liking connected with some district of nature,
whose agent and interpreter he is; as Linnæus,
of plants; Huber, of bees; Fries, of lichens;
Van Mons, of pears; Dalton, of atomic forms;
Euclid, of lines; Newton, of fluxions.

A man is a centre for nature, running out
threads of relation through every thing, fluid
and solid, material and elemental. The earth
rolls; every clod and stone comes to the me-
ridian: so every organ, function, acid, crystal,
grain of dust, has its relation to the brain. It
waits long, but its turn comes. Each plant has
its parasite, and each created thing its lover and
poet. Justice has already been done to steam,
to iron, to wood, to coal, to loadstone, to iodine,
to corn and cotton; but how few materials are
yet used by our arts! The mass of creatures
and of qualities are still hid and expectant.[1] It
would seem as if each waited, like the enchanted
princess in fairy tales, for a destined human de-
liverer. Each must be disenchanted and walk
forth to the day in human shape. In the history of discovery, the ripe and latent truth
seems to have fashioned a brain for itself.[2] A

magnet must be made man in some Gilbert, or Swedenborg, or Oersted, before the general mind can come to entertain its powers.[1]

If we limit ourselves to the first advantages, a sober grace adheres to the mineral and botanic kingdoms, which, in the highest moments, comes up as the charm of nature, — the glitter of the spar, the sureness of affinity, the veracity of angles. Light and darkness, heat and cold, hunger and food, sweet and sour, solid, liquid and gas, circle us round in a wreath of pleasures, and, by their agreeable quarrel, beguile the day of life. The eye repeats every day the first eulogy on things, — " He saw that they were good." We know where to find them ; and these performers are relished all the more, after a little experience of the pretending races. We are entitled also to higher advantages. Something is wanting to science until it has been humanized. The table of logarithms is one thing, and its vital play in botany, music, optics and architecture, another. There are advancements to numbers, anatomy, architecture, astronomy, little suspected at first, when, by union with intellect and will, they ascend into the life and reappear in conversation, character and politics.[2]

But this comes later. We speak now only of our acquaintance with them in their own sphere and the way in which they seem to fascinate and draw to them some genius who occupies himself with one thing, all his life long. The possibility of interpretation lies in the identity of the observer with the observed.[1] Each material thing has its celestial side; has its translation, through humanity, into the spiritual and necessary sphere where it plays a part as indestructible as any other. And to these, their ends, all things continually ascend. The gases gather to the solid firmament: the chemic lump arrives at the plant, and grows; arrives at the quadruped, and walks; arrives at the man, and thinks. But also the constituency determines the vote of the representative. He is not only representative, but participant. Like can only be known by like. The reason why he knows about them is that he is of them; he has just come out of nature, or from being a part of that thing.[2] Animated chlorine knows of chlorine, and incarnate zinc, of zinc. Their quality makes his career; and he can variously publish their virtues, because they compose him. Man, made of the dust of the world, does not forget his origin; and all that is yet inanimate will one

day speak and reason. Unpublished nature will
have its whole secret told. Shall we say that
quartz mountains will pulverize into innumerable Werners, Von Buchs and Beaumonts, and
the laboratory of the atmosphere holds in solution I know not what Berzeliuses and Davys?

Thus we sit by the fire and take hold on the
poles of the earth. This *quasi* omnipresence
supplies the imbecility of our condition. In
one of those celestial days when heaven and
earth meet and adorn each other, it seems a
poverty that we can only spend it once: we
wish for a thousand heads, a thousand bodies,
that we might celebrate its immense beauty in
many ways and places. Is this fancy? Well, in
good faith, we are multiplied by our proxies.
How easily we adopt their labors! Every ship
that comes to America got its chart from Columbus. Every novel is a debtor to Homer.
Every carpenter who shaves with a fore-plane
borrows the genius of a forgotten inventor.
Life is girt all round with a zodiac of sciences,
the contributions of men who have perished to
add their point of light to our sky. Engineer,
broker, jurist, physician, moralist, theologian,
and every man, inasmuch as he has any science,
— is a definer and map-maker of the latitudes

and longitudes of our condition. These road-
makers on every hand enrich us. We must ex-
tend the area of life and multiply our relations.
We are as much gainers by finding a new property in the old earth as by acquiring a new
planet.[1]

We are too passive in the reception of these
material or semi-material aids. We must not be
sacks and stomachs. To ascend one step, — we
are better served through our sympathy. Activity is contagious. Looking where others look,
and conversing with the same things, we catch
the charm which lured them. Napoleon said,
" You must not fight too often with one enemy,
or you will teach him all your art of war." Talk
much with any man of vigorous mind, and we
acquire very fast the habit of looking at things
in the same light, and on each occurrence we
anticipate his thought.

Men are helpful through the intellect and the
affections. Other help I find a false appearance.
If you affect to give me bread and fire, I perceive that I pay for it the full price, and at last
it leaves me as it found me, neither better nor
worse: but all mental and moral force is a positive good. It goes out from you, whether you
will or not, and profits me whom you never

thought of.¹ I cannot even hear of personal vigor of any kind, great power of performance, without fresh resolution. We are emulous of all that man can do. Cecil's saying of Sir Walter Raleigh, "I know that he can toil terribly," is an electric touch. So are Clarendon's portraits, — of Hampden, "who was of an industry and vigilance not to be tired out or wearied by the most laborious, and of parts not to be imposed on by the most subtle and sharp, and of a personal courage equal to his best parts;" — of Falkland, "who was so severe an adorer of truth, that he could as easily have given himself leave to steal, as to dissemble." We cannot read Plutarch without a tingling of the blood; and I accept the saying of the Chinese Mencius: "A sage is the instructor of a hundred ages. When the manners of Loo are heard of, the stupid become intelligent, and the wavering, determined."

[This is the moral of biography; yet it is hard for departed men to touch the quick like our own companions, whose names may not last as long. What is he whom I never think of? Whilst in every solitude are those who succor our genius and stimulate us in wonderful manners. There is a power in love to divine an-

other's destiny better than that other can, and,
by heroic encouragements, hold him to his task.
What has friendship so signal as its sublime
attraction to whatever virtue is in us? We will
never more think cheaply of ourselves, or of
life.[1] We are piqued to some purpose, and the
industry of the diggers on the railroad will not
again shame us.[2]

Under this head too falls that homage, very
pure as I think, which all ranks pay to the hero
of the day, from Coriolanus and Gracchus down
to Pitt, Lafayette, Wellington, Webster, La-
martine. Hear the shouts in the street! The
people cannot see him enough. They delight
in a man. Here is a head and a trunk! What
a front! what eyes! Atlantean shoulders, and
the whole carriage heroic, with equal inward
force to guide the great machine![3] This pleasure of full expression to that which, in their
private experience, is usually cramped and ob-
structed, runs also much higher, and is the secret
of the reader's joy in literary genius. Nothing
is kept back. There is fire enough to fuse the
mountain of ore. Shakspeare's principal merit
may be conveyed in saying that he of all men
best understands the English language, and can
say what he will. Yet these unchoked channels

and floodgates of expression are only health or fortunate constitution. Shakspeare's name suggests other and purely intellectual benefits.

Senates and sovereigns have no compliment, with their medals, swords and armorial coats, like the addressing to a human being thoughts out of a certain height, and presupposing his intelligence.' This honor, which is possible in personal intercourse scarcely twice in a lifetime, genius perpetually pays; contented if now and then in a century the proffer is accepted. The indicators of the values of matter are degraded to a sort of cooks and confectioners, on the appearance of the indicators of ideas. Genius is the naturalist or geographer of the supersensible regions, and draws their map; and, by acquainting us with new fields of activity, cools our affection for the old. These are at once accepted as the reality, of which the world we have conversed with is the show.

We go to the gymnasium and the swimming-school to see the power and beauty of the body; there is the like pleasure and a higher benefit from witnessing intellectual feats of all kinds; as feats of memory, of mathematical combination, great power of abstraction, the transmutings of the imagination, even versatility and concentration, — as these acts expose the invisible organs and members of the mind, which respond, member for member, to the parts of the body. For we thus enter a new gymnasium, and learn to choose men by their truest marks, taught, with Plato, " to choose those who can, without aid from the eyes or any other sense, proceed to truth and to being." Foremost among these activities are the summersaults, spells and resurrections wrought by the imagination. When this wakes, a man seems to multiply ten times or a thousand times his force. It opens the delicious sense of indeterminate size and inspires an audacious mental habit. We are as elastic as the gas of gunpowder, and a sentence in a book, or a word dropped in conversation, sets free our fancy, and instantly our heads are bathed with galaxies, and our feet tread the floor of the Pit.¹ And this benefit is real because we are entitled to these enlargements, and once having passed the bounds shall never again be quite the miserable pedants we were.

The high functions of the intellect are so allied that some imaginative power usually appears in all eminent minds, even in arithmeticians of the first class, but especially in meditative men of an intuitive habit of thought. This

class serve us, so that they have the perception
of identity and the perception of reaction. The
eyes of Plato, Shakspeare, Swedenborg, Goethe,
never shut on either of these laws. The perception of these laws is a kind of metre of the
mind. Little minds are little through failure to
see them.

Even these feasts have their surfeit. Our delight in reason degenerates into idolatry of the
herald. Especially when a mind of powerful
method has instructed men, we find the examples of oppression. The dominion of Aristotle,
the Ptolemaic astronomy, the credit of Luther,
of Bacon, of Locke ; — in religion the history
of hierarchies, of saints, and the sects which
have taken the name of each founder, are in
point. Alas! every man is such a victim. The
imbecility of men is always inviting the impu-
dence of power. It is the delight of vulgar talent to dazzle and to blind the beholder. But
true genius seeks to defend us from itself. True
genius will not impoverish, but will liberate, and
add new senses.[1] If a wise man should appear
in our village he would create, in those who
conversed with him, a new consciousness of
wealth, by opening their eyes to unobserved
advantages ; he would establish a sense of im-

movable equality, calm us with assurances that we could not be cheated; as every one would discern the checks and guaranties of condition. The rich would see their mistakes and poverty, the poor their escapes and their resources.

But nature brings all this about in due time. Rotation is her remedy. The soul is impatient of masters and eager for change. Housekeepers say of a domestic who has been valuable, " She had lived with me long enough." We are tendencies, or rather, symptoms, and none of us complete. We touch and go, and sip the foam of many lives. Rotation is the law of nature. When nature removes a great man, people explore the horizon for a successor; but none comes, and none will. His class is extinguished with him. In some other and quite different field the next man will appear; not Jefferson, not Franklin, but now a great salesman, then a road-contractor, then a student of fishes, then a buffalo-hunting explorer, or a semi-savage Western general. Thus we make a stand against our rougher masters; but against the best there is a finer remedy. The power which they communicate is not theirs. When we are exalted by ideas, we do not owe this to Plato, but to the idea, to which also Plato was debtor.[1]

⌊I must not forget that we have a special debt to a single class. Life is a scale of degrees. Between rank and rank of our great men are wide intervals.⌉ Mankind have in all ages attached themselves to a few persons who either by the quality of that idea they embodied or by the largeness of their reception were entitled to the position of leaders and law-givers. These teach us the qualities of primary nature, — admit us to the constitution of things. We swim, day by day, on a river of delusions and are effectually amused with houses and towns in the air, of which the men about us are dupes. But life is a sincerity. In lucid intervals we say, ' Let there be an entrance opened for me into realities ; ' I have worn the fool's cap too long.' We will know the meaning of our economies and politics. Give us the cipher, and if persons and things are scores of a celestial music, let us read off the strains. We have been cheated of our reason ; yet there have been sane men, who enjoyed a rich and related existence. What they know, they know for us. With each new mind, a new secret of nature transpires ; nor can the Bible be closed until the last great man is born. These men correct the delirium of the animal spirits, make us considerate and engage us to

new aims and powers. The veneration of mankind selects these for the highest place. Witness
the multitude of statues, pictures and memorials
which recall their genius in every city, village,
house and ship : —

> " Ever their phantoms arise before us,
> Our loftier brothers, but one in blood;
> At bed and table they lord it o'er us
> With looks of beauty and words of good." [1]

How to illustrate the distinctive benefit of
ideas, the service rendered by those who intro-
duce moral truths into the general mind? — I
am plagued, in all my living, with a perpetual
tariff of prices. If I work in my garden and
prune an apple-tree, I am well enough entertained, and could continue indefinitely in the
like occupation. But it comes to mind that a
day is gone, and I have got this precious nothing done. I go to Boston or New York and
run up and down on my affairs : they are sped,
but so is the day.[2] I am vexed by the recollec-
tion of this price I have paid for a trifling advantage. I remember the *peau d'âne* on which
whoso sat should have his desire, but a piece
of the skin was gone for every wish.[3] I go to a
convention of philanthropists. Do what I can,
I cannot keep my eyes off the clock. But if

there should appear in the company some gentle
soul who knows little of persons or parties, of
Carolina or Cuba, but who announces a law that
disposes these particulars, and so certifies me of
the equity which checkmates every false player,
bankrupts every self-seeker, and apprises me of
my independence on any conditions of country,
or time, or human body, — that man liberates
me; I forget the clock. I pass out of the sore
relation to persons. I am healed of my hurts.
I am made immortal by apprehending my possession of incorruptible goods. Here is great
competition of rich and poor. We live in a
market, where is only so much wheat, or wool,
or land; and if I have so much more, every
other must have so much less. I seem to have
no good without breach of good manners. Nobody is glad in the gladness of another, and our
system is one of war, of an injurious superiority.
Every child of the Saxon race is educated to
wish to be first. It is our system; and a man
comes to measure his greatness by the regrets,
envies and hatreds of his competitors. But in
these new fields there is room : here are no self-
esteems, no exclusions.

I admire great men of all classes, those who
stand for facts, and for thoughts; I like rough

and smooth, "Scourges of God," and "Darlings
of the human race." I like the first Cæsar; [1]
and Charles V., of Spain; and Charles XII., of
Sweden; Richard Plantagenet; and Bonaparte,
in France. I applaud a sufficient man, an officer
equal to his office; captains, ministers, senators.
I like a master standing firm on legs of iron,
well-born, rich, handsome, eloquent, loaded with
advantages, drawing all men by fascination into
tributaries and supporters of his power. [2] Sword
and staff, or talents sword-like or staff-like, carry
on the work of the world. But I find him
greater when he can abolish himself and all heroes, by letting in this element of reason, irre-
spective of persons, this subtilizer and irresistible upward force, into our thought, destroying
individualism; the power so great that the po-
tentate is nothing. Then he is a monarch who
gives a constitution to his people; a pontiff who
preaches the equality of souls and releases his
servants from their barbarous homages; an emperor who can spare his empire.

But I intended to specify, with a little mi-
nuteness, two or three points of service. Nature
never spares the opium or nepenthe, but wherever she mars her creature with some deformity

or defect, lays her poppies plentifully on the
bruise, and the sufferer goes joyfully through
life, ignorant of the ruin and incapable of seeing
it, though all the world point their finger at it
every day. The worthless and offensive members of society, whose existence is a social pest,
invariably think themselves the most ill-used
people alive, and never get over their astonishment at the ingratitude and selfishness of their
contemporaries. Our globe discovers its hidden
virtues, not only in heroes and archangels, but
in gossips and nurses. Is it not a rare contriv-
ance that lodged the due inertia in every creature, the conserving, resisting energy, the anger
at being waked or changed? Altogether independent of the intellectual force in each is the
pride of opinion, the security that we are right.
Not the feeblest grandame, not a mowing idiot,'
but uses what spark of perception and faculty is
left, to chuckle and triumph in his or her opin-
ion over the absurdities of all the rest.| Differ-
ence from me is the measure of absurdity. Not
one has a misgiving of being wrong.]Was it
not a bright thought that made things cohere
with this bitumen, fastest of cements? But, in
the midst of this chuckle of self-gratulation,
some figure goes by which Thersites too can

love and admire. This is he that should marshal us the way we were going. There is no
end to his aid. Without Plato we should almost lose our faith in the possibility of a reasonable book.[1] We seem to want but one, but
we want one. [We love to associate with heroic
persons, since our receptivity is unlimited; and,
with the great, our thoughts and manners easily
become great. We are all wise in capacity,
though so few in energy. There needs but one
wise man in a company and all are wise, so rapid
is the contagion.)

[Great men are thus a collyrium to clear our
eyes from egotism and enable us to see other
people and their works.[2] But there are vices
and follies incident to whole populations and
ages.) Men resemble their contemporaries even
more than their progenitors. It is observed in
old couples, or in persons who have been house-
mates for a course of years, that they grow like,
and if they should live long enough we should
not be able to know them apart. Nature ab-
hors these complaisances which threaten to melt
the world into a lump, and hastens to break up
such maudlin agglutinations. The like assimilation goes on between men of one town, of one
sect, of one political party; and the ideas of the

time are in the air, and infect all who breathe it.
Viewed from any high point, this city of New
York, yonder city of London, the Western civilization, would seem a bundle of insanities. We
keep each other in countenance and exasperate
by emulation the frenzy of the time. The shield
against the stingings of conscience is the universal practice, or our contemporaries. Again,
it is very easy to be as wise and good as your
companions. We learn of our contemporaries
what they know without effort, and almost
through the pores of the skin. We catch it by
sympathy, or as a wife arrives at the intellectual
and moral elevations of her husband. But we
stop where they stop. Very hardly can we take
another step. The great, or such as hold of nature and transcend fashions by their fidelity to
universal ideas, are saviors from these federal
errors, and defend us from our contemporaries.
They are the exceptions which we want, where
all grows like. A foreign greatness is the anti-
dote for cabalism.

Thus we feed on genius, and refresh ourselves
from too much conversation with our mates,
and exult in the depth of nature in that direction in which he leads us. What indemnification
is one great man for populations of pigmies!

Every mother wishes one son a genius, though all the rest should be mediocre. But a new danger appears in the excess of influence of the great man. His attractions warp us from our place. We have become underlings and intellectual suicides. Ah! yonder in the horizon is our help; — other great men, new qualities, counterweights and checks on each other. We cloy of the honey of each peculiar greatness. Every hero becomes a bore at last. Perhaps Voltaire was not bad-hearted, yet he said of the good Jesus, even, " I pray you, let me never hear that man's name again." [1] They cry up the virtues of George Washington, — " Damn George Washington ! " is the poor Jacobin's whole speech and confutation. But it is human nature's indispensable defence. The centripetence augments the centrifugence. [2] We balance one man with his opposite, and the health of the state depends on the see-saw.

There is however a speedy limit to the use of heroes. Every genius is defended from approach by quantities of unavailableness. They are very attractive, and seem at a distance our own : but we are hindered on all sides from approach. The more we are drawn, the more we are repelled. There is something not solid in

the good that is done for us. The best discovery the discoverer makes for himself. It has
something unreal for his companion until he too
has substantiated it. It seems as if the Deity
dressed each soul which he sends into nature in
certain virtues and powers not communicable to
other men, and sending it to perform one more
turn through the circle of beings,' wrote, " *Not
transferable* " and " *Good for this trip only*," on
these garments of the soul. There is somewhat
deceptive about the intercourse of minds. The
boundaries are invisible, but they are never
crossed. There is such good will to impart,
and such good will to receive, that each threatens
to become the other; but the law of individ-
uality collects its secret strength: you are you,
and I am I, and so we remain.

For nature wishes every thing to remain itself; and whilst every individual strives to grow
and exclude and to exclude and grow, to the
extremities of the universe, and to impose the
law of its being on every other creature, Nature
steadily aims to protect each against every other.
Each is self-defended. Nothing is more marked
than the power by which individuals are guarded
from individuals, in a world where every benefactor becomes so easily a malefactor only by

continuation of his activity into places where it is not due; where children seem so much at the mercy of their foolish parents, and where almost all men are too social and interfering. We rightly speak of the guardian angels of children. How superior in their security from infusions of evil persons, from vulgarity and second thought! They shed their own abundant beauty on the objects they behold. Therefore they are not at the mercy of such poor educators as we adults. If we huff and chide them they soon come not to mind it and get a self-reliance; and if we indulge them to folly, they learn the limitation elsewhere.

We need not fear excessive influence. A more generous trust is permitted. Serve the great. Stick at no humiliation. Grudge no office thou canst render. Be the limb of their body, the breath of their mouth. Compromise thy egotism. Who cares for that, so thou gain aught wider and nobler? Never mind the taunt of Boswellism: the devotion may easily be greater than the wretched pride which is guarding its own skirts. Be another: not thyself, but a Platonist; not a soul, but a Christian; not a naturalist, but a Cartesian; not a poet, but a Shaksperian. In vain, the wheels of ten-

dency will not stop, nor will all the forces of
inertia, fear, or of love itself hold thee there.
On, and forever onward!¹ The microscope
observes a monad or wheel-insect among the
infusories circulating in water. Presently a dot
appears on the animal, which enlarges to a slit,
and it becomes two perfect animals. The ever-
proceeding detachment appears not less in all
thought and in society. Children think they
cannot live without their parents. But, long
before they are aware of it, the black dot has
appeared and the detachment taken place. Any
accident will now reveal to them their independence.

But *great men :* — the word is injurious. Is
there caste? is there fate? What becomes of the
promise to virtue? The thoughtful youth la-
ments the superfœtation of nature. 'Generous
and handsome,' he says, 'is your hero; but
look at yonder poor Paddy, whose country is
his wheelbarrow; look at his whole nation of
Paddies.' Why are the masses, from the dawn
of history down, food for knives and powder?
The idea dignifies a few leaders, who have sentiment, opinion, love, self-devotion; and they
make war and death sacred; — but what for the

wretches whom they hire and kill? The cheapness of man is every day's tragedy. It is as real a loss that others should be low as that we should be low; for we must have society.

Is it a reply to these suggestions to say, Society is a Pestalozzian school: all are teachers and pupils in turn? We are equally served by receiving and by imparting. Men who know the same things are not long the best company for each other. But bring to each an intelligent person of another experience, and it is as if you let off water from a lake by cutting a lower basin. It seems a mechanical advantage, and great benefit it is to each speaker, as he can now paint out his thought to himself. We pass very fast, in our personal moods, from dignity to dependence. And if any appear never to assume the chair, but always to stand and serve, it is because we do not see the company in a sufficiently long period for the whole rotation of parts to come about. As to what we call the masses, and common men,—there are no common men. All men are at last of a size; and true art is only possible on the conviction that every talent has its apotheosis somewhere. Fair play and an open field and freshest laurels to all who have won them! But heaven reserves an equal scope for every creature. Each is uneasy until he has produced his private ray unto the concave sphere and beheld his talent also in its last nobility and exaltation.

The heroes of the hour are relatively great; of a faster growth; or they are such in whom, at the moment of success, a quality is ripe which is then in request. Other days will demand other qualities. Some rays escape the common observer, and want a finely adapted eye. Ask the great man if there be none greater. His companions are; and not the less great but the more that society cannot see them. Nature never sends a great man into the planet without confiding the secret to another soul.

One gracious fact emerges from these studies, — that there is true ascension in our love. The reputations of the nineteenth century will one day be quoted to prove its barbarism. The genius of humanity is the real subject whose biography is written in our annals. We must infer much, and supply many chasms in the record. The history of the universe is symptomatic, and life is mnemonical. No man, in all the procession of famous men, is reason or illumination or that essence we were looking for; but is an exhibition, in some quarter, of new possibilities. Could we one day complete the immense figure which these flagrant points compose !¹ The study of many individuals leads us to an elemental region wherein the individual is lost, or wherein all touch by their summits. Thought and feeling that break out there cannot be impounded by any fence of personality. This is the key to the power of the greatest men, — their spirit diffuses itself. A new quality of mind travels by night and by day, in concentric circles from its origin, and publishes itself by unknown methods : the union of all minds appears intimate ; what gets admission to one, cannot be kept out of any other ; the smallest acquisition of truth or of energy, in any quarter, is so much good to the commonwealth of souls. If the disparities of talent and position vanish when the individuals are seen in the duration which is necessary to complete the career of each,² even more swiftly the seeming injustice disappears when we ascend to the central identity of all the individuals, and know that they are made of the substance which ordaineth and doeth.

The genius of humanity is the right point of view of history. The qualities abide; the men who exhibit them have now more, now less, and pass away; the qualities remain on another brow. No experience is more familiar. Once you saw phœnixes : they are gone; the world is not therefore disenchanted. The vessels on which you read sacred emblems turn out to be common pottery ; but the sense of the pictures is sacred, and you may still read them transferred to the walls of the world.¹ For a time our teachers serve us personally, as metres or milestones of progress. Once they were angels of knowledge and their figures touched the sky. Then we drew near, saw their means, culture and limits; and they yielded their place to other geniuses. Happy, if a few names remain so high that we have not been able to read them nearer, and age and comparison have not robbed them of a ray. But at last we shall cease to look in men for completeness, and shall content ourselves with their social and delegated quality. All that respects the individual is temporary and prospective, like the individual himself, who is ascending out of his limits into a catholic existence. We have never come at the true and best benefit of any genius so long as we believe him an original force. In the moment when he ceases to help us as a cause, he begins to help us more as an effect. Then he appears as an exponent of a vaster mind and will. The opaque self becomes transparent with the light of the First Cause.

Yet, within the limits of human education and agency, we may say great men exist that there may be greater men. The destiny of organized nature is amelioration, and who can tell its limits? It is for man to tame the chaos; on every side, whilst he lives, to scatter the seeds of science and of song, that climate, corn, animals, men, may be milder, and the germs of love and benefit may be multiplied.[1]

II

PLATO; OR, THE PHILOSOPHER

PLATO; OR, THE PHI-
LOSOPHER

A MONG secular books, Plato only is entitled to Omar's fanatical compliment to
the Koran, when he said, "Burn the libraries;
for their value is in this book." [1] These sentences contain the culture of nations; these are
the corner-stone of schools; these are the foun-
tain-head of literatures. [2] A discipline it is in
logic, arithmetic, taste, symmetry, poetry, language, rhetoric, ontology, morals or practical
wisdom. There was never such range of speculation. Out of Plato come all things that are
still written and debated among men of thought.
Great havoc makes he among our originalities.
We have reached the mountain from which all
these drift boulders were detached. [3] The Bible
of the learned for twenty-two hundred years,
every brisk young man who says in succession
fine things to each reluctant generation,— Boe-
thius, Rabelais, Erasmus, Bruno, Locke, Rousseau, Alfieri, Coleridge, — is some reader of
Plato, translating into the vernacular, wittily,
his good things. Even the men of grander pro-

portion suffer some deduction from the misfortune (shall I say?) of coming after this exhausting generalizer. St. Augustine, Copernicus, Newton, Behmen, Swedenborg, Goethe, are
likewise his debtors and must say after him.
For it is fair to credit the broadest generalizer
with all the particulars deducible from his thesis.

Plato is philosophy, and philosophy, Plato,
— at once the glory and the shame of mankind,
since neither Saxon nor Roman have availed to
add any idea to his categories. No wife, no
children had he, and the thinkers of all civilized
nations are his posterity and are tinged with his
mind. How many great men Nature is incessantly sending up out of night, to be *his men*, —
Platonists! the Alexandrians, a constellation of
genius; the Elizabethans, not less; Sir Thomas
More, Henry More, John Hales, John Smith,
Lord Bacon, Jeremy Taylor, Ralph Cudworth,
Sydenham, Thomas Taylor; Marcilius Fici-
nus and Picus Mirandola. Calvinism is in his
Phædo: Christianity is in it. Mahometanism
draws all its philosophy, in its hand-book of
morals, the Akhlak-y-Jalaly,' from him. Mys-
ticism finds in Plato all its texts. This citizen
of a town in Greece is no villager nor patriot.
An Englishman reads and says; 'how English!'

a German, — 'how Teutonic!' an Italian, —
'how Roman and how Greek!' As they say
that Helen of Argos had that universal beauty
that every body felt related to her, so Plato
seems to a reader in New England an American
genius. His broad humanity transcends all sec-
tional lines.

This range of Plato instructs us what to think
of the vexed question concerning his reputed
works, — what are genuine, what spurious. It
is singular that wherever we find a man higher
by a whole head than any of his contemporaries,
it is sure to come into doubt what are his real
works. Thus Homer, Plato, Raffaelle, Shakspeare. For these men magnetize their contemporaries, so that their companions can do for
them what they can never do for themselves;
and the great man does thus live in several
bodies, and write, or . paint or act, by many
hands; and after some time it is not easy to say
what is the authentic work of the master and what
is only of his school.

Plato, too, like every great man, consumed
his own times. What is a great man but one of
great affinities, who takes up into himself all
arts, sciences, all knowables, as his food? He
can spare nothing; he can dispose of every thing.

What is not good for virtue, is good for knowledge. Hence his contemporaries tax him with
plagiarism. But the inventor only knows how
to borrow; and society is glad to forget the innumerable laborers who ministered to this archi-
tect, and reserves all its gratitude for him.
When we are praising Plato, it seems we are
praising quotations from Solon and Sophron
and Philolaus. Be it so. Every book is a quotation; and every house is a quotation out of all
forests and mines and stone quarries; and every
man is a quotation from all his ancestors.[1] And
this grasping inventor puts all nations under
contribution.

Plato absorbed the learning of his times, —
Philolaus, Timæus, Heraclitus, Parmenides, and
what else; then his master, Socrates; and finding himself still capable of a larger synthesis, —
beyond all example then or since, — he travelled into Italy, to gain what Pythagoras had
for him; then into Egypt, and perhaps still
farther East, to import the other element, which
Europe wanted, into the European mind. This
breadth entitles him to stand as the representative of philosophy. He says, in the Republic,
" Such a genius as philosophers must of necessity have, is wont but seldom in all its parts to

meet in one man, but its different parts generally spring up in different persons." Every man
who would do anything well, must come to it
from a higher ground. A philosopher must be
more than a philosopher. Plato is clothed with
the powers of a poet, stands upon the highest
place of the poet, and (though I doubt he wanted
the decisive gift of lyric expression), mainly is
not a poet because he chose to use the poetic
gift to an ulterior purpose.[1]

Great geniuses have the shortest biographies.
Their cousins can tell you nothing about them.
They lived in their writings, and so their house
and street life was trivial and commonplace. If
you would know their tastes and complexions,
the most admiring of their readers most resembles them. Plato especially has no external biography. If he had lover, wife, or children, we
hear nothing of them. He ground them all into
paint.[2] As a good chimney burns its smoke, so
a philosopher converts the value of all his fortunes into his intellectual performances.

He was born 427 A. C., about the time of
the death of Pericles ; was of patrician connection in his times and city, and is said to have had
an early inclination for war, but, in his twentieth
year, meeting with Socrates, was easily dissuaded

'from this pursuit and remained for ten years his scholar, until the death of Socrates. He then went to Megara, accepted the invitations of Dion and of Dionysius to the court of Sicily, and went thither three times, though very capriciously treated. He travelled into Italy; then into Egypt, where he stayed a long time; some say three, — some say thirteen years. It is said he went farther, into Babylonia: this is uncertain. Returning to Athens, he gave lessons in the Academy to those whom his fame drew thither; and died, as we have received it, in the act of writing, at eighty-one years.

But the biography of Plato is interior. We are to account for the supreme elevation of this man in the intellectual history of our race, — how it happens that in proportion to the culture of men they become his scholars; that, as our Jewish Bible has implanted itself in the table-talk and household life of every man and woman in the European and American nations, so the writings of Plato have preoccupied every school of learning, every lover of thought, every church, every poet, — making it impossible to think, on certain levels, except through him. He stands between the truth and every man's mind, and has almost impressed language and the primary

forms of thought with his name and seal. I am
struck, in reading him, with the extreme modernness of his style and spirit. Here is the germ of
that Europe we know so well, in its long history
of arts and arms; here are all its traits, already
discernible in the mind of Plato, — and in none
before him. It has spread itself since into a
hundred histories, but has added no new element.
This perpetual modernness is the measure of
merit in every work of art; since the author
of it was not misled by any thing short-lived or
local, but abode by real and abiding traits. How
Plato came thus to be Europe, and philosophy,
and almost literature, is the problem for us to
solve.

This could not have happened without a
sound, sincere and catholic man, able to honor,
at the same time, the ideal, or laws of the mind,
and fate, or the order of nature. The first period
of a nation, as of an individual, is the period of
unconscious strength. Children cry, scream and
stamp with fury, unable to express their desires.
As soon as they can speak and tell their want
and the reason of it, they become gentle. In adult
life, whilst the perceptions are obtuse, men and
women talk vehemently and superlatively, blun-
der and quarrel : their manners are full of des-

peration; their speech is full of oaths. As soon
as, with culture, things have cleared up a little,
and they see them no longer in lumps and
masses but accurately distributed, they desist
from that weak vehemence and explain their
meaning in detail. If the tongue had not been
framed for articulation, man would still be a
beast in the forest. The same weakness and
want, on a higher plane, occurs daily in the
education of ardent young men and women.
'Ah! you don't understand me; I have never
met with any one who comprehends me:' and
they sigh and weep, write verses and walk alone,
— fault of power to express their precise meaning. In a month or two, through the favor of
their good genius, they meet some one so related as to assist their volcanic estate, and, good
communication being once established, they are
thenceforward good citizens. It is ever thus.
The progress is to accuracy, to skill, to truth,
from blind force.

There is a moment in the history of every nation, when, proceeding out of this brute youth,
the perceptive powers reach their ripeness and
have not yet become microscopic: so that man,
at that instant, extends across the entire scale,
and, with his feet still planted on the immense

forces of night, converses by his eyes and brain
with solar and stellar creation. That is the moment of adult health, the culmination of power.[1]

Such is the history of Europe, in all points ;
and such in philosophy. Its early records, almost perished, are of the immigrations from
Asia, bringing with them the dreams of bar-
barians ; a confusion of crude notions of morals
and of natural philosophy, gradually subsiding
through the partial insight of single teachers.

Before Pericles came the Seven Wise Masters, and we have the beginnings of geometry,
metaphysics and ethics : then the partialists, —
deducing the origin of things from flux or water,
or from air, or from fire, or from mind. All
mix with these causes mythologic pictures. At
last comes Plato, the distributor, who needs no
barbaric paint, or tattoo, or whooping; for he
can define. He leaves with Asia the vast and
superlative ; he is the arrival of accuracy and intelligence. " He shall be as a god to me, who
can rightly divide and define."

This defining is philosophy. Philosophy is
the account which the human mind gives to itself of the constitution of the world. Two cardinal facts lie forever at the base ; the one, and
the two. — 1. Unity, or Identity ; and, 2. Va-

riety.¹ We unite all things by perceiving the
law which pervades them; by perceiving the
superficial differences and the profound resemblances. But every mental act, — this very perception of identity or oneness, recognizes the
difference of things. Oneness and otherness.
It is impossible to speak or to think without
embracing both.

The mind is urged to ask for one cause of
many effects; then for the cause of that; and
again the cause, diving still into the profound:
self-assured that it shall arrive at an absolute
and sufficient one, — a one that shall be all.
" In the midst of the sun is the light, in the
midst of the light is truth, and in the midst of
truth is the imperishable being," say the Vedas.
All philosophy, of East and West, has the same
centripetence. Urged by an opposite necessity,
the mind returns from the one to that which
is not one, but other or many; from cause to
effect; and affirms the necessary existence of
variety, the self-existence of both, as each is
involved in the other. These strictly-blended
elements it is the problem of thought to separate and to reconcile. Their existence is mutually contradictory and exclusive; and each so
fast slides into the other that we can never say

what is one, and what it is not. The Proteus
is as nimble in the highest as in the lowest
grounds; when we contemplate the one, the
true, the good, — as in the surfaces and extremities of matter.

In all nations there are minds which incline
to dwell in the conception of the fundamental
Unity. The raptures of prayer and ecstasy of
devotion lose all being in one Being. This
tendency finds its highest expression in the
religious writings of the East, and chiefly in
the Indian Scriptures, in the Vedas, the Bhagavat Geeta, and the Vishnu Purana.[1] Those
writings contain little else than this idea, and
they rise to pure and sublime strains in cele-
brating it.

The Same, the Same: friend and foe are of
one stuff; the ploughman, the plough and the
furrow are of one stuff; and the stuff is such
and so much that the variations of form are un-
important.[2] "You are fit" (says the supreme
Krishna to a sage) "to apprehend that you are
not distinct from me. That which I am, thou
art, and that also is this world, with its gods
and heroes and mankind. Men contemplate
distinctions, because they are stupefied with
ignorance." "The words *I* and *mine* consti-

tute ignorance. What is the great end of all, you shall now learn from me. It is soul,—one in all bodies, pervading, uniform, perfect, pre-eminent over nature, exempt from birth, growth and decay, omnipresent, made up of true knowledge, independent, unconnected with unrealities, with name, species and the rest, in time past, present and to come. The knowledge that this spirit, which is essentially one, is in one's own and in all other bodies, is the wisdom of one who knows the unity of things. As one diffusive air, passing through the perforations of a flute, is distinguished as the notes of a scale, so the nature of the Great Spirit is single, though its forms be manifold, arising from the consequences of acts.' When the difference of the investing form, as that of god or the rest, is destroyed, there is no distinction." "The whole world is but a manifestation of Vishnu, who is identical with all things, and is to be regarded by the wise as not differing from, but as the same as themselves. I neither am going nor coming; nor is my dwelling in any one place ; nor art thou, thou ; nor are others, others ; nor am I, I." As if he had said, ' All is for the soul, and the soul is Vishnu; and animals and stars are transient paintings; and light is whitewash; and durations are deceptive; and form is imprisonment; and heaven itself a decoy.' [1] That which the soul seeks is resolution into being above form, out of Tartarus and out of heaven, — liberation from nature.

If speculation tends thus to a terrific unity, in which all things are absorbed, action tends directly backwards to diversity. The first is the course or gravitation of mind; the second is the power of nature. Nature is the manifold. The unity absorbs, and melts or reduces. Nature opens and creates. These two principles reappear and interpenetrate all things, all thought; the one, the many. One is being; the other, intellect: one is necessity; the other, freedom: one, rest; the other, motion: one, power; the other, distribution: one, strength; the other, pleasure: one, consciousness; the other, definition: one, genius; the other, talent: one, earnestness; the other, knowledge: one, possession; the other, trade: one, caste; the other, culture: one, king; the other, democracy: and, if we dare carry these generalizations a step higher, and name the last tendency of both, we might say, that the end of the one is escape from organization, — pure science; and

the end of the other is the highest instrumentality, or use of means, or executive deity.

Each student adheres, by temperament and
by habit, to the first or to the second of these
gods of the mind. By religion, he tends to
unity ; by intellect, or by the senses, to the
many. A too rapid unification, and an excessive appliance to parts and 'particulars, are the
twin dangers of speculation.

To this partiality the history of nations corre-
sponded. The country of unity, of immovable
institutions, the seat of a philosophy delighting
in abstractions, of men faithful in doctrine and
in practice to the idea of a deaf, unimplorable,
immense fate, is Asia ; and it realizes this faith
in the social institution of caste. On the other
side, the genius of Europe is active and creative : it resists caste by culture ; its philosophy
was a discipline ; it is a land of arts, inventions,
trade, freedom. If the East loved infinity, the
West delighted in boundaries.

European civility is the triumph of talent, the
extension of system, the sharpened understanding, adaptive skill, delight in forms, delight in
manifestation, in comprehensible results. Pericles, Athens, Greece, had been working in this
element with the joy of genius not yet chilled

by any foresight of the detriment of an excess.
They saw before them no sinister political economy; no ominous Malthus; no Paris or London; no pitiless subdivision of classes, — the
doom of the pin-makers, the doom of the weavers, of dressers, of stockingers, of carders, of
spinners, of colliers; no Ireland; no Indian
caste, superinduced by the efforts of Europe to
throw it off. The understanding was in its
health and prime. Art was in its splendid
novelty. They cut the Pentelican marble as if
it were snow, and their perfect works in architecture and sculpture seemed things of course,
not more difficult than the completion of a new
ship at the Medford yards, or new mills at
Lowell. These things are in course, and may
be taken for granted. The Roman legion, By-
zantine legislation, English trade, the saloons
of Versailles, the cafés of Paris, the steam-mill,
steamboat, steam-coach, may all be seen in perspective; the town-meeting, the ballot-box, the
newspaper and cheap press.

Meantime, Plato, in Egypt and in Eastern
pilgrimages, imbibed the idea of one Deity, in
which all things are absorbed. The unity of
Asia and the detail of Europe; the infinitude
of the Asiatic soul and the defining, result-lov-

ing, machine-making, surface-seeking, opera-
going Europe, — Plato came to join, and, by
contact, to enhance the energy of each. The
excellence of Europe and Asia are in his brain.
Metaphysics and natural philosophy expressed
the genius of Europe; he substructs the religion of Asia, as the base.

In short, a balanced soul was born, perceptive of the two elements.[1] It is as easy to be
great as to be small. The reason why we do
not at once believe in admirable souls is because
they are not in our experience. In actual life,
they are so rare as to be incredible; but primarily there is not only no presumption against
them, but the strongest presumption in favor
of their appearance. But whether voices were
heard in the sky, or not; whether his mother
or his father dreamed that the infant man-child
was the son of Apollo; whether a swarm of
bees settled on his lips, or not; — a man who
could see two sides of a thing was born. The
wonderful synthesis so familiar in nature; the
upper and the under side of the medal of Jove;
the union of impossibilities, which reappears in
every object; its real and its ideal power, —
was now also transferred entire to the consciousness of a man.

The balanced soul came. If he loved abstract truth, he saved himself by propounding the most popular of all principles, the absolute good, which rules rulers, and judges the judge. If he made transcendental distinctions, he fortified himself by drawing all his illustrations from sources disdained by orators and polite conversers; from mares and puppies; from pitchers and soupladles; from cooks and criers; the shops of potters, horse-doctors, butchers and fishmongers. He cannot forgive in himself a partiality, but is resolved that the two poles of thought shall appear in his statement. His argument and his sentence are self-poised and spherical. The two poles appear; yes, and become two hands, to grasp and appropriate their own.

Every great artist has been such by synthesis. Our strength is transitional, alternating; or, shall I say, a thread of two strands. The sea-shore, sea seen from shore, shore seen from sea; the taste of two metals in contact; and our enlarged powers at the approach and at the departure of a friend; the experience of poetic creativeness, which is not found in staying at home, nor yet in travelling, but in transitions from one to the other, which must therefore be adroitly managed to present as much transitional surface as possible; this command of two elements must explain the power and the charm of Plato. Art expresses the one or the same by the different. Thought seeks to know unity in unity; poetry to show it by variety; that is, always by an object or symbol. Plato keeps the two vases, one of æther and one of pigment, at his side, and invariably uses both. Things added to things, as statistics, civil history, are inventories. Things used as language are inexhaustibly attractive. Plato turns incessantly the obverse and the reverse of the medal of Jove.

To take an example: — The physical philosophers had sketched each his theory of the world; the theory of atoms, of fire, of flux, of spirit; theories mechanical and chemical in their genius. Plato, a master of mathematics, studious of all natural laws and causes, feels these, as second causes, to be no theories of the world but bare inventories and lists. To the study of nature he therefore prefixes the dogma, — " Let us declare the cause which led the Supreme Ordainer to produce and compose the universe. He was good; and he who is good has no kind of envy. Exempt from envy, he wished that all things should be as much as possible like himself. Whosoever, taught by wise men, shall admit

this as the prime cause of the origin and foundation of the world, will be in the truth." [1] "All
things are for the sake of the good, and it is the
cause of every thing beautiful." This dogma
animates and impersonates his philosophy.

The synthesis which makes the character of
his mind appears in all his talents. Where there
is great compass of wit, we usually find excellen-
cies that combine easily in the living man, but in
description appear incompatible. The mind of
Plato is not to be exhibited by a Chinese cata-
logue, but is to be apprehended by an original
mind in the exercise of its original power. In
him the freest abandonment is united with the
precision of a geometer. His daring imagination
gives him the more solid grasp of facts; as the
birds of highest flight have the strongest alar
bones. His patrician polish, his intrinsic elegance, edged by an irony so subtle that it stings
and paralyzes, adorn the soundest health and
strength of frame. According to the old sentence, "If Jove should descend to the earth, he
would speak in the style of Plato."

With this palatial air there is, for the direct
aim of several of his works and running through
the tenor of them all, a certain earnestness, which
mounts, in the Republic and in the Phædo, to

piety. He has been charged with feigning sick-
ness at the time of the death of Socrates. But
the anecdotes that have come down from the
times attest his manly interference before the people in his master's behalf, since even the savage
cry of the assembly to Plato is preserved; and
the indignation towards popular government, in
many of his pieces, expresses a personal exas-
peration. He has a probity, a native reverence
for justice and honor, and a humanity which
makes him tender for the superstitions of the
people. Add to this, he believes that poetry,
prophecy and the high insight are from a wisdom of which man is not master; that the gods
never philosophize, but by a celestial mania
these miracles are accomplished.[1] Horsed on
these winged steeds, he sweeps the dim regions,
visits worlds which flesh cannot enter; he saw
the souls in pain, he hears the doom of the judge,
he beholds the penal metempsychosis, the Fates,
with the rock and shears, and hears the intoxi-
cating hum of their spindle.

But his circumspection never forsook him.
One would say he had read the inscription on
the gates of Busyrane, — " Be bold ; " and on
the second gate, — " Be bold, be bold, and
evermore be bold; "[2] and then again had paused

well at the third gate, — "Be not too bold."
His strength is like the momentum of a falling
planet, and his discretion the return of its due
and perfect curve, — so excellent is his Greek
love of boundary and his skill in definition. In
reading logarithms one is not more secure than
in following Plato in his flights. Nothing can
be colder than his head, when the lightnings
of his imagination are playing in the sky. He
has finished his thinking before he brings it to
the reader, and he abounds in the surprises of
a literary master. He has that opulence which
furnishes, at every turn, the precise weapon he
needs. As the rich man wears no more garments, drives no more horses, sits in no more
chambers than the poor, — but has that one
dress, or equipage, or instrument, which is fit
for the hour and the need; so Plato, in his
plenty, is never restricted, but has the fit word.
There is indeed no weapon in all the armory
of wit which he did not possess and use, —
epic, analysis, mania, intuition, music, satire and
irony, down to the customary and polite. His
illustrations are poetry and his jests illustrations.
Socrates' profession of obstetric art is good philosophy ; ¹ and his finding that word " cookery,"
and " adulatory art," for rhetoric, in the Gorgias,

does us a substantial service still. No orator can
measure in effect with him who can give good
nicknames.

What moderation and understatement and
checking his thunder in mid volley! He has
good-naturedly furnished the courtier and citizen with all that can be said against the schools.
" For philosophy is an elegant thing, if any one
modestly meddles with it ; but if he is conversant with it more than is becoming, it cor-
rupts the man." He could well afford to be
generous, — he, who from the sunlike centrality and reach of his vision, had a faith without
cloud. Such as his perception, was his speech :
he plays with the doubt and makes the most
of it : he paints and quibbles ; and by and by
comes a sentence that moves the sea and land.
The admirable earnest comes not only at intervals, in the perfect yes and no of the dialogue,
but in bursts of light. " I, therefore, Callicles,
am persuaded by these accounts, and consider
how I may exhibit my soul before the judge in
a healthy condition. Wherefore, disregarding
the honors that most men value, and looking
to the truth, I shall endeavor in reality to live
as virtuously as I can ; and when I die, to die
so. And I invite all other men, to the utmost

of my power ; and you too I in turn invite to
this contest, which, I affirm, surpasses all con-
tests here." [1]

He is a great average man ; one who, to the
best thinking, adds a proportion and equality
in his faculties, so that men see in him their
own dreams and glimpses made available and
made to pass for what they are. A great common-sense is his warrant and qualification to be
the world's interpreter. He has reason, as all
the philosophic and poetic class have : but he
has also what they have not,—this strong solving sense to reconcile his poetry with the appearances of the world, and build a bridge from
the streets of cities to the Atlantis. He omits
never this graduation, but slopes his thought,
however picturesque the precipice on one side,
to an access from the plain. He never writes
in ecstasy, or catches us up into poetic raptures.

Plato apprehended the cardinal facts. He
could prostrate himself on the earth and cover
his eyes whilst he adored that which cannot be
numbered, or gauged, or known, or named:
that of which every thing can be affirmed and
denied : that "which is entity and nonentity." [2]
He called it super-essential. He even stood

ready, as in the Parmenides, to demonstrate
that it was so, — that this Being exceeded the
limits of intellect. No man ever more fully
acknowledged the Ineffable.' Having paid his
homage, as for the human race, to the Illimitable, he then stood erect, and for the human
race affirmed, ' And yet things are knowable ! '
— that is, the Asia in his mind was first heartily
honored, — the ocean of love and power, before form, before will, before knowledge, the
Same, the Good, the One; and now, refreshed
and empowered by this worship, the instinct of
Europe, namely, culture, returns ; and he cries,
' Yet things are knowable ! ' They are knowable, because being from one, things correspond.
There is a scale ; and the correspondence of
heaven to earth, of matter to mind, of the part
to the whole, is our guide. As there is a science
of stars, called astronomy ; a science of quantities, called mathematics ; a science of qualities, called chemistry ; so there is a science of
sciences, — I call it Dialectic, — which is the
Intellect discriminating the false and the true.
It rests on the observation of identity and diversity ; for to judge is to unite to an object
the notion which belongs to it. The sciences,
even the best, — mathematics and astronomy,

—are like sportsmen, who seize whatever prey offers, even without being able to make any use of it. Dialectic must teach the use of them. " This is of that rank that no intellectual man will enter on any study for its own sake, but only with a view to advance himself in that one sole science which embraces all." [1]

" The essence or peculiarity of man is to comprehend a whole; or that which in the diversity of sensations can be comprised under a rational unity." " The soul which has never perceived the truth, cannot pass into the human form." [2] I announce to men the Intellect. I announce the good of being interpenetrated by the mind that made nature: this benefit, namely, that it can understand nature, which it made and maketh. Nature is good, but intellect is better: as the law-giver is before the law-receiver. I give you joy, O sons of men! that truth is altogether wholesome; that we have hope to search out what might be the very self of everything. The misery of man is to be baulked of the sight of essence and to be stuffed with conjectures; but the supreme good is reality; the supreme beauty is reality; and all virtue and all felicity depend on this science of the real: for courage is nothing else than know-

ledge ; the fairest fortune that can befall man is
to be guided by his dæmon to that which is
truly his own. This also is the essence of justice, — to attend every one his own : nay, the
notion of virtue is not to be arrived at except
through direct contemplation of the divine essence. Courage then ! for " the persuasion that
we must search that which we do not know,
will render us, beyond comparison, better, braver
and more industrious than if we thought it impossible to discover what we do not know, and
useless to search for it." He secures a position
not to be commanded, by his passion for reality ; valuing philosophy only as it is the pleasure of conversing with real being.

Thus, full of the genius of Europe, he said,
Culture. He saw the institutions of Sparta and
recognized, more genially one would say than
any since, the hope of education. He delighted
in every accomplishment, in every graceful and
useful and truthful performance ; above all in
the splendors of genius and intellectual achievement. " The whole of life, O Socrates," said
Glauco, " is, with the wise, the measure of hearing such discourses as these." What a price he
sets on the feats of talent, on the powers of
Pericles, of Isocrates, of Parmenides ! What

price above price on the talents themselves!
He called the several faculties, gods, in his
beautiful personation. What value he gives to
the art of gymnastic in education; what to geometry;[1] what to music; what to astronomy,
whose appeasing and medicinal power he celebrates! In the Timæus he indicates the highest
employment of the eyes. "By us it is asserted
that God invented and bestowed sight on us for
this purpose, — that on surveying the circles of
intelligence in the heavens, we might properly
employ those of our own minds, which, though
disturbed when compared with the others that
are uniform, are still allied to their circulations;
and that having thus learned, and being naturally possessed of a correct reasoning faculty,
we might, by imitating the uniform revolutions
of divinity, set right our own wanderings and
blunders." And in the Republic, — "By each
of these disciplines a certain organ of the soul
is both purified and reanimated which is blinded
and buried by studies of another kind; an organ better worth saving than ten thousand eyes,
since truth is perceived by this alone."

He said, Culture; but he first admitted its
basis, and gave immeasurably the first place to
advantages of nature. His patrician tastes laid

stress on the distinctions of birth. In the doctrine of the organic character and disposition is
the origin of caste. "Such as were fit to govern, into their composition the informing Deity
mingled gold; into the military, silver; iron
and brass for husbandmen and artificers." The
East confirms, itself, in all ages, in this faith.
The Koran is explicit on this point of caste.
"Men have their metal, as of gold and silver.
Those of you who were the worthy ones in the
state of ignorance, will be the worthy ones in
the state of faith, as soon as you embrace it."
Plato was not less firm. "Of the five orders
of things, only four can be taught to the gener-
ality of men." In the Republic he insists on
the temperaments of the youth,' as first of the
first.

A happier example of the stress laid on nature is in the dialogue with the young Theages,
who wishes to receive lessons from Socrates.
Socrates declares that if some have grown wise
by associating with him, no thanks are due to
him; but, simply, whilst they were with him
they grew wise, not because of him; he pretends not to know the way of it. "It is adverse
to many, nor can those be benefited by associating with me whom the Dæmon opposes; so

that it is not possible for me to live with these. With many however he does not prevent me from conversing, who yet are not at all benefited by associating with me. Such, O Theages, is the association with me ; for, if it pleases the God, you will make great and rapid proficiency : you will not, if he does not please. Judge whether it is not safer to be instructed by some one of those who have power over the benefit which they impart to men, than by me, who benefit or not, just as it may happen." As if he had said, ' I have no system. I cannot be answerable for you. You will be what you must. If there is love between us, inconceivably deli-cious and profitable will our intercourse be ; if not, your time is lost and you will only annoy me. I shall seem to you stupid, and the repu-tation I have, false. Quite above us, beyond the will of you or me, is this secret affinity or repulsion laid. All my good is magnetic, and I educate, not by lessons, but by going about my business.'

He said, Culture; he said, Nature; and he failed not to add, ' There is also the divine.' There is no thought in any mind but it quickly tends to convert itself into a power and organ-izes a huge instrumentality of means. Plato, lover of limits, loved the illimitable, saw the enlargement and nobility which come from truth itself and good itself, and attempted as if on the part of the human intellect, once for all to do it adequate homage, — homage fit for the immense soul to receive, and yet homage becoming the intellect to render. He said then, ' Our faculties run out into infinity, and return to us thence. We can define but a little way; but here is a fact which will not be skipped, and which to shut our eyes upon is suicide. All things are in a scale ; and, begin where we will, ascend and ascend. All things are symbolical;' and what we call results are beginnings.'

A key to the method and completeness of Plato is his twice bisected line. After he has illustrated the relation between the absolute good and true and the forms of the intelligible world, he says : " Let there be a line cut in two unequal parts. Cut again each of these two main parts, — one representing the visible, the other the intelligible world, — and let these two new sections represent the bright part and the dark part of each of these worlds. You will have, for one of the sections of the visible world, images, that is, both shadows and reflections ; — for the other section, the objects of these images, that is, plants, animals, and the works of art and nature. Then divide the intelligible world in like manner; the one section will be of opinions and hypotheses, and the other section of truths." [1] To these four sections, the four operations of the soul correspond,—conjecture, faith, understanding, reason. As every pool reflects the image of the sun, so every thought and thing restores us an image and creature of the supreme Good. The universe is perforated by a million channels for his activity. All things mount and mount.

All his thought has this ascension; in Phædrus, teaching that beauty is the most lovely of all things, exciting hilarity and shedding desire and confidence through the universe wherever it enters, and it enters in some degree into all things : — but that there is another, which is as much more beautiful than beauty as beauty is than chaos ; namely, wisdom, which our wonderful organ of sight cannot reach unto, but which, could it be seen, would ravish us with its perfect reality.[2] He has the same regard to it as the source of excellence in works of art. When an artificer, he says, in the fabrication of any work, looks to that which always subsists according to *the same* ; and, employing a model of this kind, expresses its idea and power in his work, — it must follow that his production should be beautiful. But when he beholds that which is born and dies, it will be far from beautiful.

Thus ever: the Banquet is a teaching in the same spirit, familiar now to all the poetry and to all the sermons of the world, that the love of the sexes is initial, and symbolizes at a distance the passion of the soul for that immense lake of beauty it exists to seek.[1] This faith in the Divinity is never out of mind, and constitutes the ground of all his dogmas. Body cannot teach wisdom; — God only. In the same mind he constantly affirms that virtue cannot be taught; that it is not a science, but an inspiration; that the greatest goods are produced to us through mania and are assigned to us by a divine gift.

This leads me to that central figure which he has established in his Academy as the organ through which every considered opinion shall be announced, and whose biography he has likewise so labored that the historic facts are lost in the light of Plato's mind. Socrates and Plato are the double star which the most powerful instruments will not entirely separate. Socrates again, in his traits and genius, is the best example of that synthesis which constitutes Plato's extraordinary power. Socrates, a man of humble stem,

but honest enough ; of the commonest history ;
of a personal homeliness so remarkable as to be
a cause of wit in others : — the rather that his
broad good nature and exquisite taste for a joke
invited the sally, which was sure to be paid. The
players personated him on the stage ; the potters
copied his ugly face on their stone jugs. He was
a cool fellow, adding to his humor a perfect temper and a knowledge of his man, be he who he
might whom he talked with, which laid the companion open to certain defeat in any debate, —
and in debate he immoderately delighted. The
young men are prodigiously fond of him and invite him to their feasts, whither he goes for conversation. He can drink, too ; has the strongest
head in Athens ; and after leaving the whole party
under the table, goes away as if nothing had happened, to begin new dialogues with somebody
that is sober. In short, he was what our country-
people call *an old one.*

He affected a good many citizen-like tastes,
was monstrously fond of Athens, hated trees,
never willingly went beyond the walls, knew the
old characters, valued the bores and philistines,
thought every thing in Athens a little better than
anything in any other place. He was plain as a
Quaker in habit and speech, affected low phrases,

and illustrations from cocks and quails, soup-
pans and sycamore-spoons, grooms and farriers,
and unnamable offices, — especially if he talked
with any superfine person. He had a Franklin-
like wisdom. Thus he showed one who was
afraid to go on foot to Olympia, that it was no
more than his daily walk within doors, if continuously extended, would easily reach.

Plain old uncle as he was, with his great ears,
an immense talker, — the rumor ran that on one
or two occasions, in the war with Bœotia, he had
shown a determination which had covered the retreat of a troop ; and there was some story that
under cover of folly, he had, in the city government, when one day he chanced to hold a seat
there, evinced a courage in opposing singly the
popular voice, which had well-nigh ruined him.
He is very poor ; but then he is hardy as a soldier, and can live on a few olives ; usually, in the
strictest sense, on bread and water, except when
entertained by his friends. His necessary expenses were exceedingly small, and no one could
live as he did. He wore no under garment ; his
upper garment was the same for summer and
winter, and he went barefooted ; and it is said
that to procure the pleasure, which he loves, of
talking at his ease all day with the most elegant

and cultivated young men, he will now and then
return to his shop and carve statues, good or bad,
for sale. However that be, it is certain that he
had grown to delight in nothing else than this
conversation; and that, under his hypocritical
pretence of knowing nothing, he attacks and
brings down all the fine speakers, all the fine
philosophers of Athens, whether natives or stran-
gers from Asia Minor and the islands. Nobody
can refuse to talk with him, he is so honest and
really curious to know; a man who was willingly
confuted if he did not speak the truth, and who
willingly confuted others asserting what was false;
and not less pleased when confuted than when
confuting; for he thought not any evil happened
to men of such a magnitude as false opinion respecting the just and unjust. A pitiless dispu-
tant, who knows nothing, but the bounds of whose
conquering intelligence no man had ever reached;
whose temper was imperturbable; whose dreadful logic was always leisurely and sportive; so
careless and ignorant as to disarm the wariest and
draw them, in the pleasantest manner, into horrible doubts and confusion. But he always knew
the way out; knew it, yet would not tell it. No
escape; he drives them to terrible choices by his
dilemmas, and tosses the Hippiases and Gor-

giases with their grand reputations, as a boy tosses
his balls. The tyrannous realist! — Meno has
discoursed a thousand times, at length, on virtue, before many companies, and very well, as it
appeared to him; but at this moment he cannot even tell what it is, — this cramp-fish of a
Socrates has so bewitched him.

This hard-headed humorist, whose strange
conceits, drollery and *bonhommie* diverted the
young patricians, whilst the rumor of his sayings and quibbles gets abroad every day, —
turns out, in the sequel, to have a probity as invincible as his logic, and to be either insane, or
at least, under cover of this play, enthusiastic in
his religion. When accused before the judges
of subverting the popular creed, he affirms the
immortality of the soul, the future reward and
punishment; and refusing to recant, in a caprice
of the popular government was condemned to
die, and sent to the prison. Socrates entered the
prison and took away all ignominy from the
place, which could not be a prison whilst he was
there. Crito bribed the jailer; but Socrates would
not go out by treachery. "Whatever inconvenience ensue, nothing is to be preferred before
justice. These things I hear like pipes and
drums, whose sound makes me deaf to every

thing you say." The fame of this prison, the
fame of the discourses there and the drinking of
the hemlock are one of the most precious passages in the history of the world.

The rare coincidence, in one ugly body, of the
droll and the martyr, the keen street and market
debater with the sweetest saint known to any
history at that time, had forcibly struck the mind
of Plato, so capacious of these contrasts; and
the figure of Socrates by a necessity placed itself
in the foreground of the scene, as the fittest dispenser of the intellectual treasures he had to communicate. It was a rare fortune that this Æsop
of the mob and this robed scholar should meet,
to make each other immortal in their mutual
faculty. The strange synthesis in the character
of Socrates capped the synthesis in the mind of
Plato. Moreover by this means he was able, in
the direct way and without envy to avail himself
of the wit and weight of Socrates, to which unquestionably his own debt was great; and these
derived again their principal advantage from the
perfect art of Plato.

It remains to say that the defect of Plato in
power is only that which results inevitably from
his quality. He is intellectual in his aim; and
therefore, in expression, literary. Mounting into

heaven, diving into the pit, expounding the laws
of the state, the passion of love, the remorse of
crime, the hope of the parting soul, — he is literary, and never otherwise. It is almost the sole
deduction from the merit of Plato that his writings have not, — what is no doubt incident to
this regnancy of intellect in his work, — the vital
authority which the screams of prophets and the
sermons of unlettered Arabs and Jews possess.
There is an interval; and to cohesion, contact
is necessary.[1]

I know not what can be said in reply to this
criticism but that we have come to a fact in the
nature of things : an oak is not an orange.
The qualities of sugar remain with sugar, and
those of salt with salt.

In the second place, he has not a system.
The dearest defenders and disciples are at fault.
He attempted a theory of the universe, and his
theory is not complete or self-evident. One
man thinks he means this, and another that;
he has said one thing in one place, and the reverse of it in another place. He is charged with
having failed to make the transition from ideas
to matter. Here is the world, sound as a nut,
perfect, not the smallest piece of chaos left,
never a stitch nor an end, not a mark of haste,

or botching, or second thought; but the theory of the world is a thing of shreds and patches.

The longest wave is quickly lost in the sea. Plato would willingly have a Platonism, a known and accurate expression for the world, and it should be accurate. It shall be the world passed through the mind of Plato, — nothing less. Every atom shall have the Platonic tinge; every atom, every relation or quality you knew before, you shall know again and find here, but now ordered; not nature, but art. And you shall feel that Alexander indeed overran, with men and horses, some countries of the planet; but countries, and things of which countries are made, elements, planet itself, laws of planet and of men, have passed through this man as bread into his body, and become no longer bread, but body: so all this mammoth morsel has become Plato. He has clapped copyright on the world. This is the ambition of individualism. But the mouthful proves too large. *Boa constrictor* has good will to eat it, but he is foiled. He falls abroad in the attempt; and biting, gets strangled: the bitten world holds the biter fast by his own teeth. There he perishes: unconquered nature lives on and forgets him. So it fares with all: so must it fare with Plato. In view of

eternal nature, Plato turns out to be philosophical exercitations. He argues on this side and
on that. The acutest German, the lovingest
disciple, could never tell what Platonism was ;
indeed, admirable texts can be quoted on both
sides of every great question from him.[1]

These things we are forced to say if we must
consider the effort of Plato or of any philosopher to dispose of nature, — which will not be
disposed of. No power of genius has ever yet
had the smallest success in explaining existence.
The perfect enigma remains. But there is an
injustice in assuming this ambition for Plato.
Let us not seem to treat with flippancy his ven-
erable name. Men, in proportion to their intellect, have admitted his transcendent claims.
The way to know him is to compare him, not
with nature, but with other men. How many
ages have gone by, and he remains unap-
proached ! A chief structure of human wit, like
Karnac, or the mediæval cathedrals, or the Etru-
rian remains, it requires all the breath of human
faculty to know it. I think it is trueliest seen
when seen with the most respect. His sense
deepens, his merits multiply, with study. When
we say, Here is a fine collection of fables ; or
when we praise the style, or the common sense,

or arithmetic, we speak as boys, and much of our impatient criticism of the dialectic, I suspect, is no better.

The criticism is like our impatience of miles, when we are in a hurry; but it is still best that a mile should have seventeen hundred and sixty yards. The great-eyed Plato proportioned the lights and shades after the genius of our life.[1]

PLATO: NEW READINGS

THE publication, in Mr. Bohn's " Serial Library," of the excellent translations of Plato, which we esteem one of the chief benefits the cheap press has yielded, gives us an occasion to take hastily a few more notes of the elevation and bearings of this fixed star ; or to add a · bulletin, like the journals, of *Plato at the latest dates*.

Modern science, by the extent of its generalization, has learned to indemnify the student of man for the defects of individuals by tracing growth and ascent in races ; and, by the simple expedient of lighting up the vast background, generates a feeling of complacency and hope. The human being has the saurian and the plant in his rear. His arts and sciences, the easy issue of his brain, look glorious when prospectively beheld from the distant brain of ox, crocodile and fish. It seems as if nature, in regarding the geologic night behind her, when, in five or six millenniums, she had turned out five or six men, as Homer, Phidias, Menu and Columbus, was no wise discontented with the result. These

Plato

samples attested the virtue of the tree. These
were a clear amelioration of trilobite and saurus,
and a good basis for further proceeding. With
this artist, time and space are cheap, and she is
insensible to what you say of tedious preparation. She waited tranquilly the flowing periods
of paleontology, for the hour to be struck when
man should arrive. Then periods must pass
before the motion of the earth can be suspected;
then before the map of the instincts and the
cultivable powers can be drawn. But as of races,
so the succession of individual men is fatal and
beautiful, and Plato has the fortune in the history of mankind to mark an epoch.[1]

Plato's fame does not stand on a syllogism, or
on any masterpieces of the Socratic reasoning, or
on any thesis, as for example the immortality of
the soul. He is more than an expert, or a schoolman, or a geometer, or the prophet of a peculiar
message. He represents the privilege of the intellect, the power, namely, of carrying up every
fact to successive platforms and so disclosing in
every fact a germ of expansion. These expansions are in the essence of thought. The naturalist would never help us to them by any discoveries of the extent of the universe, but is as poor
when cataloguing the resolved nebula of Orion,

as when measuring the angles of an acre. But
the Republic of Plato, by these expansions, may
be said to require and so to anticipate the astronomy of Laplace. The expansions are organic.
The mind does not create what it perceives, any
more than the eye creates the rose. In ascribing
to Plato the merit of announcing them, we only
say, Here was a more complete man, who could
apply to nature the whole scale of the senses, the
understanding and the reason. These expansions
or extensions consist in continuing the spiritual
sight where the horizon falls on our natural
vision, and by this second sight discovering the
long lines of law which shoot in every direction.
Everywhere he stands on a path which has no
end, but runs continuously round the universe.[1]
Therefore every word becomes an exponent of
nature. Whatever he looks upon discloses a second sense, and ulterior senses. His perception
of the generation of contraries, of death out of
life and life out of death, — that law by which,
in nature, decomposition is recomposition, and
putrefaction and cholera are only signals of a new
creation; his discernment of the little in the large
and the large in the small; studying the state in
the citizen and the citizen in the state; and leaving it doubtful whether he exhibited the Repub-

lic as an allegory on the education of the private soul; his beautiful definitions of ideas, of time, of form, of figure, of the line, sometimes hypothetically given, as his defining of virtue, courage, justice, temperance; his love of the apologue, and his apologues themselves; the cave of Trophonius; the ring of Gyges; the charioteer and two horses; the golden, silver, brass and iron temperaments; Theuth and Thamus; and the visions of Hades and the Fates,[1] — fables which have imprinted themselves in the human memory like the signs of the zodiac; his soliform eye and his boniform soul;[2] his doctrine of assimilation; his doctrine of reminiscence; his clear vision of the laws of return, or reaction, which secure instant justice throughout the universe, instanced everywhere, but specially in the doctrine, "what comes from God to us, returns from us to God," and in Socrates' belief that the laws below are sisters of the laws above.

More striking examples are his moral conclusions. Plato affirms the coincidence of science and virtue; for vice can never know itself and virtue, but virtue knows both itself and vice. The eye attested that justice was best, as long as it was profitable; Plato affirms that it is profitable throughout; that the profit is intrinsic, though

the just conceal his justice from gods and men;
that it is better to suffer injustice than to do
it; that the sinner ought to covet punishment;
that the lie was more hurtful than homicide; and
that ignorance, or the involuntary lie, was more
calamitous than involuntary homicide; that the
soul is unwillingly deprived of true opinions,
and that no man sins willingly; that the order
or proceeding of nature was from the mind to
the body, and, though a sound body cannot restore an unsound mind, yet a good soul can,
by its virtue, render the body the best possible.
The intelligent have a right over the ignorant,
namely, the right of instructing them. The right
punishment of one out of tune is to make him
play in tune; the fine which the good, refusing
to govern, ought to pay, is, to be governed by a
worse man; that his guards shall not handle gold
and silver, but shall be instructed that there is
gold and silver in their souls, which will make
men willing to give them every thing which they
need.

This second sight explains the stress laid on
geometry. He saw that the globe of earth was
not more lawful and precise than was the supersensible; that a celestial geometry was in place
there, as a logic of lines and angles here below;

that the world was throughout mathematical;
the proportions are constant of oxygen, azote
and lime; there is just so much water and slate
and magnesia ; not less are the proportions constant of the moral elements.[1]

This eldest Goethe, hating varnish and falsehood, delighted in revealing the real at the base
of the accidental; in discovering connection, continuity and representation everywhere, hating
insulation ; and appears like the god of wealth
among the cabins of vagabonds, opening power
and capability in everything he touches. Ethical
science was new and vacant when Plato could
write thus : — " Of all whose arguments are left
to the men of the present time, no one has ever
yet condemned injustice, or praised justice,
otherwise than as respects the repute, honors and
emoluments arising therefrom ; while, as respects
either of them in itself, and subsisting by its own
power in the soul of the possessor, and concealed
both from gods and men, no one has yet sufficiently investigated, either in poetry or prose
writings, — how, namely, that injustice is the
greatest of all the evils that the soul has within
it, and justice the greatest good."

His definition of ideas, as what is simple, permanent, uniform and self-existent, forever dis-

criminating them from the notions of the understanding, marks an era in the world. He was
born to behold the self-evolving power of spirit,
endless, generator of new ends ; a power which
is the key at once to the centrality and the eva-
nescence of things. Plato is so centred that he
can well spare all his dogmas. Thus the fact of
knowledge and ideas reveals to him the fact of
eternity ; and the doctrine of reminiscence he
offers as the most probable particular explication.
Call that fanciful, — it matters not : the connection between our knowledge and the abyss of
being is still real, and the explication must be
not less magnificent.'

He has indicated every eminent point in speculation. He wrote on the scale of the mind itself,
so that all things have symmetry in his tablet.
He put in all the past, without weariness, and
descended into detail with a courage like that he
witnessed in nature. One would say that his fore-
runners had mapped out each a farm or a district
or an island, in intellectual geography, but that
Plato first drew the sphere. He domesticates the
soul in nature : man is the microcosm. All the
circles of the visible heaven represent as many
circles in the rational soul. There is no lawless
particle, and there is nothing casual in the action

of the human mind. The names of things, too, are fatal, following the nature of things. All the gods of the Pantheon are, by their names, significant of a profound sense. The gods are the ideas. Pan is speech, or manifestation; Saturn, the contemplative; Jove, the regal soul; and Mars, passion. Venus is proportion; Calliope, the soul of the world; Aglaia, intellectual illustration.

These thoughts, in sparkles of light, had appeared often to pious and to poetic souls; but this well-bred, all-knowing Greek geometer comes with command, gathers them all up into rank and gradation, the Euclid of holiness, and marries the two parts of nature. Before all men, he saw the intellectual values of the moral sentiment. He describes his own ideal, when he paints, in Timæus, a god leading things from disorder into order. He kindled a fire so truly in the centre that we see the sphere illuminated, and can distinguish poles, equator and lines of latitude, every arc and node: a theory so averaged, so modulated, that you would say the winds of ages had swept through this rhythmic structure, and not that it was the brief extempore blotting of one short-lived scribe.[1] Hence it has happened that a very well-marked class of souls, namely those who delight in giving a spiritual, that is, an ethico-intellectual expression to every truth, by exhibiting an ulterior end which is yet legitimate to it, — are said to Platonize. Thus, Michael Angelo is a Platonist in his sonnets: Shakspeare is a Platonist when he writes, —

> " Nature is made better by no mean,
>   But nature makes that mean,"

or, —

> " He, that can endure
> To follow with allegiance a fallen lord,
> Does conquer him that did his master conquer,
> And earns a place in the story."

Hamlet is a pure Platonist, and 't is the magnitude only of Shakspeare's proper genius that hinders him from being classed as the most eminent of this school. Swedenborg, throughout his prose poem of " Conjugal Love," is a Platonist.

His subtlety commended him to men of thought. The secret of his popular success is the moral aim which endeared him to mankind. " Intellect," he said, " is king of heaven and of earth; " but in Plato, intellect is always moral. His writings have also the sempiternal youth of poetry. For their arguments, most of them, might have been couched in sonnets : and poetry has never soared higher than in the Timæus and the Phædrus. As the poet, too, he is only contemplative. He did not, like Pythagoras, break himself with an institution. All his painting in the Republic must be esteemed mythical, with intent to bring out, sometimes in violent colors, his thought. You cannot institute, without peril of charlatanism.

It was a high scheme, his absolute privilege for the best (which, to make emphatic, he expressed by community of women), as the premium which he would set on grandeur. There shall be exempts of two kinds: first, those who by demerit have put themselves below protection, — outlaws ; and secondly, those who by eminence of nature and desert are out of the reach of your rewards. Let such be free of the city and above the law. We confide them to themselves ; let them do with us as they will. Let none presume to measure the irregularities of Michael Angelo and Socrates by village scales.

In his eighth book of the Republic, he throws a little mathematical dust in our eyes. I am sorry to see him, after such noble superiorities, permitting the lie to governors. Plato plays Providence a little with the baser sort, as people allow themselves with their dogs and cats.

III

SWEDENBORG; OR, THE MYSTIC

SWEDENBORG; OR, THE MYSTIC

⟨A MONG eminent persons, those who are most dear to men are not of the class which the economist calls producers : they have nothing in their hands ; they have not culti- vated corn, nor made bread ; they have not led out a colony, nor invented a loom. A higher class, in the estimation and love of this city- building market-going race of mankind, are the poets, who, from the intellectual kingdom, feed the thought and imagination with ideas and pic- tures which raise men out of the world of corn and money, and console them for the short- comings of the day and the meanness of labor and traffic. ⟩ Then, also, the philosopher has his value, who flatters the intellect of this laborer by engaging him with subtleties which instruct him in new faculties. Others may build cities ; he is to understand them and keep them in awe. But there is a class who lead us into another region, — the world of morals or of will. What is singular about this region of thought is its claim. Wherever the sentiment of right comes in, it takes precedence of every thing else. For

other things, I make poetry of them ; but the
moral sentiment makes poetry of me.'

I have sometimes thought that he would
render the greatest service to modern criticism,
who should draw the line of relation that subsists between Shakspeare and Swedenborg. The
human mind stands ever in perplexity, demanding intellect, demanding sanctity, impatient
equally of each without the other. The reconciler has not yet appeared. If we tire of the
saints, Shakspeare is our city of refuge. Yet the
instincts presently teach that the problem of essence must take precedence of all others; — the
questions of Whence ? What ? and Whither ?
and the solution of these must be in a life, and
not in a book. A drama or poem is a proximate
or oblique reply ; but Moses, Menu, Jesus,
work directly on this problem. The atmosphere
of moral sentiment is a region of grandeur which
reduces all material magnificence to toys, yet
opens to every wretch that has reason the doors
of the universe. Almost with a fierce haste it
lays its empire on the man. In the language of
the Koran, " God said, The heaven and the earth
and all that is between them, think ye that we
created them in jest, and that ye shall not return
to us ? " It is the kingdom of the will, and by

Swedenborg

9
o
r.

r
\
s

inspiring the will, which is the seat of personality, seems to convert the universe into a person;—

> " The realms of being to no other bow,
> Not only all are thine, but all are Thou."

All men are commanded by the saint. The Koran makes a distinct class of those who are by nature good, and whose goodness has an influence on others, and pronounces this class to be the aim of creation: the other classes are admitted to the feast of being, only as following in the train of this. And the Persian poet exclaims to a soul of this kind, —

> " Go boldly forth, and feast on being's banquet ;
> Thou art the called, — the rest admitted with thee."

The privilege of this caste is an access to the secrets and structure of nature by some higher method than by experience. In common parlance, what one man is said to learn by experience, a man of extraordinary sagacity is said, without experience, to divine. The Arabians say, that Abul Khain, the mystic, and Abu Ali Seena, the philosopher, conferred together ; and, on parting, the philosopher said, " All that he sees, I know ; " and the mystic said, " All that he knows, I see." ' If one should ask the reason of this intuition, the solution would lead

us into that property which Plato denoted as
Reminiscence, and which is implied by the Bra-
mins in the tenet of Transmigration. The soul
having been often born, or, as the Hindoos
say, "travelling the path of existence through
thousands of births," having beheld the things
which are here, those which are in heaven and
those which are beneath, there is nothing of
which she has not gained the knowledge : no
wonder that she is able to recollect, in regard to
any one thing, what formerly she knew. "For,
all things in nature being linked and related,
and the soul having heretofore known all, nothing hinders but that any man who has recalled
to mind, or according to the common phrase
has learned, one thing only, should of himself
recover all his ancient knowledge, and find out
again all the rest, if he have but courage and
faint not in the midst of his researches. For
inquiry and learning is reminiscence all." How
much more, if he that inquires be a holy and
godlike soul ! For by being assimilated to the
original soul, by whom and after whom all things
subsist, the soul of man does then easily flow
into all things, and all things flow into it : they
mix ; and he is present and sympathetic with
their structure and law.'

This path is difficult, secret and beset with terror. The ancients called it *ecstasy* or absence, —a getting out of their bodies to think. All religious history contains traces of the trance of saints, —a beatitude, but without any sign of joy ; earnest, solitary, even sad ; " the flight," Plotinus called it, " of the alone to the alone;" Μύησις, the closing of the eyes, — whence our word, *Mystic*. The trances of Socrates, Plotinus, Porphyry, Behmen, Bunyan, Fox, Pascal, Guyon, Swedenborg, will readily come to mind. But what as readily comes to mind is the accompaniment of disease. This beatitude comes in terror, and with shocks to the mind of the receiver.

" It o'erinforms the tenement of clay," [1]

and drives the man mad ; or gives a certain violent bias which taints his judgment. In the chief examples of religious illumination somewhat morbid has mingled, in spite of the unquestionable increase of mental power. Must the highest good drag after it a quality which neutralizes and discredits it ? —

" Indeed, it takes
From our achievements, when performed at height,
The pith and marrow of our attribute." [2]

Shall we say, that the economical mother dis-

burses so much earth and so much fire, by weight
and meter, to make a man, and will not add a
pennyweight, though a nation is perishing for
a leader? Therefore the men of God purchased
their science by folly or pain. If you will have
pure carbon, carbuncle, or diamond, to make the
brain transparent, the trunk and organs shall be
so much the grosser: instead of porcelain they
are potter's earth, clay, or mud.

In modern times no such remarkable example
of this introverted mind has occurred as in
Emanuel Swedenborg, born in Stockholm, in
1688. This man, who appeared to his contemporaries a visionary and elixir of moonbeams, no
doubt led the most real life of any man then in
the world : and now, when the royal and ducal
Frederics, Christians and Brunswicks of that
day have slid into oblivion, he begins to spread
himself into the minds of thousands. As happens in great men, he seemed, by the variety and
amount of his powers, to be a composition of
several persons, — like the giant fruits which are
matured in gardens by the union of four or five
single blossoms. His frame is on a larger scale
and possesses the advantages of size. As it is
easier to see the reflection of the great sphere in
large globes, though defaced by some crack or

blemish, than in drops of water, so men of large calibre, though with some eccentricity or madness, like Pascal or Newton, help us more than balanced mediocre minds.

His youth and training could not fail to be extraordinary. Such a boy could not whistle or dance, but goes grubbing into mines and mountains, prying into chemistry and optics, physiology, mathematics and astronomy, to find images fit for the measure of his versatile and capacious brain. He was a scholar from a child, and was educated at Upsala. At the age of twenty-eight he was made Assessor of the Board of Mines by Charles XII. In 1716, he left home for four years and visited the universities of England, Holland, France and Germany. He performed a notable feat of engineering in 1718, at the siege of Frederikshald, by hauling two galleys, five boats and a sloop, some fourteen English miles overland, for the royal service. In 1721 he journeyed over Europe to examine mines and smelting works. He published in 1716 his Dædalus Hyperboreus, and from this time for the next thirty years was employed in the composition and publication of his scientific works. With the like force he threw himself into theology. In 1743, when he was fifty-four years old, what is called his illumination began. All his metallurgy and transportation of ships overland was absorbed into this ecstasy. He ceased to publish any more scientific books, withdrew from his practical labors and devoted himself to the writing and publication of his voluminous theological works, which were printed at his own expense, or at that of the Duke of Brunswick or other prince, at Dresden, Leipsic, London, or Amsterdam. Later, he resigned his office of Assessor: the salary attached to this office continued to be paid to him during his life. His duties had brought him into intimate acquaintance with King Charles XII., by whom he was much consulted and honored. The like favor was continued to him by his successor. At the Diet of 1751, Count Hopken says, the most solid memorials on finance were from his pen. In Sweden he appears to have attracted a marked regard. His rare science and practical skill, and the added fame of second sight and extraordinary religious knowledge and gifts, drew to him queens, nobles, clergy, shipmasters and people about the ports through which he was wont to pass in his many voyages. The clergy interfered a little with the importation and publication of his religious works, but he seems to have kept the friendship of men in power. He was never married. He had great modesty and gentleness of bearing. His habits were simple; he lived on bread, milk and vegetables; he lived in a house situated in a large garden; he went several times to England, where he does not seem to have attracted any attention whatever from the learned or the eminent; and died at London, March 29, 1772, of apoplexy, in his eighty-fifth year. He is described, when in London, as a man of a quiet, clerical habit, not averse to tea and coffee, and kind to children. He wore a sword when in full velvet dress, and, whenever he walked out, carried a gold-headed cane. There is a common portrait of him in antique coat and wig, but the face has a wandering or vacant air.

The genius which was to penetrate the science of the age with a far more subtle science; to pass the bounds of space and time, venture into the dim spirit-realm, and attempt to establish a new religion in the world, — began its lessons in quarries and forges, in the smelting-pot and crucible, in ship-yards and dissecting-rooms. No one man is perhaps able to judge of the merits of his works on so many subjects. One is glad to learn that his books on mines and metals are

held in the highest esteem by those who understand these matters. It seems that he anticipated much science of the nineteenth century;
anticipated, in astronomy, the discovery of the
seventh planet, — but, unhappily, not also of
the eighth; anticipated the views of modern
astronomy in regard to the generation of earths
by the sun; in magnetism, some important experiments and conclusions of later students; in
chemistry, the atomic theory; in anatomy, the
discoveries of Schlichting, Monro and Wilson;
and first demonstrated the office of the lungs.
His excellent English editor magnanimously
lays no stress on his discoveries, since he was too
great to care to be original; and we are to judge,
by what he can spare, of what remains.

A colossal soul, he lies vast abroad on his
times, uncomprehended by them, and requires a
long focal distance to be seen; suggests, as Aristotle, Bacon, Selden,[1] Humboldt, that a certain
vastness of learning, or *quasi* omnipresence of
the human soul in nature, is possible. His superb
speculation, as from a tower, over nature and
arts, without ever losing sight of the texture and
sequence of things, almost realizes his own picture, in the " Principia," of the original integrity
of man. Over and above the merit of his partic-

ular discoveries, is the capital merit of his self-equality. A drop of water has the properties of the sea, but cannot exhibit a storm. There is beauty of a concert, as well as of a flute ; strength of a host, as well as of a hero ; and, in Swedenborg, those who are best acquainted with modern books will most admire the merit of mass. One of the missouriums and mastodons of literature, he is not to be measured by whole colleges of ordinary scholars. His stalwart presence would flutter the gowns of an university. Our books are false by being fragmentary : their sentences are *bonmots*, and not parts of natural discourse ; childish expressions of surprise or pleasure in nature ; or, worse, owing a brief notoriety to their petulance, or aversion from the order of nature ; — being some curiosity or oddity, designedly not in harmony with nature and purposely framed to excite surprise, as jugglers do by concealing their means. But Swedenborg is systematic and respective of the world in every sentence ; all the means are orderly given ; his faculties work with astronomic punctuality, and this admirable writing is pure from all pertness or egotism.

Swedenborg was born into an atmosphere of great ideas. It is hard to say what was his own :

yet his life was dignified by noblest pictures of
the universe. The robust Aristotelian method,
with its breadth and adequateness, shaming our
sterile and linear logic by its genial radiation,
conversant with series and degree, with effects
and ends, skilful to discriminate power from
form, essence from accident, and opening, by
its terminology and definition, high roads into
nature, had trained a race of athletic philosophers. Harvey had shown the circulation of the
blood; Gilbert had shown that the earth was a
magnet; Descartes, taught by Gilbert's magnet,
with its vortex, spiral and polarity, had filled
Europe with the leading thought of vortical
motion, as the secret of nature.[1] Newton, in the
year in which Swedenborg was born, published
the " Principia," and established the universal
gravity. Malpighi, following the high doctrines
of Hippocrates, Leucippus and Lucretius, had
given emphasis to the dogma that nature works
in leasts, — " tota in minimis existit natura." [2]
Unrivalled dissectors, Swammerdam, Leuwenhoek, Winslow, Eustachius, Heister, Vesalius,
Boerhaave, had left nothing for scalpel or microscope to reveal in human or comparative anatomy :[3] Linnæus, his contemporary, was affirming, in his beautiful science, that " Nature is

always like herself: "'and, lastly, the nobility of method, the largest application of principles, had been exhibited by Leibnitz and Christian Wolff, in cosmology; whilst Locke and Grotius had drawn the moral argument. What was left for a genius of the largest calibre but to go over their ground and verify and unite? It is easy to see, in these minds, the origin of Swedenborg's studies, and the suggestion of his problems. He had a capacity to entertain and vivify these volumes of thought. Yet the proximity of these geniuses, one or other of whom had introduced all his leading ideas, makes Swedenborg another example of the difficulty, even in a highly fertile genius, of proving originality, the first birth and annunciation of one of the laws of nature.

He named his favorite views the doctrine of Forms, the doctrine of Series and Degrees, the doctrine of Influx, the doctrine of Correspondence. His statement of these doctrines deserves to be studied in his books. Not every man can read them, but they will reward him who can. His theologic works are valuable to illustrate these. His writings would be a sufficient library to a lonely and athletic student; and the " Economy of the Animal Kingdom " is one of those books which, by the sustained dignity of thinking, is an honor to the human race. He had studied spars and metals to some purpose. His varied and solid knowledge makes his style lustrous with points and shooting spiculæ of thought, and resembling one of those winter mornings when the air sparkles with crystals. The grandeur of the topics makes the grandeur of the style. He was apt for cosmology, because of that native perception of identity which made mere size of no account to him. In the atom of magnetic iron he saw the quality which would generate the spiral motion of sun and planet.

The thoughts in which he lived were, the universality of each law in nature; the Platonic doctrine of the scale or degrees; the version or conversion of each into other, and so the correspondence of all the parts; the fine secret that little explains large, and large, little; the centrality of man in nature, and the connection that subsists throughout all things: he saw that the human body was strictly universal, or an instrument through which the soul feeds and is fed by the whole of matter; so that he held, in exact antagonism to the skeptics, that "the wiser a man is, the more will he be a worshipper of the Deity." In short, he was a believer in the Identity-philosophy, which he held not idly, as the dreamers of Berlin or Boston, but which he experimented with and established through years of labor, with the heart and strength of the rudest Viking that his rough Sweden ever sent to , battle.

This theory dates from the oldest philosophers, and derives perhaps its best illustration from the newest. It is this, that Nature iterates her means perpetually on successive planes. In the old aphorism, *nature is always self-similar*. In the plant, the eye or germinative point opens to a leaf, then to another leaf, with a power of transforming the leaf into radicle, stamen, pistil, petal, bract, sepal, or seed. The whole art of the plant is still to repeat leaf on leaf without end, the more or less of heat, light, moisture and food determining the form it shall assume. In the animal, nature makes a vertebra, or a spine of vertebræ, and helps herself still by a new spine, with a limited power of modifying its form, — spine on spine, to the end of the world. A poetic anatomist, in our own day, teaches that a snake, being a horizontal line, and man, being an erect line, constitute a right angle; and between the lines of this mystical quadrant all animated beings find their place: and he assumes the hair-worm, the span-worm, or the snake, as the type or prediction of the spine. Manifestly, at the end of the spine, Nature puts out smaller spines, as arms; at the end of the arms, new spines, as hands; at the other end, she repeats the process, as legs and feet. At the top of the column she puts out another spine, which doubles or loops itself over, as a span-worm, into a ball, and forms the skull, with extremities again : the hands being now the upper jaw, the feet the lower jaw, the fingers and toes being represented this time by upper and lower teeth.[1] This new spine is destined to high uses. It is a new man on the shoulders of the last. It can almost shed its trunk and manage to live alone, according to the Platonic idea in the Timæus. Within it, on a higher plane, all that was done in the trunk repeats itself. Nature recites her lesson once more in a higher mood. The mind is a finer body, and resumes its functions of feeding, digesting, absorbing, excluding and generating, in a new and ethereal element. Here in the brain is all the process of alimentation repeated, in the acquiring, comparing, digesting and assimilating of experience. Here again is the mystery of generation repeated. In the brain are male and female faculties ; here is marriage, here is fruit. And there is no limit to this ascending scale, but series on series. Every thing, at the end of one use, is taken up into the next, each series punctually repeating every organ and process of the last. We are adapted to infinity. We are hard to please, and love nothing which ends; and in nature is no end, but every thing at the end of one use is lifted into a superior, and the ascent of these things climbs into dæmonic and celestial natures.[1] Creative force, like a musical composer, goes on unweariedly repeating a simple air or theme, now high, now low, in solo, in chorus, ten thousand times reverberated, till it fills earth and heaven with the chant.

Gravitation, as explained by Newton, is good, but grander when we find chemistry only an extension of the law of masses into particles, and that the atomic theory shows the action of chemistry to be mechanical also. Metaphysics shows us a sort of gravitation operative also in the mental phenomena; and the terrible tabulation of the French statists brings every piece of whim and humor to be reducible also to exact numerical ratios. If one man in twenty thousand, or in thirty thousand, eats shoes or marries his grandmother, then in every twenty thousand or thirty thousand is found one man who eats shoes or marries his grandmother. What

we call gravitation, and fancy ultimate, is one
fork of a mightier stream for which we have yet
no name. Astronomy is excellent; but it must
come up into life to have its full value, and not
remain there in globes and spaces. The globule
of blood gyrates around its own axis in the human
veins, as the planet in the sky; and the circles
of intellect relate to those of the heavens. Each
law of nature has the like universality; eating,
sleep or hybernation, rotation, generation, meta-
morphosis, vortical motion, which is seen in
eggs as in planets. These grand rhymes or returns in nature, — the dear, best-known face
startling us at every turn, under a mask so unexpected that we think it the face of a stranger,
and carrying up the semblance into divine
forms, — delighted the prophetic eye of Swedenborg; and he must be reckoned a leader in
that revolution, which, by giving to science an
idea, has given to an aimless accumulation of
experiments, guidance and form and a beating
heart.

I own with some regret that his printed works
amount to about fifty stout octavos, his scientific works being about half of the whole number;
and it appears that a mass of manuscript still
unedited remains in the royal library at Stock-

holm. The scientific works have just now been translated into English, in an excellent edition.

Swedenborg printed these scientific books in the ten years from 1734 to 1744, and they remained from that time neglected ; and now, after their century is complete, he has at last found a pupil in Mr. Wilkinson, in London, a philosophic critic, with a coequal vigor of understanding and imagination comparable only to Lord Bacon's, who has restored his master's buried books to the day, and transferred them, with every advantage, from their forgotten Latin into English, to go round the world in our commercial and conquering tongue. This startling reappearance of Swedenborg, after a hundred years, in his pupil, is not the least remarkable fact in his history. Aided it is said by the munificence of Mr. Clissold, and also by his literary skill, this piece of poetic justice is done. The admirable preliminary discourses with which Mr. Wilkinson has enriched these volumes, throw all the contemporary philosophy of England into shade, and leave me nothing to say on their proper grounds.[1]

The " Animal Kingdom " is a book of wonderful merits. It was written with the highest end, — to put science and the soul, long es-

tranged from each other, at one again. It was
an anatomist's account of the human body, in
the highest style of poetry. Nothing can exceed
the bold and brilliant treatment of a subject
usually so dry and repulsive.[1] He saw nature
" wreathing through an everlasting spiral, with
wheels that never dry, on axles that never creak,"
and sometimes sought " to uncover those secret
recesses where Nature is sitting at the fires in the
depths of her laboratory ; " whilst the picture
comes recommended by the hard fidelity with
which it is based on practical anatomy. It is remarkable that this sublime genius decides peremptorily for the analytic, against the synthetic
method ; and, in a book whose genius is a daring
poetic synthesis, claims to confine himself to a
rigid experience.

He knows, if he only, the flowing of nature,
and how wise was that old answer of Amasis to
him who bade him drink up the sea, — "Yes,
willingly, if you will stop the rivers that flow
in." [2] Few knew as much about nature and her
subtle manners, or expressed more subtly her
goings. He thought as large a demand is made
on our faith by nature, as by miracles. "He
noted that in her proceeding from first principles through her several subordinations, there

was no state through which she did not pass, as
if her path lay through all things." "For as
often as she betakes herself upward from visible
phenomena, or, in other words, withdraws herself inward, she instantly as it were disappears,
while no one knows what has become of her, or
whither she is gone: so that it is necessary to
take science as a guide in pursuing her steps."

The pursuing the inquiry under the light of
an end or final cause gives wonderful animation,
a sort of personality to the whole writing. This
book announces his favorite dogmas. The ancient doctrine of Hippocrates, that the brain is a
gland; and of Leucippus, that the atom may be
known by the mass; or, in Plato, the macrocosm
by the microcosm; and, in the verses of Lucretius, —

> Ossa videlicet e pauxillis atque minutis
> Ossibus sic et de pauxillis atque minutis
> Visceribus viscus gigni, sanguenque creari
> Sanguinis inter se multis coeuntibus guttis;
> Ex aurique putat micis consistere posse
> Aurum, et de terris terram concrescere parvis;
> Ignibus ex igneis, humorem humoribus esse.[1]

> " The principle of all things, entrails made
> Of smallest entrails; bone, of smallest bone;
> Blood, of small sanguine drops reduced to one;

Gold, of small grains ; earth, of small sands compacted ;
Small drops to water, sparks to fire contracted : ''

and which Malpighi had summed in his maxim
that "nature exists entire in leasts," — is a favorite thought of Swedenborg. "It is a constant
law of the organic body that large, compound,
or visible forms exist and subsist from smaller,
simpler and ultimately from invisible forms,
which act similarly to the larger ones, but more
perfectly and more universally ; and the least
forms so perfectly and universally as to involve
an idea representative of their entire universe."
The unities of each organ are so many little
organs, homogeneous with their compound : the
unities of the tongue are little tongues ; those of
the stomach, little stomachs ; those of the heart
are little hearts. This fruitful idea furnishes a
key to every secret. What was too small for the
eye to detect was read by the aggregates ; what
was too large, by the units. There is no end to
his application of the thought. "Hunger is an
aggregate of very many little hungers, or losses
of blood by the little veins all over the body."
It is a key to his theology also. "Man is a kind
of very minute heaven, corresponding to the
world of spirits and to heaven. Every particular
idea of man, and every affection, yea, every

smallest part of his affection, is an image and effigy of him. A spirit may be known from only a single thought. God is the grand man."

The hardihood and thoroughness of his study of nature required a theory of forms also. " Forms ascend in order from the lowest to the highest. The lowest form is angular, or the terrestrial and corporeal. The second and next higher form is the circular, which is also called the perpetual-angular, because the circumference of a circle is a perpetual angle. The form above this is the spiral, parent and measure of circular forms: its diameters are not rectilinear, but variously circular, and have a spherical surface for centre ; therefore it is called the perpetual-circular. The form above this is the vortical, or perpetual-spiral : next, the perpetual-vortical, or celestial : last, the perpetual-celestial, or spiritual."

Was it strange that a genius so bold should take the last step also, should conceive that he might attain the science of all sciences, to unlock the meaning of the world? In the first volume of the " Animal Kingdom," he broaches the subject in a remarkable note : — " In our doctrine of Representations and Correspondences we shall treat of both these symbolical

and typical resemblances, and of the astonishing
things which occur, I will not say in the living
body only, but throughout nature, and which
correspond so entirely to supreme and spiritual
things that one would swear that the physical
world was purely symbolical of the spiritual
world; insomuch that if we choose to express
any natural truth in physical and definite vocal
terms, and to convert these terms only into the
corresponding and spiritual terms, we shall by
this means elicit a spiritual truth or theological
dogma, in place of the physical truth or precept: although no mortal would have predicted
that any thing of the kind could possibly arise
by bare literal transposition; inasmuch as the
one precept, considered separately from the
other, appears to have absolutely no relation to
it. I intend hereafter to communicate a number
of examples of such correspondences, together
with a vocabulary containing the terms of spiritual things, as well as of the physical things for
which they are to be substituted. This symbolism pervades the living body."

The fact thus explicitly stated is implied in
all poetry, in allegory, in fable, in the use of
emblems and in the structure of language.
Plato knew it, as is evident from his twice bi-

sected line in the sixth book of the Republic. Lord Bacon had found that truth and nature differed only as seal and print; and he instanced some physical propositions, with their translation into a moral or political sense. Behmen, and all mystics, imply this law in their dark riddle-writing. The poets, in as far as they are poets, use it; but it is known to them only as the magnet was known for ages, as a toy. Swedenborg first put the fact into a detached and scientific statement, because it was habitually present to him, and never not seen. It was involved, as we explained already, in the doctrine of identity and iteration, because the mental series exactly tallies with the material series. It required an insight that could rank things in order and series; or rather it required such rightness of position that the poles of the eye should coincide with the axis of the world. The earth had fed its mankind through five or six millenniums, and they had sciences, religions, philosophies, and yet had failed to see the correspondence of meaning between every part and every other part. And, down to this hour, literature has no book in which the symbolism of things is scientifically opened. One would say that as soon as men had the first hint that

every sensible object, — animal, rock, river, air,
— nay, space and time, subsists not for itself,
nor finally to a material end, but as a picture-
language to tell another story of beings and
duties, other science would be put by, and a
science of such grand presage would absorb all
faculties : that each man would ask of all objects what they mean : Why does the horizon
hold me fast, with my joy and grief, in this
centre? Why hear I the same sense from count-
less differing voices, and read one never quite
expressed fact in endless picture-language? Yet
whether it be that these things will not be intellectually learned, or that many centuries must
elaborate and compose so rare and opulent a
soul, — there is no comet, rock-stratum, fossil,
fish, quadruped, spider, or fungus, that, for itself, does not interest more scholars and classi-
fiers than the meaning and upshot of the frame
of things.[1]

But Swedenborg was not content with the
culinary use of the world. In his fifty-fourth
year these thoughts held him fast, and his profound mind admitted the perilous opinion, too
frequent in religious history, that he was an ab-
normal person, to whom was granted the privilege of conversing with angels and spirits ; and

this ecstasy connected itself with just this office of explaining the moral import of the sensible world. To a right perception, at once broad and minute, of the order of .nature, he added the comprehension of the moral laws in their widest social aspects ; but whatever he saw, through some excessive determination to form in his constitution, he saw not abstractly, but in pictures, heard it in dialogues, constructed it in events. When he attempted to announce the law most sanely, he was forced to couch it in parable.

Modern psychology offers no similar example of a deranged balance. The principal powers continued to maintain a healthy action, and to a reader who can make due allowance in the report for the reporter's peculiarities, the results are still instructive, and a more striking testimony to the sublime laws he announced than any that balanced dulness could afford. He attempts to give some account of the *modus* of the new state, affirming that " his presence in the spiritual world is attended with a certain separation, but only as to the intellectual part of his mind, not as to the will part ; " and he affirms that " he sees, with the internal sight, the things that are in another life, more clearly than he sees the things which are here in the world."

Having adopted the belief that certain books of the Old and New Testaments were exact allegories, or written in the angelic and ecstatic mode, he employed his remaining years in extricating from the literal, the universal sense. He had borrowed from Plato the fine fable of "a most ancient people, men better than we and dwelling nigher to the gods;"[1] and Swedenborg added that they used the earth symbolically; that these, when they saw terrestrial objects, did not think at all about them, but only about those which they signified. The correspondence between thoughts and things henceforward occupied him. "The very organic form resembles the end inscribed on it." A man is in general and in particular an organized justice or injustice, selfishness or gratitude. And the cause of this harmony he assigned in the Arcana: "The reason why all and single things, in the heavens and on earth, are representative, is because they exist from an influx of the Lord, through heaven." This design of exhibiting such correspondences, which, if adequately executed, would be the poem of the world, in which all history and science would play an essential part, was narrowed and defeated by the exclusively theologic direction which his inquiries took. His perception of nature is not human and universal, but is mystical and Hebraic. He fastens each natural object to a theologic notion ; — a horse signifies carnal understanding ; a tree, perception ; the moon, faith ; a cat means this ; an ostrich that ; an artichoke this other ; — and poorly tethers every symbol to a several ecclesiastic sense. The slippery Proteus is not so easily caught. In nature, each individual symbol plays innumerable parts, as each particle of matter circulates in turn through every system. The central identity enables any one symbol to express successively all the qualities and shades of real being. In the transmission of the heavenly waters, every hose fits every hydrant. Nature avenges herself speedily on the hard pedantry that would chain her waves. She is no literalist. Every thing must be taken genially, and we must be at the top of our condition to understand any thing rightly.[1]

His theological bias thus fatally narrowed his interpretation of nature, and the dictionary of symbols is yet to be written. But the interpreter whom mankind must still expect, will find no predecessor who has approached so near to the true problem.

Swedenborg styles himself in the title-page

of his books, "Servant of the Lord Jesus
Christ;" and by force of intellect, and in effect,
he is the last Father in the Church, and is not
likely to have a successor. No wonder that his
depth of ethical wisdom should give him influence as a teacher. To the withered traditional
church, yielding dry catechisms, he let in nature
again, and the worshipper, escaping from the
vestry of verbs and texts, is surprised to find
himself a party to the whole of his religion.
His religion thinks for him and is of universal
application. He turns it on every side; it fits
every part of life, interprets and dignifies every
circumstance.[1] Instead of a religion which visited him diplomatically three or four times, —
when he was born, when he married, when he fell
sick and when he died, and, for the rest, never
interfered with him, — here was a teaching which
accompanied him all day, accompanied him even
into sleep and dreams; into his thinking, and
showed him through what a long ancestry his
thoughts descend; into society, and showed by
what affinities he was girt to his equals and his
counterparts; into natural objects, and showed
their origin and meaning, what are friendly, and
what are hurtful; and opened the future world
by indicating the continuity of the same laws.

His disciples allege that their intellect is invigorated by the study of his books.

There is no such problem for criticism as his theological writings, their merits are so commanding, yet such grave deductions must be made. Their immense and sandy diffuseness is like the prairie or the desert, and their incongruities are like the last deliration. He is superfluously explanatory, and his feeling of the ignorance of men, strangely exaggerated. Men take truths of this nature very fast. Yet he abounds in assertions, he is a rich discoverer, and of things which most import us to know. His thought dwells in essential resemblances, like the resemblance of a house to the man who built it. He saw things in their law, in likeness of function, not of structure. There is an invariable method and order in his delivery of his truth, the habitual proceeding of the mind from inmost to outmost. What earnestness and weightiness, — his eye never roving, without one swell of vanity, or one look to self in any common form of literary pride! a theoretic or speculative man, but whom no practical man in the universe could affect to scorn. Plato is a gownsman; his garment, though of purple, and almost sky-woven, is an academic robe and hinders action with its voluminous folds. But this mystic is awful to Cæsar. Lycurgus himself would bow.

The moral insight of Swedenborg, the correction of popular errors, the announcement of ethical laws, take him out of comparison with any other modern writer and entitle him to a place, vacant for some ages, among the lawgivers of mankind. That slow but commanding influence which he has acquired, like that of other religious geniuses, must be excessive also, and have its tides, before it subsides into a permanent amount. Of course what is real and universal cannot be confined to the circle of those who sympathize strictly with his genius, but will pass forth into the common stock of wise and just thinking. The world has a sure chemistry, by which it extracts what is excellent in its children and lets fall the infirmities and limitations of the grandest mind.[1]

That metempsychosis which is familiar in the old mythology of the Greeks, collected in Ovid and in the Indian Transmigration, and is there *objective*, or really takes place in bodies by alien will, — in Swedenborg's mind has a more philosophic character. It is subjective, or depends entirely upon the thought of the person. All

things in the universe arrange themselves to each
person anew, according to his ruling love. Man
is such as his affection and thought are. Man is
man by virtue of willing, not by virtue of knowing and understanding. As he is, so he sees.
The marriages of the world are broken up. In-
teriors associate all in the spiritual world. Whatever the angels looked upon was to them celestial.
Each Satan appears to himself a man; to those
as bad as he, a comely man; to the purified, a
heap of carrion. Nothing can resist states: every
thing gravitates: like will to like: what we call
poetic justice takes effect on the spot. We have
come into a world which is a living poem. Every
thing is as I am. Bird and beast is not bird and
beast, but emanation and effluvia of the minds
and wills of men there present. Every one makes
his own house and state. The ghosts are tor-
mented with the fear of death and cannot remember that they have died. They who are in evil
and falsehood are afraid of all others. Such as
have deprived themselves of charity, wander and
flee: the societies which they approach discover
their quality and drive them away. The covet-
ous seem to themselves to be abiding in cells
where their money is deposited, and these to be
infested with mice. They who place merit in

good works seem to themselves to cut wood. " I asked such, if they were not wearied? They replied, that they have not yet done work enough to merit heaven."

He delivers golden sayings which express with singular beauty the ethical laws; as when he uttered that famed sentence, that " In heaven the angels are advancing continually to the spring-time of their youth, so that the oldest angel appears the youngest:" " The more angels, the more room:" "The perfection of man is the love of use:" " Man, in his perfect form, is heaven:" "What is from Him, is Him:" " Ends always ascend as nature descends." And the truly poetic account of the writing in the inmost heaven, which, as it consists of in-flexions according to the form of heaven, can be read without instruction. He almost justifies his claim to preternatural vision, by strange insights of the structure of the human body and mind. " It is never permitted to any one, in heaven, to stand behind another and look at the back of his head; for then the influx which is from the Lord is disturbed." The angels, from the sound of the voice, know a man's love; from the articulation of the sound, his wisdom; and from the sense of the words, his science.

In the " Conjugal Love," he has unfolded the science of marriage. Of this book one would say that with the highest elements it has failed of success. It came near to be the Hymn of Love, which Plato attempted in the " Banquet;" the love, which, Dante says, Casella sang among the angels in Paradise; [1] and which, as rightly celebrated, in its genesis, fruition and effect, might well entrance the souls, as it would lay open the genesis of all institutions, customs and manners. The book had been grand if the Hebraism had been omitted and the law stated without Gothicism, as ethics, and with that scope for ascension of state which the nature of things requires. It is a fine Platonic development of the science of marriage; teaching that sex is universal, and not local; virility in the male qualifying every organ, act, and thought; and the feminine in woman. Therefore in the real or spiritual world the nuptial union is not momentary, but incessant and total; and chastity not a local, but a universal virtue; unchastity being discovered as much in the trading, or planting, or speaking, or philosophizing, as in generation; and that, though the virgins he saw in heaven were beautiful, the wives were incomparably more beautiful, and went on increasing in beauty evermore.

Yet Swedenborg, after his mode, pinned his theory to a temporary form. He exaggerates the circumstance of marriage ; and though he finds false marriages on earth, fancies a wiser choice in heaven. But of progressive souls, all loves and friendships are momentary. *Do you love me?* means, Do you see the same truth? If you do, we are happy with the same happiness : but presently one of us passes into the perception of new truth ; — we are divorced, and no tension in nature can hold us to each other. I know how delicious is this cup of love, — I existing for you, you existing for me ; but it is a child's clinging to his toy ; an attempt to eternize the fireside and nuptial chamber ; to keep the picture-alphabet through which our first lessons are prettily conveyed. The Eden of God is bare and grand: like the out-door landscape remembered from the evening fireside, it seems cold and desolate whilst you cower over the coals, but once abroad again, we pity those who can forego the magnificence of nature for candle-light and cards. Perhaps the true subject of the " Conjugal Love " is *Conversation*, whose laws are profoundly set forth. It is false, if literally applied to marriage. For God is the bride or bridegroom of the soul. Heaven is not the pairing of two, but the communion of all souls. We meet, and dwell an instant under the temple of one thought, and part, as though we parted not, to join another thought in other fellowships of joy. So far from there being anything divine in the low and proprietary sense of *Do you love me?* it is only when you leave and lose me by casting yourself on a sentiment which is higher than both of us, that I draw near and find myself at your side; and I am repelled if you fix your eye on me and demand love. In fact, in the spiritual world we change sexes every moment. You love the worth in me; then I am your husband: but it is not me, but the worth, that fixes the love; and that worth is a drop of the ocean of worth that is beyond me. Meantime I adore the greater worth in another, and so become his wife. He aspires to a higher worth in another spirit, and is wife or receiver of that influence.'

Whether from a self-inquisitorial habit that he grew into from jealousy of the sins to which men of thought are liable, he has acquired, in disentangling and demonstrating that particular form of moral disease, an acumen which no conscience can resist. I refer to his feeling of the profanation of thinking to what is good, " from scien-

tifics." " To reason about faith, is to doubt and
deny." He was painfully alive to the difference
between knowing and doing, and this sensibility
is incessantly expressed. Philosophers are, therefore, vipers, cockatrices, asps, hemorrhoids, pres-
ters, and flying serpents; literary men are con-
jurors and charlatans.

But this topic suggests a sad afterthought, that
here we find the seat of his own pain. Possibly
Swedenborg paid the penalty of introverted faculties. Success, or a fortunate genius, seems to
depend on a happy adjustment of heart and
brain; on a due proportion, hard to hit, of moral
and mental power, which perhaps obeys the law
of those chemical ratios which make a proportion in volumes necessary to combination, as
when gases will combine in certain fixed rates,
but not at any rate. It is hard to carry a full
cup; and this man, profusely endowed in heart
and mind, early fell into dangerous discord with
himself. In his Animal Kingdom he surprised
us by declaring that he loved analysis, and not
synthesis; and now, after his fiftieth year, he
falls into jealousy of his intellect; and though
aware that truth is not solitary nor is goodness
solitary, but both must ever mix and marry, he
makes war on his mind, takes the part of the con-

science against it, and, on all occasions, traduces
and blasphemes it. The violence is instantly
avenged. Beauty is disgraced, love is unlovely,
when truth, the half part of heaven, is denied,
as much as when a bitterness in men of talent
leads to satire and destroys the judgment. He
is wise, but wise in his own despite. There is
an air of infinite grief and the sound of wailing
all over and through this lurid universe. A
vampyre sits in the seat of the prophet and turns
with gloomy appetite to the images of pain. Indeed, a bird does not more readily weave its nest,
or a mole bore into the ground, than this seer
of the souls substructs a new hell and pit, each
more abominable than the last, round every new
crew of offenders. He was let down through a
column that seemed of brass, but it was formed
of angelic spirits, that he might descend safely
amongst the unhappy, and witness the vastation
of souls and hear there, for a long continuance,
their lamentations : he saw their tormentors,
who increase and strain pangs to infinity ; he saw
the hell of the jugglers, the hell of the assassins,
the hell of the lascivious; the hell of robbers,
who kill and boil men ; the infernal tun of the
deceitful ; the excrementitious hells ; the hell of
the revengeful, whose faces resembled a round,

broad cake, and their arms rotate like a wheel. Except Rabelais and Dean Swift nobody ever had such science of filth and corruption.

These books should be used with caution. It is dangerous to sculpture these evanescing images of thought. True in transition, they become false if fixed. It requires, for his just apprehension, almost a genius equal to his own. But when his visions become the stereotyped language of multitudes of persons of all degrees of age and capacity, they are perverted. The wise people of the Greek race were accustomed to lead the most intelligent and virtuous young men, as part of their education, through the Eleusinian mysteries, wherein, with much pomp and graduation, the highest truths known to ancient wisdom were taught. An ardent and contemplative young man, at eighteen or twenty years, might read once these books of Swedenborg, these mysteries of love and conscience, and then throw them aside for ever.[1] Genius is ever haunted by similar dreams, when the hells and the heavens are opened to it. But these pictures are to be held as mystical, that is, as a quite arbitrary and accidental picture of the truth, — not as the truth. Any other symbol would be as good ; then this is safely seen.

Swedenborg's system of the world wants central spontaneity; it is dynamic, not vital, and lacks power to generate life. There is no individual in it. The universe is a gigantic crystal, all whose atoms and laminæ lie in uninterrupted order and with unbroken unity, but cold and still. What seems an individual and a will, is none. There is an immense chain of intermediation, extending from centre to extremes, which bereaves every agency of all freedom and character.[1] The universe, in his poem, suffers under a magnetic sleep, and only reflects the mind of the magnetizer. Every thought comes into each mind by influence from a society of spirits that surround it, and into these from a higher society, and so on. All his types mean the same few things. All his figures speak one speech. All his interlocutors Swedenborgize. Be they who they may, to this complexion must they come at last. This Charon ferries them all over in his boat; kings, counsellors, cavaliers, doctors, Sir Isaac Newton, Sir Hans Sloane, King George II., Mahomet, or whomsoever, and all gather one grimness of hue and style. Only when Cicero comes by, our gentle seer sticks a little at saying he talked with Cicero, and with a touch of human relenting remarks, "one

whom it was given me to believe was Cicero;"
and when the *soi disant* Roman opens his
mouth, Rome and eloquence have ebbed away,
— it is plain theologic Swedenborg like the rest.
His heavens and hells are dull; fault of want
of individualism. The thousand-fold relation
of men is not there. The interest that attaches
in nature to each man, because he is right by his
wrong, and wrong by his right; because he de-
fies all dogmatizing and classification, so many
allowances and contingences and futurities are
to be taken into account; strong by his vices,
often paralyzed by his virtues;—sinks into
entire sympathy with his society. This want re-
acts to the centre of the system. Though the
agency of "the Lord" is in every line referred
to by name, it never becomes alive. There is no
lustre in that eye which gazes from the centre
and which should vivify the immense depend-
ency of beings.[1]

The vice of Swedenborg's mind is its theologic determination. Nothing with him has the
liberality of universal wisdom, but we are always
in a church. That Hebrew muse, which taught
the lore of right and wrong to men, had the
same excess of influence for him it has had for
the nations. The mode, as well as the essence,

was sacred. Palestine is ever the more valuable as a chapter in universal history, and ever the less an available element in education.[1] The genius of Swedenborg, largest of all modern souls in this department of thought, wasted itself in the endeavor to reanimate and conserve what had already arrived at its natural term, and, in the great secular Providence, was retiring from its prominence, before Western modes of thought and expression. Swedenborg and Behmen both failed by attaching themselves to the Christian symbol, instead of to the moral sentiment, which carries innumerable christianities, humanities, divinities, in its bosom.

The excess of influence shows itself in the incongruous importation of a foreign rhetoric. 'What have I to do,' asks the impatient reader, 'with jasper and sardonyx, beryl and chalcedony; what with arks and passovers, ephahs and ephods; what with lepers and emerods; what with heave-offerings and unleavened bread, chariots of fire, dragons crowned and horned, behemoth and unicorn? Good for Orientals, these are nothing to me. The more learning you bring to explain them, the more glaring the impertinence. The more coherent and elaborate the system, the less I like it. I say, with the Spartan, "Why do you speak so much to the purpose, of that which is nothing to the purpose?"[1] My learning is such as God gave me in my birth and habit, in the delight and study of my eyes and not of another man's. Of all absurdities, this of some foreigner proposing to take away my rhetoric and substitute his own, and amuse me with pelican and stork, instead of thrush and robin; palm-trees and shittim-wood, instead of sassafras and hickory, — seems the most needless.'

Locke said, "God, when he makes the prophet, does not unmake the man." Swedenborg's history points the remark. The parish disputes in the Swedish church between the friends and foes of Luther and Melancthon, concerning "faith alone" and "works alone," intrude themselves into his speculations upon the economy of the universe, and of the celestial societies. The Lutheran bishop's son, for whom the heavens are opened, so that he sees with eyes and in the richest symbolic forms the awful truth of things, and utters again in his books, as under a heavenly mandate, the indisputable secrets of moral nature, — with all these grandeurs resting upon him, remains the Lutheran bishop's son; his judgments are those

of a Swedish polemic, and his vast enlargements
purchased by adamantine limitations. He carries his controversial memory with him in his
visits to the souls. He is like Michael Angelo,
who, in his frescoes, put the cardinal who had
offended him to roast under a mountain of devils; or like Dante, who avenged, in vindictive
melodies, all his private wrongs; or perhaps
still more like Montaigne's parish priest, who,
if a hail-storm passes over the village, thinks
the day of doom is come, and the cannibals already have got the pip. Swedenborg confounds
us not less with the pains of Melancthon and
Luther and Wolfius, and his own books, which
he advertises among the angels.

Under the same theologic cramp, many of his
dogmas are bound. His cardinal position in
morals is that evils should be shunned as sins.
But he does not know what evil is, or what good
is, who thinks any ground remains to be occupied, after saying that evil is to be shunned as
evil. I doubt not he was led by the desire to
insert the element of personality of Deity. But
nothing is added. One man, you say, dreads
erysipelas, — show him that this dread is evil:
or, one dreads hell, — show him that *dread* is
evil. He who loves goodness, harbors angels,

reveres reverence and lives with God. The less we have to do with our sins the better. No man can afford to waste his moments in compunctions. "That is active duty," say the Hindoos, "which is not for our bondage; that is knowledge, which is for our liberation: all other duty is good only unto weariness."

Another dogma, growing out of this pernicious theologic limitation, is his Inferno. Swedenborg has devils. Evil, according to old philosophers, is good in the making. That pure malignity can exist is the extreme proposition of unbelief. It is not to be entertained by a rational agent; it is atheism; it is the last profanation. Euripides rightly said, —

"Goodness and being in the gods are one;
He who imputes ill to them makes them none." [1]

To what a painful perversion had Gothic theology arrived, that Swedenborg admitted no conversion for evil spirits! But the divine effort is never relaxed; the carrion in the sun will convert itself to grass and flowers; and man, though in brothels, or jails, or on gibbets, is on his way to all that is good and true. [2] Burns, with the wild humor of his apostrophe to poor "auld Nickie Ben,"

"O wad ye tak a thought, and mend!"

has the advantage of the vindictive theologian. Every thing is superficial and perishes but love and truth only. The largest is always the truest sentiment, and we feel the more generous spirit of the Indian Vishnu, — "I am the same to all mankind. There is not one who is worthy of my love or hatred. They who serve me with adoration, — I am in them, and they in me. If one whose ways are altogether evil serve me alone, he is as respectable as the just man ; he is altogether well employed ; he soon becometh of a virtuous spirit and obtaineth eternal happiness."

For the anomalous pretension of Revelations of the other world, — only his probity and genius can entitle it to any serious regard. His revelations destroy their credit by running into detail. If a man say that the Holy Ghost has informed him that the Last Judgment (or the last of the judgments) took place in 1757; or that the Dutch, in the other world, live in a heaven by themselves, and the English in a heaven by themselves; I reply that the Spirit which is holy is reserved, taciturn, and deals in laws. The rumors of ghosts and hobgoblins gossip and tell fortunes. The teachings of the high Spirit are abstemious, and, in regard to

particulars, negative. Socrates's Genius did not
advise him to act or to find, but if he purposed
to do somewhat not advantageous, it dissuaded
him. "What God is," he said, "I know not;
what he is not, I know." The Hindoos have
denominated the Supreme Being, the "Internal
Check." The illuminated Quakers explained
their Light, not as somewhat which leads to any
action, but it appears as an obstruction to any
thing unfit.' But the right examples are private
experiences, which are absolutely at one on this
point. Strictly speaking, Swedenborg's revelation is a confounding of planes, — a capital offence in so learned a categorist. This is to carry
the law of surface into the plane of substance,
to carry individualism and its fopperies into the
realm of essences and generals, — which is dislo-
cation and chaos.

The secret of heaven is kept from age to age.
No imprudent, no sociable angel ever dropt an
early syllable to answer the longings of saints,
the fears of mortals. We should have listened
on our knees to any favorite, who, by stricter
obedience, had brought his thoughts into parallelism with the celestial currents and could hint
to human ears the scenery and circumstance of
the newly parted soul. But it is certain that it

must tally with what is best in nature. It must not be inferior in tone to the already known works of the artist who sculptures the globes of the firmament and writes the moral law. It must be fresher than rainbows, stabler than mountains, agreeing with flowers, with tides and the rising and setting of autumnal stars. Melodious poets shall be hoarse as street ballads when once the penetrating key-note of nature and spirit is sounded, — the earth-beat, sea-beat, heart-beat, which makes the tune to which the sun rolls, and the globule of blood, and the sap of trees.

In this mood we hear the rumor that the seer has arrived, and his tale is told. But there is no beauty, no heaven : for angels, goblins. The sad muse loves night and death and the pit. His Inferno is mesmeric. His spiritual world bears the same relation to the generosities and joys of truth of which human souls have already made us cognizant, as a man's bad dreams bear to his ideal life.[1] It is indeed very like, in its endless power of lurid pictures, to the phenomena of dreaming, which nightly turns many an honest gentleman, benevolent but dyspeptic, into a wretch, skulking like a dog about the outer yards and kennels of creation. When he mounts into the heaven, I do not hear its language. A man should not tell me that he has walked among the angels; his proof is that his eloquence makes me one. Shall the archangels be less majestic and sweet than the figures that have actually walked the earth? These angels that Swedenborg paints give us no very high idea of their discipline and culture : they are all country parsons : their heaven is a *fête champêtre*, an evangelical picnic, or French distribution of prizes to virtuous peasants. Strange, scholastic, didactic, passionless, bloodless man, who denotes classes of souls as a botanist disposes of a carex, and visits doleful hells as a stratum of chalk or hornblende! He has no sympathy. He goes up and down the world of men, a modern Rhadamanthus in gold-headed cane and peruke, and with nonchalance and the air of a referee, distributes souls. The warm, many-weathered, passionate-peopled world is to him a grammar of hieroglyphs, or an emblematic freemason's procession. How different is Jacob Behmen! *he* is tremulous with emotion and listens awe-struck, with the gentlest humanity, to the Teacher whose lessons he conveys; and when he asserts that, "in some sort, love is greater than God," his heart beats so high that the thumping against his leathern coat is

audible across the centuries. 'T is a great difference. Behmen is healthily and beautifully wise,
notwithstanding the mystical narrowness and in-
communicableness.[1] Swedenborg is disagreeably
wise, and with all his accumulated gifts, paralyzes and repels.

It is the best sign of a great nature that it
opens a foreground, and, like the breath of morning landscapes, invites us onward. Swedenborg
is retrospective, nor can we divest him of his
mattock and shroud. Some minds are for ever
restrained from descending into nature ; others
are for ever prevented from ascending out of it.
With a force of many men, he could never break
the umbilical cord which held him to nature, and
he did not rise to the platform of pure genius.

It is remarkable that this man, who, by his
perception of symbols, saw the poetic construction of things and the primary relation of mind
to matter, remained entirely devoid of the whole
apparatus of poetic expression, which that perception creates. He knew the grammar and rudiments of the Mother-Tongue, — how could he
not read off one strain into music ? Was he like
Saadi, who, in his vision, designed to fill his lap
with the celestial flowers, as presents for his
friends ; but the fragrance of the roses so intoxi-

cated him that the skirt dropped from his hands?
or is reporting a breach of the manners of that
heavenly society? or was it that he saw the vision
intellectually, and hence that chiding of the intellectual that pervades his books? Be it as it
may, his books have no melody, no emotion,
no humor, no relief to the dead prosaic level.
In his profuse and accurate imagery is no pleasure, for there is no beauty. We wander forlorn
in a lack-lustre landscape. No bird ever sang in
all these gardens of the dead. The entire want
of poetry in so transcendent a mind betokens
the disease, and like a hoarse voice in a beautiful person, is a kind of warning. I think, sometimes, he will not be read longer. His great name
will turn a sentence. His books have become a
monument. His laurel so largely mixed with
cypress, a charnel-breath so mingles with the
temple incense, that boys and maids will shun
the spot.

Yet in this immolation of genius and fame
at the shrine of conscience, is a merit sublime
beyond praise. He lived to purpose: he gave
a verdict. He elected goodness as the clue to
which the soul must cling in all this labyrinth
of nature. Many opinions conflict as to the true
centre. In the shipwreck, some cling to running

rigging, some to cask and barrel, some to spars, some to mast; the pilot chooses with science, — I plant myself here; all will sink before this; " he comes to land who sails with me." ! Do not rely on heavenly favor, or on compassion to folly, or on prudence, on common sense, the old usage and main chance of men : nothing can keep you, — not fate, nor health, nor admirable intellect ; none can keep you, but rectitude only, rectitude for ever and ever ! And with a tenacity that never swerved in all his studies, inventions, dreams, he adheres to this brave choice. I think of him as of some transmigrating votary of Indian legend, who says 'Though I be dog, or jackal, or pismire, in the last rudiments of nature, under what integument or ferocity, I cleave to right, as the sure ladder that leads up to man and to God.' ²

Swedenborg has rendered a double service to mankind, which is now only beginning to be known. By the science of experiment and use, he made his first steps : he observed and published the laws of nature; and ascending by just degrees from events to their summits and causes, he was fired with piety at the harmonies he felt, and abandoned himself to his joy and worship. This was his first service. If the glory was too

bright for his eyes to bear, if he staggered under
the trance of delight, the more excellent is the
spectacle he saw, the realities of being which
beam and blaze through him, and which no infirmities of the prophet are suffered to obscure;
and he renders a second passive service to men,
not less than the first, perhaps, in the great circle
of being, — and, in the retributions of spiritual
nature, not less glorious or less beautiful to himself.

IV

MONTAIGNE; OR, THE SKEPTIC

MONTAIGNE; OR, THE SKEPTIC

EVERY fact is related on one side to sensation, and on the other to morals. The game of thought is, on the appearance of one of these two sides, to find the other: given the upper, to find the under side. Nothing so thin but has these two faces, and when the observer has seen the obverse, he turns it over to see the reverse.[1] Life is a pitching of this penny,— heads or tails. We never tire of this game, because there is still a slight shudder of astonishment at the exhibition of the other face, at the contrast of the two faces. A man is flushed with success, and bethinks himself what this good luck signifies. He drives his bargain in the street; but it occurs that he also is bought and sold. He sees the beauty of a human face, and searches the cause of that beauty, which must be more beautiful. He builds his fortunes, maintains the laws, cherishes his children; but he asks himself, Why? and whereto? This head and this tail are called, in the language of philosophy, Infinite and Finite; Relative and Absolute; Apparent and Real; and many fine names beside.

Each man is born with a predisposition to one or the other of these sides of nature; and it will easily happen that men will be found devoted to one or the other. One class has the perception of difference, and is conversant with facts and surfaces, cities and persons, and the bringing certain things to pass; — the men of talent and action. Another class have the perception of identity, and are men of faith and philosophy, men of genius.[1]

Each of these riders drives too fast. Plotinus believes only in philosophers; Fenelon, in saints; Pindar and Byron, in poets. Read the haughty language in which Plato and the Platonists speak of all men who are not devoted to their own shining abstractions: other men are rats and mice. The literary class is usually proud and exclusive. The correspondence of Pope and Swift describes mankind around them as monsters; and that of Goethe and Schiller, in our own time, is scarcely more kind.[2]

It is easy to see how this arrogance comes. The genius is a genius by the first look he casts on any object. Is his eye creative? Does he not rest in angles and colors, but beholds the design? — he will presently undervalue the actual object. In powerful moments, his thought has

Montaigne

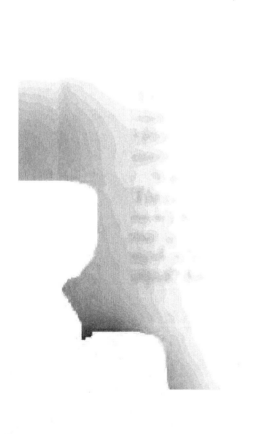

Voicy du grand Montaigne vne entiere figure
Le Peinctre a peinct le corps, et luy son bel esprit:
Le premier par son art égale la Nature
Mais l'aultre la surpasse en-toutce qu'il escrit.
Thomas de Leu fecit.

dissolved the works of art and nature into their causes, so that the works appear heavy and faulty. He has a conception of beauty which the sculptor cannot embody. Picture, statue, temple, railroad, steam-engine, existed first in an artist's mind, without flaw, mistake, or friction, which impair the executed models.[1] So did the Church, the State, college, court, social circle, and all the institutions. It is not strange that these men, remembering what they have seen and hoped of ideas, should affirm disdainfully the superiority of ideas. Having at some time seen that the happy soul will carry all the arts in power, they say, Why cumber ourselves with superfluous realizations? and like dreaming beggars they assume to speak and act as if these values were already substantiated.

On the other part, the men of toil and trade and luxury, — the animal world, including the animal in the philosopher and poet also, and the practical world, including the painful drudgeries which are never excused to philosopher or poet any more than to the rest, — weigh heavily on the other side. The trade in our streets believes in no metaphysical causes, thinks nothing of the force which necessitated traders and a trading planet to exist: no, but sticks to cotton, sugar, wool and salt. The ward meetings, on election days, are not softened by any misgiving of the value of these ballotings.¹ Hot life is streaming in a single direction. To the men of this world, to the animal strength and spirits, to the men of practical power, whilst immersed in it, the man of ideas appears out of his reason. They alone have reason.

Things always bring their own philosophy with them, that is, prudence. No man acquires property without acquiring with it a little arithmetic also. In England, the richest country that ever existed, property stands for more, compared with personal ability, than in any other. After dinner, a man believes less, denies more : verities have lost some charm. After dinner, arithmetic is the only science: ideas are disturbing, incendiary, follies of young men, repudiated by the solid portion of society : and a man comes to be valued by his athletic and animal qualities. Spence relates that Mr. Pope was with Sir Godfrey Kneller one day, when his nephew, a Guinea trader, came in. " Nephew," said Sir Godfrey, " you have the honor of seeing the two greatest men in the world." " I don't know how great men you may be," said the Guinea man, " but I don't like your looks. I have often bought a

man much better than both of you, all muscles
and bones, for ten guineas." Thus the men of
the senses revenge themselves on the professors
and repay scorn for scorn. The first had leaped
to conclusions not yet ripe, and say more than
is true; the others make themselves merry with
the philosopher, and weigh man by the pound.
They believe that mustard bites the tongue, that
pepper is hot, friction-matches incendiary, re-
volvers are to be avoided, and suspenders hold
up pantaloons; that there is much sentiment in
a chest of tea; and a man will be eloquent, if
you give him good wine. Are you tender and
scrupulous, — you must eat more mince-pie.
They hold that Luther had milk in him when
he said, —

> " Wer nicht liebt Wein, Weiber, Gesang,
>   Der bleibt ein Narr sein Leben lang ; " —

and when he advised a young scholar, perplexed
with fore-ordination and free-will, to get well
drunk. " The nerves," says Cabanis, " they are
the man." My neighbor, a jolly farmer, in the
tavern bar-room, thinks that the use of money
is sure and speedy spending. For his part, he
says, he puts his down his neck and gets the
good of it.

The inconvenience of this way of thinking is

that it runs into indifferentism and then into disgust. Life is eating us up. We shall be fables presently. Keep cool : it will be all one a hundred years hence. Life's well enough, but we shall be glad to get out of it, and they will all be glad to have us. Why should we fret and drudge? Our meat will taste to-morrow as it did yesterday, and we may at last have had enough of it. "Ah," said my languid gentleman at Oxford, "there's nothing new or true,—and no matter."

With a little more bitterness, the cynic moans; our life is like an ass led to market by a bundle of hay being carried before him ; he sees nothing but the bundle of hay. "There is so much trouble in coming into the world," said Lord Bolingbroke, "and so much more, as well as meanness, in going out of it, that 't is hardly worth while to be here at all." I knew a philosopher of this kidney who was accustomed briefly to sum up his experience of human nature in saying, " Mankind is a damned rascal:" ' and the natural corollary is pretty sure to follow, — ' The world lives by humbug, and so will I.'

The abstractionist and the materialist thus mutually exasperating each other, and the scoffer expressing the worst of materialism, there arises

a third party to occupy the middle ground between these two, the skeptic, namely. He finds
both wrong by being in extremes. He labors to
plant his feet, to be the beam of the balance.
He will not go beyond his card. He sees the
one-sidedness of these men of the street; he will
not be a Gibeonite; he stands for the intellectual
faculties, a cool head and whatever serves to keep
it cool; no unadvised industry, no unrewarded
self-devotion, no loss of the brains in toil. Am
I an ox, or a dray?—You are both in extremes,
he says. You that will have all solid, and a world
of pig-lead, deceive yourselves grossly. You believe yourselves rooted and grounded on adamant; and yet, if·we uncover the last facts of
our knowledge, you are spinning like bubbles
in a river, you know not whither or whence, and
you are bottomed and capped and wrapped in
delusions.[1] Neither will he be betrayed to a book
and wrapped in a gown.[2] The studious class are
their own victims; they are thin and pale, their
feet are cold, their heads are hot, the night is
without sleep, the day a fear of interruption, —
pallor, squalor, hunger and egotism. If you
come near them and see what conceits they entertain, — they are abstractionists, and spend
their days and nights in dreaming some dream;

in expecting the homage of society to some precious scheme, built on a truth, but destitute of proportion in its presentment, of justness in its application, and of all energy of will in the schemer to embody and vitalize it.[1]

But I see plainly, he says, that I cannot see. I know that human strength is not in extremes, but in avoiding extremes. I, at least, will shun the weakness of philosophizing beyond my depth. What is the use of pretending to powers we have not? What is the use of pretending to assurances we have not, respecting the other life? Why exaggerate the power of virtue? Why be an angel before your time? These strings, wound up too high, will snap. If there is a wish for immortality, and no evidence, why not say just that? If there are conflicting evidences, why not state them? If there is not ground for a candid thinker to make up his mind, yea or nay, — why not suspend the judgment? I weary of these dogmatizers. I tire of these hacks of routine, who deny the dogmas. I neither affirm nor deny. I stand here to try the case. I am here to consider, σκοπεῖν, to consider how it is. I will try to keep the balance true. Of what use to take the chair and glibly rattle off theories of society, reli-

gion and nature, when I know that practical
objections lie in the way, insurmountable by
me and by my mates? Why so talkative in
public, when each of my neighbors can pin me
to my seat by arguments I cannot refute? Why
pretend that life is so simple a game, when we
know how subtle and elusive the Proteus is?[1]
Why think to shut up all things in your nar-
row coop, when we know there are not one or
two only, but ten, twenty, a thousand things,
and unlike? Why fancy that you have all the
truth in your keeping? There is much to say
on all sides.

Who shall forbid a wise skepticism, seeing
that there is no practical question on which any
thing more than an approximate solution can be
had? Is not marriage an open question, when it
is alleged, from the beginning of the world, that
such as are in the institution wish to get out,
and such as are out wish to get in? And the
reply of Socrates, to him who asked whether he
should choose a wife, still remains reasonable,
that " whether he should choose one or not, he
would repent it." Is not the State a question?
All society is divided in opinion on the subject
of the State. Nobody loves it; great numbers
dislike it and suffer conscientious scruples to

allegiance; and the only defence set up, is the fear of doing worse in disorganizing. Is it otherwise with the Church? Or, to put any of the questions which touch mankind nearest, — shall the young man aim at a leading part in law, in politics, in trade? It will not be pretended that a success in either of these kinds is quite coincident with what is best and inmost in his mind. Shall he then, cutting the stays that hold him fast to the social state, put out to sea with no guidance but his genius? There is much to say on both sides. Remember the open question between the present order of "competition" and the friends of "attractive and associated labor." The generous minds embrace the proposition of labor shared by all; it is the only honesty; nothing else is safe.' It is from the poor man's hut alone that strength and virtue come: and yet, on the other side, it is alleged that labor impairs the form and breaks the spirit of man, and the laborers cry unanimously, 'We have no thoughts.' Culture, how indispensable! I cannot forgive you the want of accomplishments; and yet culture will instantly impair that chiefest beauty of spontaneousness. Excellent is culture for a savage; but once let him read in the book, and he is no longer able not to think of Plutarch's heroes. In short, since true fortitude of understanding consists "in not letting what we know be embarrassed by what we do not know," we ought to secure those advantages which we can command, and not risk them by clutching after the airy and unattainable. Come, no chimeras! Let us go abroad; let us mix in affairs; let us learn and get and have and climb. "Men are a sort of moving plants, and, like trees, receive a great part of their nourishment from the air. If they keep too much at home, they pine." Let us have a robust, manly life; let us know what we know, for certain; what we have, let it be solid and seasonable and our own. A world in the hand is worth two in the bush. Let us have to do with real men and women, and not with skipping ghosts.

This then is the right ground of the skeptic, — this of consideration, of self-containing; not at all of unbelief; not at all of universal denying, nor of universal doubting, — doubting even that he doubts; least of all of scoffing and profligate jeering at all that is stable and good. These are no more his moods than are those of religion and philosophy. He is the considerer, the prudent, taking in sail, counting stock, husbanding his means, believing that a man has too many enemies than that he can afford to be his own foe; that we cannot give ourselves too many advantages in this unequal conflict, with powers so vast and unweariable ranged on one side, and this little conceited vulnerable popinjay that a man is, bobbing up and down into every danger, on the other. It is a position taken up for better defence, as of more safety, and one that can be maintained; and it is one of more opportunity and range: as, when we build a house, the rule is to set it not too high nor too low, under the wind, but out of the dirt.

The philosophy we want is one of fluxions and mobility. The Spartan and Stoic schemes are too stark and stiff for our occasion. A theory of Saint John, and of non-resistance, seems, on the other hand, too thin and aerial. We want some coat woven of elastic steel, stout as the first and limber as the second. We want a ship in these billows we inhabit. An angular, dogmatic house would be rent to chips and splinters in this storm of many elements. No, it must be tight, and fit to the form of man, to live at all; as a shell must dictate the architecture of a house founded on the sea. The soul of man must be the type of our scheme, just as the body of man is the type after which a dwelling-house is built. Adaptiveness is the peculiarity of human nature. We are golden averages, volitant stabilities, compensated or periodic errors, houses founded on the sea. The wise skeptic wishes to have a near view of the best game and the chief players; what is best in the planet; art and nature, places and events; but mainly men. Every thing that is excellent in mankind, — a form of grace, an arm of iron, lips of persuasion, a brain of resources, every one skilful to play and win, — he will see and judge.

The terms of admission to this spectacle are, that he have a certain solid and intelligible way of living of his own; some method of answering the inevitable needs of human life; proof that he has played with skill and success; that he has evinced the temper, stoutness and the range of qualities which, among his contemporaries and countrymen, entitle him to fellowship and trust. For the secrets of life are not shown except to sympathy and likeness. Men do not confide themselves to boys, or coxcombs, or pedants, but to their peers. Some wise limitation, as the modern phrase is; some condition between the extremes, and having, itself, a positive quality; some stark and sufficient man, who

is not salt or sugar, but sufficiently related to the
world to do justice to Paris or London, and, at
the same time, a vigorous and original thinker,
whom cities can not overawe, but who uses them,
— is the fit person to occupy this ground of
speculation.

These qualities meet in the character of Montaigne. And yet, since the personal regard which
I entertain for Montaigne may be unduly great,
' I will, under the shield of this prince of egotists,
offer, as an apology for electing him as the representative of skepticism, a word or two to explain
how my love began and grew for this admirable
gossip.[1]

A single odd volume of Cotton's translation
of the Essays remained to me from my father's
library, when a boy. It lay long neglected, until,
after many years, when I was newly escaped from
college, I read the book, and procured the remaining volumes. I remember the delight and
wonder in which I lived with it. It seemed to
me as if I had myself written the book, in some
former life, so sincerely it spoke to my thought
and experience. It happened, when in Paris, in
1833, that, in the cemetery of Père Lachaise, I
came to a tomb of Auguste Collignon, who died
in 1830, aged sixty-eight years, and who, said

the monument, "lived to do right, and had formed himself to virtue on the Essays of Montaigne." Some years later, I became acquainted with an accomplished English poet, John Sterling;[1] and, in prosecuting my correspondence, I found that, from a love of Montaigne, he had made a pilgrimage to his chateau, still standing near Castellan, in Périgord, and, after two hundred and fifty years, had copied from the walls of his library the inscriptions which Montaigne had written there. That Journal of Mr. Sterling's, published in the Westminster Review, Mr. Hazlitt has reprinted in the *Prolegomena* to his edition of the Essays. I heard with pleasure that one of the newly-discovered autographs of William Shakspeare was in a copy of Florio's translation of Montaigne. It is the only book which we certainly know to have been in the poet's library. And, oddly enough, the duplicate copy of Florio, which the British Museum purchased with a view of protecting the Shakspeare autograph (as I was informed in the Museum), turned out to have the autograph of Ben Jonson in the fly-leaf. Leigh Hunt relates of Lord Byron, that Montaigne was the only great writer of past times whom he read with avowed satisfaction. Other coincidences, not needful to be mentioned here, concurred to make this old Gascon still new and immortal for me.

In 1571, on the death of his father, Montaigne, then thirty-eight years old, retired from the practice of law at Bordeaux, and settled himself on his estate. Though he had been a man of pleasure and sometimes a courtier, his studious habits now grew on him, and he loved the compass, staidness and independence of the country gentleman's life. He took up his economy in good earnest, and made his farms yield the most. Downright and plain-dealing, and abhorring to be deceived or to deceive, he was esteemed in the country for his sense and probity. In the civil wars of the League, which converted every house into a fort, Montaigne kept his gates open and his house without defence. All parties freely came and went, his courage and honor being universally esteemed. The neighboring lords and gentry brought jewels and papers to him for safe-keeping. Gibbon reckons, in these bigoted times, but two men of liberality in France, — Henry IV. and Montaigne.

Montaigne is the frankest and honestest of all writers. His French freedom runs into grossness; but he has anticipated all censure by the bounty of his own confessions. In his times,

books were written to one sex only, and almost
all were written in Latin; so that in a humorist
a certain nakedness of statement was permitted,
which our manners, of a literature addressed
equally to both sexes, do not allow. But though
a biblical plainness coupled with a most unca-
nonical levity may shut his pages to many sensitive readers, yet the offence is superficial. He
parades it: he makes the most of it: nobody can
think or say worse of him than he does.¹ He
pretends to most of the vices; and, if there be
any virtue in him, he says, it got in by stealth.
There is no man, in his opinion, who has not
deserved hanging five or six times; and he pretends no exception in his own behalf. "Five or
six as ridiculous stories," too, he says, "can be
told of me, as of any man living." But, with all
this really superfluous frankness, the opinion of
an invincible probity grows into every reader's
mind. "When I the most strictly and religiously
confess myself, I find that the best virtue I have
has in it some tincture of vice; and I, who am
as sincere and perfect a lover of virtue of that
stamp as any other whatever, am afraid that
Plato, in his purest virtue, if he had listened and
laid his ear close to himself, would have heard
some jarring sound of human mixture; but

faint and remote and only to be perceived by himself."

Here is an impatience and fastidiousness at color or pretence of any kind. He has been in courts so long as to have conceived a furious disgust at appearances; he will indulge himself with a little cursing and swearing; he will talk with sailors and gipsies, use flash and street ballads; he has stayed in-doors till he is deadly sick; he will to the open air, though it rain bullets. He has seen too much of gentlemen of the long robe, until he wishes for cannibals; and is so nervous, by factitious life, that he thinks the more barbarous man is, the better he is. He likes his saddle. You may read theology, and grammar, and metaphysics elsewhere. Whatever you get here shall smack of the earth and of real life, sweet, or smart, or stinging. He makes no hesitation to entertain you with the records of his disease, and his journey to Italy is quite full of that matter.[1] He took and kept this position of equilibrium. Over his name he drew an emblematic pair of scales, and wrote *Que sçais je?* under it. As I look at his effigy opposite the title-page, I seem to hear him say, 'You may play old Poz, if you will;[2] you may rail and exaggerate,—I stand here for truth, and will not, for all the states

and churches and revenues and personal reputations of Europe, overstate the dry fact, as I see
it; I will rather mumble and prose about what
I certainly know, — my house and barns; my
father, my wife and my tenants; my old lean
bald pate; my knives and forks; what meats I
eat and what drinks I prefer, and a hundred
straws just as ridiculous, — than I will write,
with a fine crow-quill, a fine romance. I like
gray days, and autumn and winter weather. I
am gray and autumnal myself, and think an un-
dress and old shoes that do not pinch my feet,
and old friends who do not constrain me, and
plain topics where I do not need to strain myself
and pump my brains, the most suitable. Our
condition as men is risky and ticklish enough.
One cannot be sure of himself and his fortune
an hour, but he may be whisked off into some
pitiable or ridiculous plight. Why should I
vapor and play the philosopher, instead of bal-
lasting, the best I can, this dancing balloon? So,
at least, I live within compass, keep myself ready
for action, and can shoot the gulf at last with
decency. If there be anything farcical in such a
life, the blame is not mine: let it lie at fate's
and nature's door.'

The Essays, therefore, are an entertaining

soliloquy on every random topic that comes into his head; treating every thing without ceremony, yet with masculine sense. There have been men with deeper insight; but, one would say, never a man with such abundance of thoughts: he is never dull, never insincere, and has the genius to make the reader care for all that he cares for.

The sincerity and marrow of the man reaches to his sentences. I know not anywhere the book that seems less written. It is the language of conversation transferred to a book. Cut these words, and they would bleed; they are vascular and alive. One has the same pleasure in it that he feels in listening to the necessary speech of men about their work, when any unusual circumstance gives momentary importance to the dialogue. For blacksmiths and teamsters do not trip in their speech; it is a shower of bullets. It is Cambridge men who correct themselves and begin again at every half sentence, and, moreover, will pun, and refine too much, and swerve from the matter to the expression.| Montaigne talks with shrewdness, knows the world and books and himself, and uses the positive degree; never shrieks, or protests, or prays: no weakness, no convulsion, no superlative: does not wish to jump out of his skin, or play any antics, or annihilate space or time, but is stout and solid; tastes every moment of the day; likes pain because it makes him feel himself and realize things; as we pinch ourselves to know that we are awake. He keeps the plain; he rarely mounts or sinks; likes to feel solid ground and the stones underneath. His writing has no enthusiasms, no aspiration; contented, self-respecting and keeping the middle of the road. There is but one exception, — in his love for Socrates. In speaking of him, for once his cheek flushes and his style rises to passion.

Montaigne died of a quinsy, at the age of sixty, in 1592. When he came to die he caused the mass to be celebrated in his chamber. At the age of thirty-three, he had been married. " But," he says, " might I have had my own will, I would not have married Wisdom herself, if she would have had me: but 't is to much purpose to evade it, the common custom and use of life will have it so. Most of my actions are guided by example, not choice." In the hour of death, he gave the same weight to custom. *Que sçais je?* What do I know?

This book of Montaigne the world has endorsed by translating it into all tongues and printing seventy-five editions of it in Europe;

and that, too, a circulation somewhat chosen, namely among courtiers, soldiers, princes, men of the world and men of wit and generosity.

Shall we say that Montaigne has spoken wisely, and given the right and permanent expression of the human mind, on the conduct of life?

We are natural believers. Truth, or the connection between cause and effect, alone interests us. We are persuaded that a thread runs through all things: all worlds are strung on it, as beads; and men, and events, and life, come to us only because of that thread: they pass and repass only that we may know the direction and continuity of that line. A book or statement which goes to show that there is no line, but random and chaos, a calamity out of nothing, a prosperity and no account of it, a hero born from a fool, a fool from a hero, — dispirits us. Seen or unseen, we believe the tie exists. Talent makes counterfeit ties; genius finds the real ones. We hearken to the man of science, because we anticipate the sequence in natural phenomena which he uncovers. We love whatever affirms, connects, preserves; and dislike what scatters or pulls down. One man appears whose nature is to all men's eyes conserving and constructive ; his presence supposes a well-ordered society, agriculture, trade, large institutions and empire. If these did not exist, they would begin to exist through his endeavors. Therefore he cheers and comforts men, who feel all this in him very readily. The nonconformist and the rebel say all manner of unanswerable things against the existing republic, but discover to our sense no plan of house or state of their own. Therefore, though the town and state and way of living, which our counsellor contemplated, might be a very modest or musty prosperity, yet men rightly go for him, and reject the reformer so long as he comes only with axe and crowbar.

But though we are natural conservers and causationists, and reject a sour, dumpish unbelief, the skeptical class, which Montaigne represents, have reason, and every man, at some time, belongs to it. Every superior mind will pass through this domain of equilibration, — I should rather say, will know how to avail himself of the checks and balances in nature, as a natural weapon against the exaggeration and formalism of bigots and blockheads.

Skepticism is the attitude assumed by the

student in relation to the particulars which
society adores, but which he sees to be reverend
only in their tendency and spirit. The ground
occupied by the skeptic is the vestibule of the
temple. Society does not like to have any
breath of question blown on the existing order.
But the interrogation of custom at all points is
an inevitable stage in the growth of every superior mind, and is the evidence of its perception
of the flowing power which remains itself in all
changes.[1]

The superior mind will find itself equally at
odds with the evils of society and with the projects that are offered to relieve them. The wise
skeptic is a bad citizen; no conservative, he
sees the selfishness of property and the drowsi-
ness of institutions. But neither is he fit to
work with any democratic party that ever was
constituted; for parties wish every one committed, and he penetrates the popular patriot-
ism. His politics are those of the "Soul's
Errand" of Sir Walter Raleigh; or of Krishna,
in the Bhagavat, "There is none who is worthy
of my love or hatred;" whilst he sentences law,
physic, divinity, commerce and custom. He is
a reformer; yet he is no better member of the
philanthropic association. It turns out that he

is not the champion of the operative, the pauper, the prisoner, the slave. It stands in his mind that our life in this world is not of quite so easy interpretation as churches and school-books say. He does not wish to take ground against these benevolences, to play the part of devil's attorney, and blazon every doubt and sneer that darkens the sun for him. But he says, There are doubts.

I mean to use the occasion, and celebrate the calendar-day of our Saint Michel de Montaigne, by counting and describing these doubts or negations. I wish to ferret them out of their holes and sun them a little. We must do with them as the police do with old rogues, who are shown up to the public at the marshal's office. They will never be so formidable when once they have been identified and registered. But I mean honestly by them, — that justice shall be done to their terrors. I shall not take Sunday objections, made up on purpose to be put down. I shall take the worst I can find, whether I can dispose of them or they of me.

I do not press the skepticism of the materialist. I know the quadruped opinion will not prevail. 'T is of no importance what bats and oxen think. The first dangerous symptom I report is, the levity of intellect; as if it were fatal to earnestness to know much. Knowledge is the knowing that we can not know. The dull pray; the geniuses are light mockers. How respectable is earnestness on every platform! but intellect kills it. Nay, San Carlo, my subtle and admirable friend, one of the most penetrating of men, finds that all direct ascension, even of lofty piety, leads to this ghastly insight and sends back the votary orphaned.[1] My astonishing San Carlo thought the lawgivers and saints infected. They found the ark empty; saw, and would not tell; and tried to choke off their approaching followers, by saying, ' Action, action, my dear fellows, is for you!' Bad as was to me this detection by San Carlo, this frost in July, this blow from a bride, there was still a worse, namely the cloy or satiety of the saints. In the mount of vision, ere they have yet risen from their knees, they say, ' We discover that this our homage and beatitude is partial and deformed: we must fly for relief to the suspected and reviled Intellect, to the Understanding, the Mephistopheles, to the gymnastics of talent.'[2]

This is hobgoblin the first; and though it has been the subject of much elegy in our nineteenth century, from Byron, Goethe and other poets

of less fame, not to mention many distinguished
private observers, — I confess it is not very af-
fecting to my imagination; for it seems to concern the shattering of baby-houses and crockery-
shops. What flutters the Church of Rome, or
of England, or of Geneva, or of Boston, may
yet be very far from touching any principle of
faith. I think that the intellect and moral sentiment are unanimous; and that though philosophy extirpates bugbears, yet it supplies the
natural checks of vice, and polarity to the soul.
I think that the wiser a man is, the more stupen-
dous he finds the natural and moral economy, and
lifts himself to a more absolute reliance.[1]

There is the power of moods, each setting at
nought all but its own tissue of facts and beliefs.
There is the power of complexions, obviously
modifying the dispositions and sentiments. The
beliefs and unbeliefs appear to be structural;
and as soon as each man attains the poise and
vivacity which allow the whole machinery to play,
he will not need extreme examples, but will
rapidly alternate all opinions in his own life.
Our life is March weather, savage and serene in
one hour. We go forth austere, dedicated, believing in the iron links of Destiny, and will not
turn on our heel to save our life: but a book,

or a bust, or only the sound of a name, shoots
a spark through the nerves, and we suddenly
believe in will : my finger-ring shall be the seal
of Solomon ; fate is for imbeciles ; all is possible
to the resolved mind. Presently a new experience gives a new turn to our thoughts : common
sense resumes its tyranny ; we say, ' Well, the
army, after all, is the gate to fame, manners and
poetry : and, look you, — on the whole, selfishness plants best, prunes best, makes the best
commerce and the best citizen.' Are the opinions of a man on right and wrong, on fate and
causation, at the mercy of a broken sleep or an
indigestion ? Is his belief in God and Duty no
deeper than a stomach evidence? And what
guaranty for the permanence of his opinions?
I like not the French celerity, — a new Church
and State once a week. This is the second negation ; and I shall let it pass for what it will.
As far as it asserts rotation of states of mind, I
suppose it suggests its own remedy, namely in
the record of larger periods. What is the mean
of many states ; of all the states? Does the
general voice of ages affirm any principle, or is
no community of sentiment discoverable in distant times and places? And when it shows the
power of self-interest, I accept that as part of

the divine law and must reconcile it with aspiration the best I can.

The word Fate, or Destiny, expresses the sense of mankind, in all ages, that the laws of the world do not always befriend, but often hurt and crush us. Fate, in the shape of *Kinde* or nature, grows over us like grass.[1] We paint Time with a scythe; Love and Fortune, blind; and Destiny, deaf. We have too little power of resistance against this ferocity which champs us up. What front can we make against these unavoidable, victorious, maleficent forces? What can I do against the influence of Race, in my history? What can I do against hereditary and constitutional habits; against scrofula, lymph, impotence? against climate, against barbarism, in my country? I can reason down or deny every thing, except this perpetual Belly : feed he must and will, and I cannot make him respectable.[2]

But the main resistance which the affirmative impulse finds, and one including all others, is in the doctrine of the Illusionists. There is a painful rumor in circulation that we have been practised upon in all the principal performances of life, and free agency is the emptiest name. We

IV

have been sopped and drugged with the air, with food, with woman, with children, with sciences, with events, which leave us exactly where they found us. The mathematics, 't is complained, leave the mind where they find it: so do all sciences; and so do all events and actions. I find a man who has passed through all the sciences, the churl he was; and, through all the offices, learned, civil and social, can detect the child. We are not the less necessitated to dedicate life to them. In fact we may come to accept it as the fixed rule and theory of our state of education, that God is a substance, and his method is illusion. The Eastern sages owned the goddess Yoganidra, the great illusory energy of Vishnu, by whom, as utter ignorance, the whole world is beguiled.

Or shall I state it thus? — The astonishment of life is the absence of any appearance of reconciliation between the theory and practice of life. Reason, the prized reality, the Law, is apprehended, now and then, for a serene and profound moment amidst the hubbub of cares and works which have no direct bearing on it; — is then lost for months or years, and again found for an interval, to be lost again. If we compute it in time, we may, in fifty years, have half a dozen

reasonable hours. But what are these cares and
works the better? A method in the world we do
not see, but this parallelism of great and little,
which never react on each other, nor discover
the smallest tendency to converge. Experiences,
fortunes, governings, readings, writings, are
nothing to the purpose; as when a man comes
into the room it does not appear whether he
has been fed on yams or buffalo, — he has contrived to get so much bone and fibre as he
wants, out of rice or out of snow. So vast is the
disproportion between the sky of law and the
pismire of performance under it, that whether
he is a man of worth or a sot is not so great a
matter as we say. Shall I add, as one juggle of
this enchantment, the stunning non-intercourse
law which makes co-operation impossible? The
young spirit pants to enter society. But all the
ways of culture and greatness lead to solitary
imprisonment. He has been often baulked. He
did not expect a sympathy with his thought
from the village, but he went with it to the
chosen and intelligent, and found no entertainment for it, but mere misapprehension, distaste
and scoffing. Men are strangely mistimed and
misapplied; and the excellence of each is an in-
flamed individualism which separates him more.

There are these, and more than these dis-
eases of thought, which our ordinary teachers
do not attempt to remove. Now shall we, because a good nature inclines us to virtue's side,
say, There are no doubts, — and lie for the
right? Is life to be led in a brave or in a cowardly manner? and is not the satisfaction of the
doubts essential to all manliness? Is the name
of virtue to be a barrier to that which is virtue?
Can you not believe that a man of earnest and
burly habit may find small good in tea, essays
and catechism, and want a rougher instruction,
want men, labor, trade, farming, war, hunger,
plenty, love, hatred, doubt and terror to make
things plain to him; and has he not a right to
insist on being convinced in his own way?
When he is convinced, he will be worth the
pains.[1]

Belief consists in accepting the affirmations
of the soul; unbelief, in denying them. Some
minds are incapable of skepticism. The doubts
they profess to entertain are rather a civility or
accommodation to the common discourse of
their company. They may well give themselves
leave to speculate, for they are secure of a return. Once admitted to the heaven of thought,
they see no relapse into night, but infinite invi-

tation on the other side. Heaven is within heaven, and sky over sky, and they are encompassed with divinities. Others there are to whom the heaven is brass, and it shuts down to the surface of the earth. It is a question of temperament, or of more or less immersion in nature. The last class must needs have a reflex or parasite faith; not a sight of realities, but an instinctive reliance on the seers and believers of realities. The manners and thoughts of believers astonish them and convince them that these have seen something which is hid from themselves. But their sensual habit would fix the believer to his last position, whilst he as inevitably advances; and presently the unbeliever, for love of belief, burns the believer.

Great believers are always reckoned infidels, impracticable, fantastic, atheistic, and really men of no account. The spiritualist finds himself driven to express his faith by a series of skepticisms. Charitable souls come with their projects and ask his co-operation. How can he hesitate? It is the rule of mere comity and courtesy to agree where you can, and to turn your sentence with something auspicious, and not freezing and sinister. But he is forced to say, 'O, these things will be as they must be: what can you do?

These particular griefs and crimes are the foliage
and fruit of such trees as we see growing. It is
vain to complain of the leaf or the berry; cut it
off, it will bear another just as bad. You must
begin your cure lower down.' The generosities
of the day prove an intractable element for him.
The people's questions are not his; their methods are not his; and against all the dictates of
good nature he is driven to say he has no pleasure in them.'

Even the doctrines dear to the hope of man,
of the divine Providence and of the immortality of the soul, his neighbors can not put the
statement so that he shall affirm it. But he denies out of more faith, and not less. He denies
out of honesty. He had rather stand charged
with the imbecility of skepticism, than with un-
truth. I believe, he says, in the moral design of
the universe; it exists hospitably for the weal
of souls; but your dogmas seem to me caricatures: why should I make believe them? Will
any say, This is cold and infidel? The wise and
magnanimous will not say so. They will exult
in his far-sighted good-will that can abandon to
the adversary all the ground of tradition and
common belief, without losing a jot of strength.
It sees to the end of all transgression. George

Fox saw that there was "an ocean of darkness and death; but withal an infinite ocean of light and love which flowed over that of darkness."[1]

The final solution in which skepticism is lost, is in the moral sentiment, which never forfeits its supremacy. All moods may be safely tried, and their weight allowed to all objections: the moral sentiment as easily outweighs them all, as any one. This is the drop which balances the sea. I play with the miscellany of facts, and take those superficial views which we call skepticism; but I know that they will presently appear to me in that order which makes skepticism impossible. A man of thought must feel the thought that is parent of the universe; that the masses of nature do undulate and flow.

This faith avails to the whole emergency of life and objects. The world is saturated with deity and with law. He is content with just and unjust, with sots and fools, with the triumph of folly and fraud.[2] He can behold with serenity the yawning gulf between the ambition of man and his power of performance, between the demand and supply of power, which makes the tragedy of all souls.

Charles Fourier announced that "the attractions of man are proportioned to his destinies;"

in other words, that every desire predicts its own satisfaction. Yet all experience exhibits the reverse of this; the incompetency of power is the universal grief of young and ardent minds. They accuse the divine Providence of a certain parsimony. It has shown the heaven and earth to every child and filled him with a desire for the whole; a desire raging, infinite; a hunger, as of space to be filled with planets; a cry of famine, as of devils for souls. Then for the satisfaction, — to each man is administered a single drop, a bead of dew of vital power, *per day*, — a cup as large as space, and one drop of the water of life in it.¹ Each man woke in the morning with an appetite that could eat the solar system like a cake; a spirit for action and passion without bounds; he could lay his hand on the morning star; he could try conclusions with gravitation or chemistry; but, on the first motion to prove his strength, — hands, feet, senses, gave way and would not serve him. He was an emperor deserted by his states, and left to whistle by himself, or thrust into a mob of emperors, all whistling: and still the sirens sang, " The attractions are proportioned to the destinies." In every house, in the heart of each maiden and of each boy, in the soul of the soaring saint, this chasm is found, — between the largest promise of ideal power, and the shabby experience.

The expansive nature of truth comes to our succor, elastic, not to be surrounded. Man helps himself by larger generalizations. The lesson of life is practically to generalize; to believe what the years and the centuries say, against the hours; to resist the usurpation of particulars; to penetrate to their catholic sense. Things seem to say one thing, and say the reverse. The appearance is immoral; the result is moral. Things seem to tend downward, to justify despondency, to promote rogues, to defeat the just; and by knaves as by martyrs the just cause is carried forward. Although knaves win in every political struggle, although society seems to be delivered over from the hands of one set of criminals into the hands of another set of criminals, as fast as the government is changed, and the march of civilization is a train of felonies, — yet, general ends are somehow answered. We see, now, events forced on which seem to retard or retrograde the civility of ages. But the world-spirit is a good swimmer, and storms and waves cannot drown him. He snaps his finger at laws: and so, throughout history, heaven seems to affect low and poor means. Through the years

and the centuries, through evil agents, through
toys and atoms, a great and beneficent tendency
irresistibly streams.[1]

Let a man learn to look for the permanent in
the mutable and fleeting; let him learn to bear
the disappearance of things he was wont to reverence without losing his reverence; let him learn
that he is here, not to work but to be worked
upon; and that, though abyss open under abyss,
and opinion displace opinion, all are at last contained in the Eternal Cause: —

> " If my bark sink, 't is to another sea."[2]

V

SHAKSPEARE; OR, THE POET

SHAKSPEARE; OR, THE POET

GREAT men are more distinguished by range and extent than by originality. If we require the originality which consists in weaving, like a spider, their web from their own bowels ; in finding clay and making bricks and building the house; no great men are original. Nor does valuable originality consist in unlikeness to other men. The hero is in the press of knights and the thick of events; and seeing what men want and sharing their desire, he adds the needful length of sight and of arm, to come at the desired point. The greatest genius is the most indebted man. A poet is no rattle-brain, saying what comes uppermost, and, because he says every thing, saying at last something good ; but a heart in unison with his time and country. There is nothing whimsical and fantastic in his production, but sweet and sad earnest, freighted with the weightiest convictions and pointed with the most determined aim which any man or class knows of in his times.'

The Genius of our life is jealous of individuals, and will not have any individual great,

except through the general. There is no choice
to genius. A great man does not wake up on
some fine morning and say, ' I am full of life, I
will go to sea and find an Antarctic continent:
to-day I will square the circle: I will ransack
botany and find a new food for man: I have a
new architecture in my mind: I foresee a new
mechanic power:' no, but he finds himself in
the river of the thoughts and events, forced onward by the ideas and necessities of his contemporaries.' He stands where all the eyes of men
look one way, and their hands all point in the
direction in which he should go. The Church
has reared him amidst rites and pomps, and he
carries out the advice which her music gave him,
and builds a cathedral needed by her chants and
processions. He finds a war raging: it educates
him, by trumpet, in barracks, and he betters the
instruction. He finds two counties groping to
bring coal, or flour, or fish, from the place of
production to the place of consumption, and he
hits on a railroad. Every master has found his
materials collected, and his power lay in his sympathy with his people and in his love of the
materials he wrought in. What an economy of
power! and what a compensation for the short-
ness of life! All is done to his hand. The world

Shakspeare

has brought him thus far on his way. The human race has gone out before him, sunk the hills, filled the hollows and bridged the rivers. Men, nations, poets, artisans, women, all have worked for him, and he enters into their labors. Choose any other thing, out of the line of tendency, out of the national feeling and history, and he would have all to do for himself: his powers would be expended in the first preparations. Great genial power, one would almost say, consists in not being original at all; in being altogether receptive; in letting the world do all, and suffering the spirit of the hour to pass unobstructed through the mind.

Shakspeare's youth fell in a time when the English people were importunate for dramatic entertainments. The court took offence easily at political allusions and attempted to suppress them. The Puritans, a growing and energetic party, and the religious among the Anglican church, would suppress them. But the people wanted them. Inn-yards, houses without roofs, and extemporaneous enclosures at country fairs were the ready theatres of strolling players. The people had tasted this new joy; and, as we could not hope to suppress newspapers now, — no, not by the strongest party, — neither then could king, prelate, or puritan, alone or united, suppress an organ which was ballad, epic, newspaper, caucus, lecture, Punch and library, at the same time. Probably king, prelate and puritan, all found their own account in it. It had become, by all causes, a national interest, — by no means conspicuous, so that some great scholar would have thought of treating it in an English history, — but not a whit less considerable because it was cheap and of no account, like a baker's-shop. The best proof of its vitality is the crowd of writers which suddenly broke into this field; Kyd, Marlow, Greene, Jonson, Chapman, Dekker, Webster, Heywood, Middleton, Peele, Ford, Massinger, Beaumont and Fletcher.

The secure possession, by the stage, of the public mind, is of the first importance to the poet who works for it.[1] He loses no time in idle experiments. Here is audience and expectation prepared. In the case of Shakspeare there is much more. At the time when he left Stratford and went up to London, a great body of stage-plays of all dates and writers existed in manuscript and were in turn produced on the boards. Here is the Tale of Troy, which the audience will bear hearing some part of, every week; the Death of Julius Cæsar, and other

stories out of Plutarch, which they never tire of;
a shelf full of English history, from the chroni-
cles of Brut and Arthur, down to the royal
Henries, which men hear eagerly; and a string
of doleful tragedies, merry Italian tales and
Spanish voyages, which all the London 'pren-
tices know. All the mass has been treated, with
more or less skill, by every playwright, and the
prompter has the soiled and tattered manu-
scripts. It is now no longer possible to say
who wrote them first. They have been the
property of the Theatre so long, and so many
rising geniuses have enlarged or altered them,
inserting a speech or a whole scene, or adding a
song, that no man can any longer claim copyright in this work of numbers. Happily, no
man wishes to. They are not yet desired in
that way. We have few readers, many specta-
tors and hearers. They had best lie where they
are.

Shakspeare, in common with his comrades,
esteemed the mass of old plays waste stock, in
which any experiment could be freely tried.
Had the *prestige* which hedges about a modern tragedy existed, nothing could have been
done. The rude warm blood of the living England circulated in the play, as in street-ballads,

IV

and gave body which he wanted to his airy and
majestic fancy. The poet needs a ground in
popular tradition on which he may work, and
which, again, may restrain his art within the due
temperance. It holds him to the people, supplies a foundation for his edifice, and in furnish-
ing so much work done to his hand, leaves him
at leisure and in full strength for the audacities
of his imagination. In short, the poet owes to
his legend what sculpture owed to the temple.
Sculpture in Egypt and in Greece grew up in
subordination to architecture. It was the orna-
ment of the temple wall: at first a rude relief
carved on pediments, then the relief became
bolder and a head or arm was projected from
the wall; the groups being still arranged with
reference to the building, which serves also as
a frame to hold the figures; and when at last
the greatest freedom of style and treatment was
reached, the prevailing genius of architecture
still enforced a certain calmness and continence
in the statue. As soon as the statue was begun
for itself, and with no reference to the temple
or palace, the art began to decline: freak, ex-
travagance and exhibition took the place of the
old temperance. This balance-wheel, which the
sculptor found in architecture, the perilous irri-

tability of poetic talent found in the accumulated dramatic materials to which the people
were already wonted, and which had a certain
excellence which no single genius, however extraordinary, could hope to create.

In point of fact it appears that Shakspeare
did owe debts in all directions, and was able to
use whatever he found ; and the amount of in-
debtedness may be inferred from Malone's laborious computations in regard to the First, Second and Third parts of Henry VI., in which,
" out of 6043 lines, 1771 were written by some
author preceding Shakspeare, 2373 by him, on
the foundation laid by his predecessors, and
1899 were entirely his own." And the proceeding investigation hardly leaves a single drama of
his absolute invention. Malone's sentence is an
important piece of external history. In Henry
VIII. I think I see plainly the cropping out of
the original rock on which his own finer stratum was laid. The first play was written by a
superior, thoughtful man, with a vicious ear.
I can mark his lines, and know well their ca-
dence. See Wolsey's soliloquy, and the following scene with Cromwell, where instead of the
metre of Shakspeare, whose secret is that the
thought constructs the tune, so that reading for

the sense will best bring out the rhythm, —
here the lines are constructed on a given tune,
and the verse has even a trace of pulpit eloquence. But the play contains through all its
length unmistakable traits of Shakspeare's hand,
and some passages, as the account of the coro-
nation, are like autographs. What is odd, the
compliment to Queen Elizabeth is in the bad
rhythm.[1]

Shakspeare knew that tradition supplies a
better fable than any invention can. If he lost
any credit of design, he augmented his resources;
and, at that day, our petulant demand for originality was not so much pressed. There was no
literature for the million. The universal reading, the cheap press, were unknown. A great
poet who appears in illiterate times, absorbs
into his sphere all the light which is any where
radiating. Every intellectual jewel, every flower
of sentiment it is his fine office to bring to his
people; and he comes to value his memory
equally with his invention.[2] He is therefore
little solicitous whence his thoughts have been
derived; whether through translation, whether
through tradition, whether by travel in distant
countries, whether by inspiration; from whatever source, they are equally welcome to his

uncritical audience. Nay, he borrows very near home. Other men say wise things as well as he; only they say a good many foolish things, and do not know when they have spoken wisely. He knows the sparkle of the true stone, and puts it in high place, wherever he finds it.[1] Such is the happy position of Homer perhaps; of Chaucer, of Saadi. They felt that all wit was their wit. And they are librarians and historiographers, as well as poets. Each romancer was heir and dispenser of all the hundred tales of the world, —

> " Presenting Thebes' and Pelops' line
> And the tale of Troy divine."[2]

The influence of Chaucer is conspicuous in all our early literature; and more recently not only Pope and Dryden have been beholden to him, but, in the whole society of English writers, a large unacknowledged debt is easily traced. One is charmed with the opulence which feeds so many pensioners. But Chaucer is a huge borrower. Chaucer, it seems, drew continually, through Lydgate and Caxton, from Guido di Colonna, whose Latin romance of the Trojan war was in turn a compilation from Dares Phrygius, Ovid and Statius. Then Petrarch, Boccaccio and the Provençal poets are his benefac-

tors: the Romaunt of the Rose is only judicious
translation from William of Lorris and John of
Meung : Troilus and Creseide, from Lollius of
Urbino : The Cock and the Fox, from the *Lais*
of Marie : The House of Fame, from the French
or Italian : and poor Gower he uses as if he were
only a brick-kiln or stone-quarry out of which to
build his house.[1] He steals by this apology, —
that what he takes has no worth where he finds
it and the greatest where he leaves it. It has
come to be practically a sort of rule in literature,
that a man having once shown himself capable
of original writing, is entitled thenceforth to
steal from the writings of others at discretion.
Thought is the property of him who can entertain it and of him who can adequately place it.
A certain awkwardness marks the use of borrowed thoughts ; but as soon as we have learned
what to do with them they become our own.

Thus all originality is relative. Every thinker
is retrospective. The learned member of the
legislature, at Westminster or at Washington,
speaks and votes for thousands. Show us the
constituency, and the now invisible channels by
which the senator is made aware of their wishes ;
the crowd of practical and knowing men, who,
by correspondence or conversation, are feeding

him with evidence, anecdotes and estimates, and
it will bereave his fine attitude and resistance of
something of their impressiveness. As Sir Robert Peel and Mr. Webster vote, so Locke and
Rousseau think, for thousands; and so there
were fountains all around Homer,[1] Menu, Saadi,
or Milton, from which they drew; friends,
lovers, books, traditions, proverbs, — all perished — which, if seen, would go to reduce the
wonder. Did the bard speak with authority?
Did he feel himself overmatched by any companion? The appeal is to the consciousness of
the writer. Is there at last in his breast a Delphi
whereof to ask concerning any thought or thing,
whether it be verily so, yea or nay? and to have
answer, and to rely on that? All the debts which
such a man could contract to other wit would
never disturb his consciousness of originality;
for the ministrations of books and of other minds
are a whiff of smoke to that most private reality
with which he has conversed.[2]

It is easy to see that what is best written or
done by genius in the world, was no man's work,
but came by wide social labor, when a thousand
wrought like one, sharing the same impulse. Our
English Bible is a wonderful specimen of the
strength and music of the English language. But

it was not made by one man, or at one time;
but centuries and churches brought it to perfection. There never was a time when there was
not some translation existing. The Liturgy, admired for its energy and pathos, is an anthology
of the piety of ages and nations, a translation of
the prayers and forms of the Catholic church, —
these collected, too, in long periods, from the
prayers and meditations of every saint and sacred
writer all over the world.¹ Grotius makes the
like remark in respect to the Lord's Prayer, that
the single clauses of which it is composed were
already in use in the time of Christ, in the Rab-
binical forms. He picked out the grains of gold.
The nervous language of the Common Law, the
impressive forms of our courts and the precision
and substantial truth of the legal distinctions,
are the contribution of all the sharp-sighted,
strong-minded men who have lived in the countries where these laws govern. The translation
of Plutarch gets its excellence by being translation on translation. There never was a time
when there was none. All the truly idiomatic
and national phrases are kept, and all others
successively picked out and thrown away. Something like the same process had gone on, long
before, with the originals of these books. The

world takes liberties with world-books. Vedas, Æsop's Fables, Pilpay, Arabian Nights, Cid, Iliad, Robin Hood, Scottish Minstrelsy, are not the work of single men. In the composition of such works the time thinks, the market thinks, the mason, the carpenter, the merchant, the farmer, the fop, all think for us. Every book supplies its time with one good word; every municipal law, every trade, every folly of the day; and the generic catholic genius who is not afraid or ashamed to owe his originality to the originality of all, stands with the next age as the recorder and embodiment of his own.[1]

We have to thank the researches of antiquaries, and the Shakspeare Society, for ascertaining the steps of the English drama, from the Mysteries celebrated in churches and by churchmen, and the final detachment from the church, and the completion of secular plays, from Ferrex and Porrex,[2] and Gammer Gurton's Needle, down to the possession of the stage by the very pieces which Shakspeare altered, remodelled and finally made his own. Elated with success and piqued by the growing interest of the problem, they have left no bookstall unsearched, no chest in a garret unopened, no file of old yellow accounts to decompose in damp and worms, so keen was the hope to discover whether the boy Shakspeare poached or not, whether he held horses at the theatre door, whether he kept school, and why he left in his will only his second-best bed to Ann Hathaway, his wife.

There is somewhat touching in the madness with which the passing age mischooses the object on which all candles shine and all eyes are turned; the care with which it registers every trifle touching Queen Elizabeth and King James, and the Essexes, Leicesters, Burleighs and Buckinghams; and lets pass without a single valuable note the founder of another dynasty, which alone will cause the Tudor dynasty to be remembered, —the man who carries the Saxon race in him by the inspiration which feeds him, and on whose thoughts the foremost people of the world are now for some ages to be nourished, and minds to receive this and not another bias. A popular player; — nobody suspected he was the poet of the human race; and the secret was kept as faithfully from poets and intellectual men as from courtiers and frivolous people.[1] Bacon, who took the inventory of the human understanding for his times, never mentioned his name. Ben Jonson, though we have strained his few words of regard and panegyric, had no suspicion of the elastic fame whose first vibrations he was attempting. He no doubt thought the praise he has conceded to him generous, and esteemed himself, out of all question, the better poet of the two.

If it need wit to know wit, according to the proverb, Shakspeare's time should be capable of recognizing it. Sir Henry Wotton was born four years after Shakspeare, and died twenty-three years after him ; and I find, among his correspondents and acquaintances, the following persons: Theodore Beza, Isaac Casaubon, Sir Philip Sidney, the Earl of Essex, Lord Bacon, Sir Walter Raleigh, John Milton, Sir Henry Vane, Isaac Walton, Dr. Donne, Abraham Cowley, Bellarmine, Charles Cotton, John Pym, John Hales, Kepler, Vieta, Albericus Gentilis, Paul Sarpi, Arminius ; with all of whom exists some token of his having communicated, without enumerating many others whom doubtless he saw, — Shakspeare, Spenser, Jonson, Beaumont, Massinger, the two Herberts, Marlow, Chapman and the rest. Since the constellation of great men who appeared in Greece in the time of Pericles, there was never any such society ; — yet their genius failed them to find out the best head in the universe.[1] Our poet's mask was impenetrable. You cannot see the mountain near.

It took a century to make it suspected; and not until two centuries had passed, after his death, did any criticism which we think adequate begin to appear. It was not possible to write the history of Shakspeare till now; for he is the father of German literature: it was with the introduction of Shakspeare into German, by Lessing, and the translation of his works by Wieland and Schlegel, that the rapid burst of German literature was most intimately connected. It was not until the nineteenth century, whose speculative genius is a sort of living Hamlet, that the tragedy of Hamlet could find such wondering readers.[1] Now, literature, philosophy and thought are Shakspearized. His mind is the horizon beyond which, at present, we do not see. Our ears are educated to music by his rhythm. Coleridge and Goethe are the only critics who have expressed our convictions with any adequate fidelity: but there is in all cultivated minds a silent appreciation of his superlative power and beauty, which, like Christianity, qualifies the period.

The Shakspeare Society have inquired in all directions, advertised the missing facts, offered money for any information that will lead to proof, — and with what result? Beside some important illustration of the history of the English stage, to which I have adverted, they have gleaned a few facts touching the property, and dealings in regard to property, of the poet. It appears that from year to year he owned a larger share in the Blackfriars' Theatre: its wardrobe and other appurtenances were his: that he bought an estate in his native village with his earnings as writer and shareholder; that he lived in the best house in Stratford; was intrusted by his neighbors with their commissions in London, as of borrowing money, and the like; that he was a veritable farmer. About the time when he was writing Macbeth, he sues Philip Rogers, in the borough-court of Stratford, for thirty-five shillings, ten pence, for corn delivered to him at different times; and in all respects appears as a good husband, with no reputation for eccentricity or excess. He was a good-natured sort of man, an actor and shareholder in the theatre, not in any striking manner distinguished from other actors and managers.[1] I admit the importance of this information. It was well worth the pains that have been taken to procure it.

But whatever scraps of information concerning his condition these researches may have rescued, they can shed no light upon that infinite invention which is the concealed magnet of his attraction for us. We are very clumsy writers of history. We tell the chronicle of parentage, birth, birth-place, schooling, school-mates, earning of money, marriage, publication of books, celebrity, death; and when we have come to an end of this gossip, no ray of relation appears between it and the goddess-born; and it seems as if, had we dipped at random into the " Modern Plutarch," and read any other life there, it would have fitted the poems as well.[1] It is the essence of poetry to spring, like the rainbow daughter of Wonder, from the invisible, to abolish the past and refuse all history. Malone, Warburton, Dyce and Collier have wasted their oil. The famed theatres, Covent Garden, Drury Lane, the Park and Tremont have vainly assisted. Betterton, Garrick, Kemble, Kean and Macready dedicate their lives to this genius; him they crown, elucidate, obey and express. The genius knows them not. The recitation begins; one golden word leaps out immortal from all this painted pedantry and sweetly torments us with invitations to its own inaccessible homes. I remember I went once to see the Hamlet of a famed performer, the pride of the English stage; and all I then heard and all I now remember of the tragedian was that in which

the tragedian had no part; simply Hamlet's
question to the ghost:—

> " What may this mean,
> That thou, dead corse, again in complete steel
> Revisit'st thus the glimpses of the moon ? "

That imagination which dilates the closet he
writes in to the world's dimension, crowds it
with agents in rank and order, as quickly reduces the big reality to be the glimpses of the
moon.¹ These tricks of his magic spoil for us
the illusions of the green-room. Can any biography shed light on the localities into which
the Midsummer Night's Dream admits me?
Did Shakspeare confide to any notary or parish recorder, sacristan, or surrogate in Stratford,
the genesis of that delicate creation? The forest of Arden, the nimble air of Scone Castle,
the moonlight of Portia's villa, " the antres vast
and desarts idle " of Othello's captivity,—where
is the third cousin, or grand-nephew, the chan-
cellor's file of accounts, or private letter, that
has kept one word of those transcendent secrets? In fine, in this drama, as in all great
works of art,— in the Cyclopæan architecture
of Egypt and India, in the Phidian sculpture,
the Gothic minsters, the Italian painting, the
Ballads of Spain and Scotland, — the Genius

draws up the ladder after him, when the creative age goes up to heaven, and gives way to a
new age, which sees the works and asks in vain
for a history.

Shakspeare is the only biographer of Shakspeare; and even he can tell nothing, except to
the Shakspeare in us, that is, to our most apprehensive and sympathetic hour.[1] He cannot step
from off his tripod and give us anecdotes of his
inspirations. Read the antique documents ex-
tricated, analyzed and compared by the assidu-
ous Dyce and Collier, and now read one of these
skyey sentences, — aerolites, — which seem to
have fallen out of heaven, and which not your
experience but the man within the breast has
accepted as words of fate, and tell me if they
match ; if the former account in any manner for
the latter ; or which gives the most historical
insight into the man.

Hence, though our external history is so
meagre, yet, with Shakspeare for biographer, instead of Aubrey and Rowe, we have really the
information which is material ; that which describes character and fortune, that which, if we
were about to meet the man and deal with him,
would most import us to know. We have his
recorded convictions on those questions which

knock for answer at every heart, — on life and death, on love, on wealth and poverty, on the prizes of life and the ways whereby we come at them; on the characters of men, and the influences, occult and open, which affect their fortunes; and on those mysterious and demoniacal powers which defy our science and which yet interweave their malice and their gift in our brightest hours. Who ever read the volume of the Sonnets without finding that the poet had there revealed, under masks that are no masks to the intelligent, the lore of friendship and of love; the confusion of sentiments in the most susceptible, and, at the same time, the most intellectual of men? What trait of his private mind has he hidden in his dramas? One can discern, in his ample pictures of the gentleman and the king, what forms and humanities pleased him; his delight in troops of friends, in large hospitality, in cheerful giving. Let Timon, let Warwick, let Antonio the merchant answer for his great heart. So far from Shakspeare's being the least known, he is the one person, in all modern history, known to us. What point of morals, of manners, of economy, of philosophy, of religion, of taste, of the conduct of life, has he not settled? What mystery has he not signified his

IV

knowledge of? What office, or function, or district of man's work, has he not remembered? What king has he not taught state, as Talma taught Napoleon? What maiden has not found him finer than her delicacy? What lover has he not outloved? What sage has he not outseen? What gentleman has he not instructed in the rudeness of his behavior?

Some able and appreciating critics think no criticism on Shakspeare valuable that does not rest purely on the dramatic merit; that he is falsely judged as poet and philosopher. I think as highly as these critics of his dramatic merit, but still think it secondary. He was a full man, who liked to talk; a brain exhaling thoughts and images, which, seeking vent, found the drama next at hand.[1] Had he been less, we should have had to consider how well he filled his place, how good a dramatist he was, — and he is the best in the world. But it turns out that what he has to say is of that weight as to withdraw some attention from the vehicle; and he is like some saint whose history is to be rendered into all languages, into verse and prose, into songs and pictures, and cut up into proverbs; so that the occasion which gave the saint's meaning the form of a conversation, or of a prayer, or of a code of

laws, is immaterial compared with the universality of its application. So it fares with the wise
Shakspeare and his book of life. He wrote the
airs for all our modern music : he wrote the text
of modern life ; the text of manners : he drew
the man of England and Europe ; the father of
the man in America ; ' he drew the man, and described the day, and what is done in it : he read
the hearts of men and women, their probity,
and their second thought and wiles ; the wiles
of innocence, and the transitions by which virtues and vices slide into their contraries : he
could divide the mother's part from the father's
part in the face of the child, or draw the fine
demarcations of freedom and of fate : he knew
the laws of repression which make the police of
nature : and all the sweets and all the terrors of
human lot lay in his mind as truly but as softly
as the landscape lies on the eye. And the importance of this wisdom of life sinks the form,
as of Drama or Epic, out of notice. 'T is like
making a question concerning the paper on which
a king's message is written.

Shakspeare is as much out of the category of
eminent authors, as he is out of the crowd. He
is inconceivably wise ; the others, conceivably.
A good reader can, in a sort, nestle into Plato's

brain and think from thence ; but not into Shakspeare's. We are still out of doors. For executive faculty, for creation, Shakspeare is unique.
No man can imagine it better. He was the far-
thest reach of subtlety compatible with an individual self, — the subtilest of authors, and only
just within the possibility of authorship. With
this wisdom of life is the equal endowment of
imaginative and of lyric power. He clothed the
creatures of his legend with form and sentiments
as if they were people who had lived under his
roof; and few real men have left such distinct
characters as these fictions. And they spoke in
language as sweet as it was fit. Yet his talents
never seduced him into an ostentation, nor did
he harp on one string. An omnipresent humanity co-ordinates all his faculties. Give a man of
talents a story to tell, and his partiality will presently appear. He has certain observations,
opinions, topics, which have some accidental
prominence, and which he disposes all to exhibit.
He crams this part and starves that other part,
consulting not the fitness of the thing, but his
fitness and strength. But Shakspeare has no
peculiarity, no importunate topic ; but all is duly
given ; no veins, no curiosities ; no cow-painter, ·
no bird-fancier, no mannerist is he : he has no

discoverable egotism : the great he tells greatly;
the small subordinately. He is wise without
emphasis or assertion ; he is strong, as nature is
strong, who lifts the land into mountain slopes
without effort and by the same rule as she floats
a bubble in the air, and likes as well to do the
one as the other. This makes that equality of
power in farce, tragedy, narrative, and love-songs;
a merit so incessant that each reader is incredu-
lous of the perception of other readers.

This power of expression, or of transferring
the inmost truth of things into music and verse,
makes him the type of the poet and has added
a new problem to metaphysics. This is that
which throws him into natural history, as a main
production of the globe, and as announcing new
eras and ameliorations. Things were mirrored
in his poetry without loss or blur : he could paint
the fine with precision, the great with compass,
the tragic and the comic indifferently and without any distortion or favor. He carried his
powerful execution into minute details, to a hair
point; finishes an eyelash or a dimple as firmly
as he draws a mountain; and yet these, like
nature's, will bear the scrutiny of the solar microscope.

In short, he is the chief example to prove

that more or less of production, more or fewer
pictures, is a thing indifferent. He had the
power to make one picture. Daguerre learned
how to let one flower etch its image on his plate
of iodine, and then proceeds at leisure to etch a
million. There are always objects; but there was
never representation. Here is perfect representation, at last; and now let the world of figures
sit for their portraits. No recipe can be given
for the making of a Shakspeare; but the possibility of the translation of things into song is
demonstrated.

His lyric power lies in the genius of the piece.
The sonnets, though their excellence is lost in
the splendor of the dramas, are as inimitable as
they; and it is not a merit of lines, but a total
merit of the piece; like the tone of voice of some
incomparable person, so is this a speech of
poetic beings, and any clause as unproducible
now as a whole poem.

Though the speeches in the plays, and single
lines, have a beauty which tempts the ear to
pause on them for their euphuism, yet the sentence is so loaded with meaning and so linked
with its foregoers and followers, that the logician
is satisfied. His means are as admirable as his
ends; every subordinate invention, by which he

helps himself to connect some irreconcilable opposites, is a poem too. He is not reduced to dismount and walk because his horses are running off with him in some distant direction: he always rides.

The finest poetry was first experience; but the thought has suffered a transformation since it was an experience. Cultivated men often attain a good degree of skill in writing verses; but it is easy to read, through their poems, their personal history: any one acquainted with the parties can name every figure; this is Andrew and that is Rachel. The sense thus remains prosaic. It is a caterpillar with wings, and not yet a butterfly. In the poet's mind the fact has gone quite over into the new element of thought, and has lost all that is exuvial. This generosity abides with Shakspeare. We say, from the truth and closeness of his pictures, that he knows the lesson by heart. Yet there is not a trace of egotism.

One more royal trait properly belongs to the poet. I mean his cheerfulness, without which no man can be a poet, — for beauty is his aim. He loves virtue, not for its obligation but for its grace: he delights in the world, in man, in woman, for the lovely light that sparkles from them. Beauty, the spirit of joy and hilarity, he

sheds over the universe. Epicurus relates that
poetry hath such charms that a lover might forsake his mistress to partake of them. And the
true bards have been noted for their firm and
cheerful temper. Homer lies in sunshine; Chaucer is glad and erect; and Saadi says, " It was
rumored abroad that I was penitent; but what
had I to do with repentance?"[1] Not less sovereign and cheerful, — much more sovereign and
cheerful, is the tone of Shakspeare. His name
suggests joy and emancipation to the heart of
men. If he should appear in any company of
human souls, who would not march in his troop?
He touches nothing that does not borrow health
and longevity from his festal style.

And now, how stands the account of man with
this bard and benefactor, when, in solitude, shutting our ears to the reverberations of his fame,
we seek to strike the balance? Solitude has
austere lessons; it can teach us to spare both
heroes and poets; and it weighs Shakspeare also,
and finds him to share the halfness and imper-
fection of humanity.

Shakspeare, Homer, Dante, Chaucer, saw the
splendor of meaning that plays over the visible
world; knew that a tree had another use than

for apples, and corn another than for meal, and
the ball of the earth, than for tillage and roads :
that these things bore a second and finer harvest
to the mind, being emblems of its thoughts, and
conveying in all their natural history a certain
mute commentary on human life.¹ Shakspeare
employed them as colors to compose his picture.
He rested in their beauty ; and never took the
step which seemed inevitable to such genius,
namely to explore the virtue which resides in
these symbols and imparts this power : — what
is that which they themselves say ? He converted the elements which waited on his command, into entertainments. He was master of
the revels to mankind. Is it not as if one should
have, through majestic powers of science, the
comets given into his hand, or the planets and
their moons, and should draw them from their
orbits to glare with the municipal fireworks on
a holiday night, and advertise in all towns,
" Very superior pyrotechny this evening" ? Are
the agents of nature, and the power to understand them, worth no more than a street ser-
enade, or the breath of a cigar ? One remem-
bers again the trumpet-text in the Koran, —
" The heavens and the earth and all that is
between them, think ye we have created them

in jest?" As long as the question is of talent
and mental power, the world of men has not his
equal to show. But when the question is, to life
and its materials and its auxiliaries, how does he
profit me? What does it signify? It is but a
Twelfth Night, or Midsummer-Night's Dream,
or Winter Evening's Tale: what signifies another picture more or less? The Egyptian verdict of the Shakspeare Societies comes to mind;
that he was a jovial actor and manager. I can
not marry this fact to his verse. Other admirable
men have led lives in some sort of keeping with
their thought; but this man, in wide contrast.
Had he been less, had he reached only the common measure of great authors, of Bacon, Milton,
Tasso, Cervantes, we might leave the fact in the
twilight of human fate: but that this man of men,
he who gave to the science of mind a new and
larger subject than had ever existed, and planted
the standard of humanity some furlongs forward
into Chaos, — that he should not be wise for
himself; — it must even go into the world's
history that the best poet led an obscure and
profane life, using his genius for the public
amusement.[1]

Well, other men, priest and prophet, Israelite,
German and Swede, beheld the same objects:

they also saw through them that which was contained. And to what purpose? The beauty straightway vanished; they read commandments, all-excluding mountainous duty; an obligation, a sadness, as of piled mountains, fell on them, and life became ghastly, joyless, a pilgrim's progress, a probation, beleaguered round with doleful histories of Adam's fall and curse behind us; with doomsdays and purgatorial and penal fires before us; and the heart of the seer and the heart of the listener sank in them.

It must be conceded that these are half-views of half-men. The world still wants its poet-priest, a reconciler, who shall not trifle, with Shakspeare the player, nor shall grope in graves, with Swedenborg the mourner; but who shall see, speak, and act, with equal inspiration. For knowledge will brighten the sunshine; right is more beautiful than private affection; and love is compatible with universal wisdom.[1]

VI

NAPOLEON; OR, THE MAN OF THE WORLD

NAPOLEON; OR, THE MAN OF THE WORLD

AMONG the eminent persons of the nine-teenth century, Bonaparte is far the best known and the most powerful; [and owes his predominance to the fidelity with which he expresses the tone of thought and belief, the aims of the masses of active and cultivated men.] It is Swedenborg's theory that every organ is made up of homogeneous particles; or as it is sometimes expressed, every whole is made of similars; that is, the lungs are composed of infinitely small lungs; the liver, of infinitely small livers; the kidney, of little kidneys,' etc. Following this analogy, if any man is found to carry with him the power and affections of vast numbers, if Napoleon is France, if Napoleon is Europe, it is because the people whom he sways are little Napoleons.

In our society there is a standing antagonism between the conservative and the democratic classes; between those who have made their fortunes, and the young and the poor who have fortunes to make; between the interests of dead labor, — that is, the labor of hands long ago still in the grave, which labor is now entombed in money stocks, or in land and buildings owned by idle capitalists, — and the interests of living labor, which seeks to possess itself of land and buildings and money stocks. The first class is timid, selfish, illiberal, hating innovation, and continually losing numbers by death. The second class is selfish also, encroaching, bold, self-relying, always outnumbering the other and recruiting its numbers every hour by births. It desires to keep open every avenue to the competition of all, and to multiply avenues: the class of business men in America, in England, in France and throughout Europe; the class of industry and skill. Napoleon is its representative. The instinct of active, brave, able men, throughout the middle class every where, has pointed out Napoleon as the incarnate Democrat. He had their virtues and their vices; above all, he had their spirit or aim. That tendency is material, pointing at a sensual success and employing the richest and most various means to that end; conversant with mechanical powers, highly intellectual, widely and accurately learned and skilful, but subordinating all intellectual and spiritual forces into means to a material success. To be the rich man, is the end. " God has

Napoleon

granted," says the Koran, "to every people a prophet in its own tongue." Paris and London and New York, the spirit of commerce, of money and material power, were also to have their prophet; and Bonaparte was qualified and sent.

Every one of the million readers of anecdotes or memoirs or lives of Napoleon, delights in the page, because he studies in it his own history.[1] Napoleon is thoroughly modern, and, at the highest point of his fortunes, has the very spirit of the newspapers. He is no saint, — to use his own word, "no capuchin," and he is no hero, in the high sense. The man in the street finds in him the qualities and powers of other men in the street. He finds him, like himself, by birth a citizen, who, by very intelligible merits, arrived at such a commanding position that he could indulge all those tastes which the common man possesses but is obliged to conceal and deny: good society, good books, fast travelling, dress, dinners, servants without number, personal weight, the execution of his ideas, the standing in the attitude of a benefactor to all persons about him, the refined enjoyments of pictures, statues, music, palaces and conventional honors, — precisely what is agreeable to

IV

the heart of every man in the nineteenth century, this powerful man possessed.

It is true that a man of Napoleon's truth of adaptation to the mind of the masses around him, becomes not merely representative but actually a monopolizer and usurper of other minds. Thus Mirabeau plagiarized every good thought, every good word that was spoken in France. Dumont relates that he sat in the gallery of the Convention and heard Mirabeau make a speech. It struck Dumont that he could fit it with a peroration, which he wrote in pencil immediately, and showed it to Lord Elgin, who sat by him. Lord Elgin approved it, and Dumont, in the evening, showed it to Mirabeau. Mirabeau read it, pronounced it admirable, and declared he would incorporate it into his harangue to-morrow, to the Assembly. " It is impossible," said Dumont, "as, unfortunately, I have shown it to Lord Elgin." " If you have shown it to Lord Elgin and to fifty persons beside, I shall still speak it to-morrow :" and he did speak it, with much effect, at the next day's session. For Mirabeau, with his overpowering personality, felt that these things which his presence inspired were as much his own as if he had said them, and that his adoption of them gave

them their weight. Much more absolute and
centralizing was the successor to Mirabeau's
popularity and to much more than his predominance in France. Indeed, a man of Napoleon's
stamp almost ceases to have a private speech
and opinion. He is so largely receptive, and is
so placed, that he comes to be a bureau for all
the intelligence, wit and power of the age and
country. He gains the battle; he makes the
code; he makes the system of weights and measures; he levels the Alps; he builds the road.
All distinguished engineers, savans, statists, report to him: so likewise do all good heads in
every kind: he adopts the best measures, sets
his stamp on them, and not these alone, but on
every happy and memorable expression. Every
sentence spoken by Napoleon and every line of
his writing, deserves reading, as it is the sense
of France.

Bonaparte was the idol of common men because he had in transcendent degree the qualities
and powers of common men. There is a certain
satisfaction in coming down to the lowest ground
of politics, for we get rid of cant and hypocrisy.
Bonaparte wrought, in common with that great
class he represented, for power and wealth, —
but Bonaparte, specially, without any scruple as

to the means. All the sentiments which em-
barrass men's pursuit of these objects, he set
aside. The sentiments were for women and children. Fontanes, in 1804, expressed Napoleon's
own sense, when in behalf of the Senate he addressed him, — " Sire, the desire of perfection is
the worst disease that ever afflicted the human
mind." The advocates of liberty and of progress are "ideologists ; " — a word of contempt
often in his mouth ; — " Necker is an ideologist : " " Lafayette is an ideologist." [1]

An Italian proverb, too well known, declares
that " if you would succeed, you must not be
too good." It is an advantage, within certain
limits, to have renounced the dominion of the
sentiments of piety, gratitude and generosity ;
since what was an impassable bar to us, and still
is to others, becomes a convenient weapon for
our purposes ; just as the river which was a
formidable barrier, winter transforms into the
smoothest of roads.

Napoleon renounced, once for all, sentiments
and affections, and would help himself with his
hands and his head. With him is no miracle and
no magic. He is a worker in brass, in iron, in
wood, in earth, in roads, in buildings, in money
and in troops, and a very consistent and wise

master-workman. He is never weak and literary, but acts with the solidity and the precision
of natural agents. He has not lost his native
sense and sympathy with things.[1] Men give way
before such a man, as before natural events. To
be sure there are men enough who are immersed
in things, as farmers, smiths, sailors and mechan-
ics generally ; and we know how real and solid
such men appear in the presence of scholars and
grammarians : but these men ordinarily lack the
power of arrangement, and are like hands without a head. But Bonaparte superadded to this
mineral and animal force, insight and generalization, so that men saw in him combined the
natural and the intellectual power, as if the sea
and land had taken flesh and begun to cipher.
Therefore the land and sea seem to presuppose
him. He came unto his own and they received
him. This ciphering operative knows what he
is working with and what is the product. He
knew the properties of gold and iron, of wheels
and ships, of troops and diplomatists, and required that each should do after its kind.

The art of war was the game in which he
exerted his arithmetic. It consisted, according
to him, in having always more forces than
the enemy, on the point where the enemy is

attacked, or where he attacks : and his whole
talent is strained by endless manœuvre and
evolution, to march always on the enemy at an
angle, and destroy his forces in detail. It is
obvious that a very small force, skilfully and
rapidly manœuvring so as always to bring two
men against one at the point of engagement,
will be an overmatch for a much larger body
of men.

The times, his constitution and his early circumstances combined to develop this pattern
democrat. He had the virtues of his class and
the conditions for their activity. That common-
sense which no sooner respects any end than it
finds the means to effect it ; the delight in the
use of means ; in the choice, simplification and
combining of means ; the directness and thoroughness of his work ; the prudence with which
all was seen and the energy with which all was
done, make him the natural organ and head of
what I may almost call, from its extent, the
modern party.[1]

Nature must have far the greatest share in
every success, and so in his. Such a man was
wanted, and such a man was born; a man of
stone and iron, capable of sitting on horseback
sixteen or seventeen hours, of going many days

together without rest or food except by snatches, and with the speed and spring of a tiger in action; a man not embarrassed by any scruples; compact, instant, selfish, prudent, and of a perception which did not suffer itself to be baulked or misled by any pretences of others, or any superstition or any heat or haste of his own.[1] " My hand of iron," he said, " was not at the extremity of my arm, it was immediately connected with my head." He respected the power of nature and fortune, and ascribed to it his superiority, instead of valuing himself, like inferior men, on his opinionativeness, and waging war with nature. His favorite rhetoric lay in allusion to his star; and he pleased himself, as well as the people, when he styled himself the " Child of Destiny."[2] " They charge me," he said, " with the commission of great crimes: men of my stamp do not commit crimes. Nothing has been more simple than my elevation, 't is in vain to ascribe it to intrigue or crime; it was owing to the peculiarity of the times and to my reputation of having fought well against the enemies of my country. I have always marched with the opinion of great masses and with events. Of what use then would crimes be to me?" Again he said, speaking of his son, " My son can not replace me; I could not replace myself. I am the creature of circumstances."

He had a directness of action never before combined with so much comprehension. He is a realist, terrific to all talkers and confused truth-obscuring persons. He sees where the matter hinges, throws himself on the precise point of resistance, and slights all other considerations. He is strong in the right manner, namely by insight. He never blundered into victory, but won his battles in his head before he won them on the field. His principal means are in himself. He asks counsel of no other. In 1796 he writes to the Directory: " I have conducted the campaign without consulting any one. I should have done no good if I had been under the necessity of conforming to the notions of another person. I have gained some advantages over superior forces and when totally destitute of every thing, because, in the persuasion that your confidence was reposed in me, my actions were as prompt as my thoughts."

History is full, down to this day, of the imbecility of kings and governors. They are a class of persons much to be pitied, for they know not what they should do. The weavers strike for bread, and the king and his ministers, knowing not what to do, meet them with bayonets. But Napoleon understood his business. Here was a man who in each moment and emergency knew what to do next. It is an immense comfort and refreshment to the spirits, not only of kings, but of citizens. Few men have any next; they live from hand to mouth, without plan, and are ever at the end of their line, and after each action wait for an impulse from abroad. Napoleon had been the first man of the world, if his ends had been purely public. As he is, he inspires confidence and vigor by the extraordinary unity of his action. He is firm, sure, self-denying, self-postponing, sacrificing every thing, — money, troops, generals, and his own safety also, to his aim ; not misled, like common adventurers, by the splendor of his own means. "Incidents ought not to govern policy," he said, " but policy, incidents." " To be hurried away by every event is to have no political system at all." His victories were only so many doors, and he never for a moment lost sight of his way onward, in the dazzle and uproar of the present circumstance. He knew what to do, and he flew to his mark. He would shorten a straight line to come at his object. Horrible anecdotes may no doubt be collected from his history, of the price at which he bought his successes; but he must not therefore be set down as cruel, but only as one who knew no impediment to his will; not bloodthirsty, not cruel, — but woe to what thing or person stood in his way! Not bloodthirsty, but not sparing of blood, — and pitiless. He saw only the object: the obstacle must give way. "Sire, General Clarke can not combine with General Junot, for the dreadful fire of the Austrian battery." — "Let him carry the battery." — "Sire, every regiment that approaches the heavy artillery is sacrificed: Sire, what orders?" — "Forward, forward!" Seruzier, a colonel of artillery, gives, in his "Military Memoirs," the following sketch of a scene after the battle of Austerlitz. — "At the moment in which the Russian army was making its retreat, painfully, but in good order, on the ice of the lake, the Emperor Napoleon came riding at full speed toward the artillery. 'You are losing time,' he cried; 'fire upon those masses; they must be engulfed: fire upon the ice!' The order remained unexecuted for ten minutes. In vain several officers and myself were placed on the slope of a hill to produce the effect: their balls and mine rolled upon the ice without breaking it up. Seeing that, I tried a

simple method of elevating light howitzers.
The almost perpendicular fall of the heavy pro-
jectiles produced the desired effect. My method
was immediately followed by the adjoining bat-
teries, and in less than no time we buried " some
" thousands of Russians and Austrians under
the waters of the lake." [1]

In the plenitude of his resources, every obstacle, seemed to vanish. " There shall be no
Alps," he said ; and he built his perfect roads,
climbing by graded galleries their steepest pre-
cipices, until Italy was as open to Paris as any
town in France. He laid his bones to, and
wrought for his crown. Having decided what
was to be done, he did that with might and main.
He put out all his strength. He risked every
thing and spared nothing, neither ammunition,
nor money, nor troops, nor generals, nor himself.

We like to see every thing do its office after
its kind, whether it be a milch-cow or a rattle-
snake ; and if fighting be the best mode of ad-
justing national differences, (as large majorities
of men seem to agree,) certainly Bonaparte was
right in making it thorough. The grand principle of war, he said, was that an army ought
always to be ready, by day and by night and at

all hours, to make all the resistance it is capable
of making. He never economized his ammunition, but, on a hostile position, rained a torrent
of iron, — shells, balls, grape-shot, — to annihi-
late all defence. On any point of resistance he
concentrated squadron on squadron in over-
whelming numbers until it was swept out of
existence. To a regiment of horse-chasseurs at
Lobenstein, two days before the battle of Jena,
Napoleon said, " My lads, you must not fear
death; when soldiers brave death, they drive
him into the enemy's ranks." In the fury of
assault, he no more spared himself. He went to
the edge of his possibility. It is plain that in
Italy he did what he could, and all that he could.
He came, several times, within an inch of ruin;
and his own person was all but lost. He was
flung into the marsh at Arcola. The Austrians
were between him and his troops, in the *mêlée*,
and he was brought off with desperate efforts.
At Lonato, and at other places, he was on the
point of being taken prisoner. He fought sixty
battles. He had never enough. Each victory
was a new weapon. " My power would fall,
were I not to support it by new achievements.
Conquest has made me what I am, and conquest
must maintain me." He felt, with every wise

man, that as much life is needed for conserva-
tion as for creation. We are always in peril,
always in a bad plight, just on the edge of destruction and only to be saved by invention and
courage.

. This vigor was guarded and tempered by the
coldest prudence and punctuality. A thunder-
bolt in the attack, he was found invulnerable in
his intrenchments. His very attack was never
the inspiration of courage, but the result of calculation. His idea of the best defence consists .
in being still the attacking party. " My ambition," he says, "was great, but was of a cold
nature." In one of his conversations with Las
Casas, he remarked, "As to moral courage, I
have rarely met with the two-o'clock-in-the-
morning kind: I mean unprepared courage;
that which is necessary on an unexpected occasion, and which, in spite of the most unforeseen
events, leaves full freedom of judgment and de-
cision: " and he did not hesitate to declare that
he was himself eminently endowed with this
two-o'clock-in-the-morning courage, and that
he had met with few persons equal to himself
in this respect.

Every thing depended on the nicety of his
combinations, and the stars were not more

punctual than his arithmetic. His personal
attention descended to the smallest particulars.
"At Montebello, I ordered Kellermann to attack with eight hundred horse, and with these
he separated the six thousand Hungarian grena-
diers, before the very eyes of the Austrian cavalry. This cavalry was half a league off and
required a quarter of an hour to arrive on the
field of action, and I have observed that it is
always these quarters of an hour that decide the
fate of a battle." "Before he fought a battle,
Bonaparte thought little about what he should
do in case of success, but a great deal about
what he should do in case of a reverse of fortune." The same prudence and good sense
mark all his behavior. His instructions to
his secretary at the Tuileries are worth remembering. "During the night, enter my chamber
as seldom as possible. Do not awake me when
you have any good news to communicate; with
that there is no hurry. But when you bring
bad news, rouse me instantly, for then there is
not a moment to be lost." It was a whimsical
economy of the same kind which dictated his
practice, when general in Italy, in regard to
his burdensome correspondence. He directed
Bourrienne to leave all letters unopened for

three weeks, and then observed with satisfaction how large a part of the correspondence had thus disposed of itself and no longer required an answer. His achievement of business was immense, and enlarges the known powers of man. There have been many working kings, from Ulysses to William of Orange, but none who accomplished a tithe of this man's performance.

To these gifts of nature, Napoleon added the advantage of having been born to a private and humble fortune. In his later days he had the weakness of wishing to add to his crowns and badges the prescription of aristocracy; but he knew his debt to his austere education, and made no secret of his contempt for the born kings, and for "the hereditary asses," as he coarsely styled the Bourbons. He said that "in their exile they had learned nothing, and forgot nothing." Bonaparte had passed through all the degrees of military service, but also was citizen before he was emperor, and so has the key to citizenship. His remarks and estimates discover the information and justness of measurement of the middle class. Those who had to deal with him found that he was not to be imposed upon, but could cipher as well as another man. This appears in all parts of his Memoirs, dictated at St. Helena. When the expenses of the empress, of his household, of his palaces, had accumulated great debts, Napoleon examined the bills of the creditors himself, detected overcharges and errors, and reduced the claims by considerable sums.

His grand weapon, namely the millions whom he directed, he owed to the representative character which clothed him. He interests us as he stands for France and for Europe; and he exists as captain and king only as far as the Revolution, or the interest of the industrious masses, found an organ and a leader in him. In the social interests, he knew the meaning and value of labor, and threw himself naturally on that side. I like an incident mentioned by one of his biographers at St. Helena. "When walking with Mrs. Balcombe, some servants, carrying heavy boxes, passed by on the road, and Mrs. Balcombe desired them, in rather an angry tone, to keep back. Napoleon interfered, saying 'Respect the burden, Madam.'"[1] In the time of the empire he directed attention to the improvement and embellishment of the markets of the capital. "The market-place," he said, "is the Louvre of the common people." The

principal works that have survived him are his
magnificent roads. He filled the troops with his
spirit, and a sort of freedom and companion-
ship grew up between him and them, which the
forms of his court never permitted between the
officers and himself. They performed, under
his eye, that which no others could do. The
best document of his relation to his troops is the
order of the day on the morning of the battle
of Austerlitz, in which Napoleon promises
the troops that he will keep his person out of
reach of fire. This declaration, which is the reverse of that ordinarily made by generals and
sovereigns on the eve of a battle, sufficiently
explains the devotion of the army to their
leader.

But though there is in particulars this identity between Napoleon and the mass of the
people, his real strength lay in their conviction
that he was their representative in his genius
and aims, not only when he courted, but when
he controlled, and even when he decimated them
by his conscriptions. He knew, as well as any
Jacobin in France, how to philosophize on liberty and equality; and when allusion was made
to the precious blood of centuries, which was
spilled by the killing of the Duc d'Enghien,

IV

he suggested, "Neither is my blood ditch-water." The people felt that no longer the throne was occupied and the land sucked of its nourishment, by a small class of legitimates, secluded from all community with the children of the soil, and holding the ideas and superstitions of a long-forgotten state of society. Instead of that vampyre, a man of themselves held, in the Tuileries, knowledge and ideas like their own, opening of course to them and their children all places of power and trust. The day of sleepy, selfish policy, ever narrowing the means and opportunities of young men, was ended, and a day of expansion and demand was come. A market for all the powers and productions of man was opened; brilliant prizes glittered in the eyes of youth and talent. The old, iron-bound, feudal France was changed into a young Ohio or New York; and those who smarted under the immediate rigors of the new monarch, pardoned them as the necessary severities of the military system which had driven out the oppressor. And even when the majority of the people had begun to ask whether they had really gained any thing under the exhausting levies of men and money of the new master, the whole talent of the country, in every rank and kindred, took his part and defended him as its natural patron. In 1814, when advised to rely on the higher classes, Napoleon said to those around him, " Gentlemen, in the situation in which I stand, my only nobility is the rabble of the Faubourgs."

Napoleon met this natural expectation. The necessity of his position required a hospitality to every sort of talent, and its appointment to trusts ; and his feeling went along with this policy. Like every superior person, he undoubtedly felt a desire for men and compeers, and a wish to measure his power with other masters, and an impatience of fools and underlings. In Italy, he sought for men and found none. "Good God !" he said, " how rare men are ! There are eighteen millions in Italy, and I have with difficulty found two, — Dandolo and Melzi." In later years, with larger experience, his respect for mankind was not increased. In a moment of bitterness he said to one of his oldest friends, " Men deserve the contempt with which they inspire me. I have only to put some gold-lace on the coat of my virtuous republicans and they immediately become just what I wish them." This impatience at levity was, however, an oblique tribute of respect to those able persons who commanded his regard not only when he found them friends and coadjutors but also when they resisted his will. He could not confound Fox and Pitt, Carnot, Lafayette and Bernadotte, with the danglers of his court; and in spite of the detraction which his systematic egotism dictated toward the great captains who conquered with and for him, ample acknowledgments are made by him to Lannes, Duroc, Kleber, Dessaix, Massena, Murat, Ney and Augereau. If he felt himself their patron and the founder of their fortunes, as when he said "I made my generals out of mud,"—he could not hide his satisfaction in receiving from them a seconding and support commensurate with the grandeur of his enterprise. In the Russian campaign he was so much impressed by the courage and resources of Marshal Ney, that he said, "I have two hundred millions in my coffers, and I would give them all for Ney." The characters which he has drawn of several of his marshals are discriminating, and though they did not content the insatiable vanity of French officers, are no doubt substantially just. And in fact every species of merit was sought and advanced under his government. "I know," he said, "the depth and draught of water of every one of my generals." Natural power was sure to be well received at his court. Seventeen men in his time were raised from common soldiers to the rank of king, marshal, duke, or general; and the crosses of his Legion of Honor were given to personal valor, and not to family connexion. "When soldiers have been baptized in the fire of a battle-field, they have all one rank in my eyes."

When a natural king becomes a titular king, every body is pleased and satisfied. The Revolution entitled the strong populace of the Faubourg St. Antoine, and every horse-boy and powder-monkey in the army, to look on Napoleon as flesh of his flesh and the creature of *his* party: but there is something in the success of grand talent which enlists an universal sympathy. For in the prevalence of sense and spirit over stupidity and malversation, all reasonable men have an interest; and as intellectual beings we feel the air purified by the electric shock, when material force is overthrown by intellectual energies. As soon as we are removed out of the reach of local and accidental partialities, Man feels that Napoleon fights for him; these are honest victories; this strong steam-engine does our work. Whatever appeals to the imagination,

by transcending the ordinary limits of human
ability, wonderfully encourages and liberates us.[1]
This capacious head, revolving and disposing
sovereignly trains of affairs, and animating such
multitudes of agents; this eye, which looked
through Europe; this prompt invention; this
inexhaustible resource: — what events! what
romantic pictures! what strange situations! —
when spying the Alps, by a sunset in the Sicilian
sea; drawing up his army for battle in sight of
the Pyramids, and saying to his troops, "From
the tops of those pyramids, forty centuries look
down on you;" fording the Red Sea; wading
in the gulf of the Isthmus of Suez. On the shore
of Ptolemais, gigantic projects agitated him.
"Had Acre fallen, I should have changed the
face of the world." His army, on the night of
the battle of Austerlitz, which was the anniver-
sary of his inauguration as Emperor, presented
him with a bouquet of forty standards taken in
the fight. Perhaps it is a little puerile, the pleasure he took in making these contrasts glaring;
as when he pleased himself with making kings
wait in his antechambers, at Tilsit, at Paris and
at Erfurt.

We can not, in the universal imbecility, inde-
cision and indolence of men, sufficiently con-

gratulate ourselves on this strong and ready actor, who took occasion by the beard, and showed us how much may be accomplished by the mere force of such virtues as all men possess in less degrees; namely, by punctuality, by personal attention, by courage and thoroughness. "The Austrians," he said, "do not know the value of time." I should cite him, in his earlier years, as a model of prudence. His power does not consist in any wild or extravagant force; in any enthusiasm like Mahomet's, or singular power of persuasion; but in the exercise of common-sense on each emergency, instead of abiding by rules and customs. The lesson he teaches is that which vigor always teaches; — that there is always room for it. To what heaps of cowardly doubts is not that man's life an answer.[1] When he appeared it was the belief of all military men that there could be nothing new in war; as it is the belief of men to-day that nothing new can be undertaken in politics, or in church, or in letters, or in trade, or in farming, or in our social manners and customs; and as it is at all times the belief of society that the world is used up. But Bonaparte knew better than society; and moreover knew that he knew better. I think all men know better

than they do ; know that the institutions we so
volubly commend are go-carts and baubles ; but
they dare not trust their presentiments. Bonaparte relied on his own sense, and did not care
a bean for other people's. The world treated his
novelties just as it treats everybody's novelties,
— made infinite objection, mustered all the im-
pediments; but he snapped his finger at their
objections. "What creates great difficulty," he
remarks, "in the profession of the land-com-
mander, is the necessity of feeding so many men
and animals. If he allows himself to be guided
by the commissaries he will never stir, and all
his expeditions will fail." An example of his
common-sense is what he says of the passage of
the Alps in winter, which all writers, one repeating after the other, had described as impracticable. "The winter," says Napoleon, "is
not the most unfavorable season for the passage
of lofty mountains. The snow is then firm, the
weather settled, and there is nothing to fear from
avalanches, the real and only danger to be apprehended in the Alps. On these high mountains there are often very fine days in December,
of a dry cold, with extreme calmness in the air."
Read his account, too, of the way in which battles
are gained. "In all battles a moment occurs

when the bravest troops, after having made the greatest efforts, feel inclined to run. That terror proceeds from a want of confidence in their own courage, and it only requires a slight opportunity, a pretence, to restore confidence to them. The art is, to give rise to the opportunity and to invent the pretence. At Arcola I won the battle with twenty-five horsemen. I seized that moment of lassitude, gave every man a trumpet, and gained the day with this handful. You see that two armies are two bodies which meet and endeavor to frighten each other; a moment of panic occurs, and that moment must be turned to advantage. When a man has been present in many actions, he distinguishes that moment without difficulty: it is as easy as casting up an addition."

This deputy of the nineteenth century added to his gifts a capacity for speculation on general topics. He delighted in running through the range of practical, of literary and of abstract questions. His opinion is always original and to the purpose. On the voyage to Egypt he liked, after dinner, to fix on three or four persons to support a proposition, and as many to oppose it. He gave a subject, and the discussions turned on questions of religion, the different kinds of

government, and the art of war. One day he
asked whether the planets were inhabited? On
another, what was the age of the world? Then
he proposed to consider the probability of the
destruction of the globe, either by water or by
fire: at another time, the truth or fallacy of
presentiments, and the interpretation of dreams.
He was very fond of talking of religion. In
1806 he conversed with Fournier, bishop of
Montpellier, on matters of theology. There
were two points on which they could not agree,
viz. that of hell, and that of salvation out of the
pale of the church. The Emperor told Josephine that he disputed like a devil on these two
points, on which the bishop was inexorable. To
the philosophers he readily yielded all that was
proved against religion as the work of men and
time, but he would not hear of materialism.
One fine night, on deck, amid a clatter of materialism, Bonaparte pointed to the stars, and
said, " You may talk as long as you please, gentlemen, but who made all that ? " He delighted
in the conversation of men of science, particularly
of Monge and Berthollet ; but the men of letters he slighted ; they were " manufacturers of
phrases." Of medicine too he was fond of talking, and with those of its practitioners whom he

most esteemed, — with Corvisart at Paris, and with Antonomarchi at St. Helena. "Believe me," he said to the last, "we had better leave off all these remedies: life is a fortress which neither you nor I know any thing about. Why throw obstacles in the way of its defence? Its own means are superior to all the apparatus of your laboratories.' Corvisart candidly agreed with me that all your filthy mixtures are good for nothing. Medicine is a collection of uncertain prescriptions, the results of which, taken collectively, are more fatal than useful to mankind. Water, air and cleanliness are the chief articles in my pharmacopœia."

His memoirs, dictated to Count Montholon and General Gourgaud at St. Helena, have great value, after all the deduction that it seems is to be made from them on account of his known disingenuousness. He has the good-nature of strength and conscious superiority.' I admire his simple, clear narrative of his battles; — good as Cæsar's; his good-natured and sufficiently respectful account of Marshal Wurmser and his other antagonists; and his own equality as a writer to his varying subject. The most agreeable portion is the Campaign in Egypt.

He had hours of thought and wisdom.' In

intervals of leisure, either in the camp or the palace, Napoleon appears as a man of genius directing on abstract questions the native appetite for truth and the impatience of words he was wont to show in war. He could enjoy every play of invention, a romance, a *bon mot*, as well as a stratagem in a campaign. He delighted to fascinate Josephine and her ladies, in a dim-lighted apartment, by the terrors of a fiction to which his voice and dramatic power lent every addition.

I call Napoleon the agent or attorney of the middle class of modern society; of the throng who fill the markets, shops, counting-houses, manufactories, ships, of the modern world, aiming to be rich. He was the agitator, the destroyer of prescription, the internal improver, the liberal, the radical, the inventor of means, the opener of doors and markets, the subverter of monopoly and abuse. Of course the rich and aristocratic did not like him. England, the centre of capital, and Rome and Austria, centres of tradition and genealogy, opposed him. The consternation of the dull and conservative classes, the terror of the foolish old men and old women of the Roman conclave, who in their despair took hold of any thing, and would cling to red-

hot iron,—the vain attempts of statists to amuse
and deceive him, of the emperor of Austria to
bribe him; and the instinct of the young, ardent
and active men every where, which pointed him
out as the giant of the middle class, make his
history bright and commanding. He had the
virtues of the masses of his constituents: he had
also their vices. I am sorry that the brilliant
picture has its reverse. But that is the fatal
quality which we discover in our pursuit of
wealth, that it is treacherous, and is bought by
the breaking or weakening of the sentiments;
and it is inevitable that we should find the same
fact in the history of this champion, who proposed to himself simply a brilliant career, without any stipulation or scruple concerning the
means.

Bonaparte was singularly destitute of generous sentiments. The highest-placed individual
in the most cultivated age and population of
the world,—he has not the merit of common
truth and honesty. He is unjust to his generals;
egotistic and monopolizing; meanly stealing the
credit of their great actions from Kellermann,
from Bernadotte; intriguing to involve his faithful Junot in hopeless bankruptcy, in order to
drive him to a distance from Paris, because the

familiarity of his manners offends the new pride
of his throne. He is a boundless liar. The
official paper, his " Moniteur," and all his bul-
letins, are proverbs for saying what he wished
to be believed; and worse, — he sat, in his premature old age, in his lonely island, coldly falsi-
fying facts and dates and characters, and giving
to history a theatrical *éclat*. Like all Frenchmen
he has a passion for stage effect. Every action
that breathes of generosity is poisoned by this
calculation. His star, his love of glory, his doctrine of the immortality of the soul, are all
French. " I must dazzle and astonish. If I were
to give the liberty of the press, my power could
not last three days." To make a great noise is
his favorite design. " A great reputation is a
great noise : the more there is made, the farther
off it is heard. Laws, institutions, monuments,
nations, all fall ; but the noise continues, and re-
sounds in after ages." His doctrine of immortality is simply fame. His theory of influence
is not flattering. "There are two levers for moving men, — interest and fear. Love is a silly
infatuation, depend upon it. Friendship is but
a name. I love nobody. I do not even love my
brothers : perhaps Joseph a little, from habit,
and because he is my elder ; and Duroc, I love

him too; but why?—because his character
pleases me: he is stern and resolute, and I believe the fellow never shed a tear. For my part
I know very well that I have no true friends.
As long as I continue to be what I am, I may
have as many pretended friends as I please.
Leave sensibility to women; but men should
be firm in heart and purpose, or they should
have nothing to do with war and government."
He was thoroughly unscrupulous. He would
steal, slander, assassinate, drown and poison, as
his interest dictated. He had no generosity, but
mere vulgar hatred; he was intensely selfish;
he was perfidious; he cheated at cards; he was
a prodigious gossip, and opened letters, and delighted in his infamous police, and rubbed his
hands with joy when he had intercepted some
morsel of intelligence concerning the men and
women about him, boasting that " he knew every
thing;" and interfered with the cutting the
dresses of the women; and listened after the
hurrahs and the compliments of the street, in-
cognito. His manners were coarse. He treated
women with low familiarity. He had the habit
of pulling their ears and pinching their cheeks
when he was in good humor, and of pulling the
ears and whiskers of men, and of striking and

horse-play with them, to his last days. It does not appear that he listened at key-holes, or at least that he was caught at it. In short, when you have penetrated through all the circles of power and splendor, you were not dealing with a gentleman, at last; but with an impostor and a rogue; and he fully deserves the epithet of *Jupiter Scapin*, or a sort of Scamp Jupiter.[1]

In describing the two parties into which modern society divides itself, — the democrat and the conservative, — I said, Bonaparte represents the democrat, or the party of men of business, against the stationary or conservative party. I omitted then to say, what is material to the statement, namely that these two parties differ only as young and old. The democrat is a young conservative; the conservative is an old democrat. The aristocrat is the democrat ripe and gone to seed; — because both parties stand on the one ground of the supreme value of property, which one endeavors to get, and the other to keep. Bonaparte may be said to represent the whole history of this party, its youth and its age; yes, and with poetic justice its fate, in his own. The counter-revolution, the counter-party, still waits for its organ and representative,

in a lover and a man of truly public and universal aims.

Here was an experiment, under the most
favorable conditions, of the powers of intellect
without conscience.[1] Never was such a leader
so endowed and so weaponed; never leader
found such aids and followers. And what was
the result of this vast talent and power, of these
immense armies, burned cities, squandered treasures, immolated millions of men, of this de-
moralized Europe? It came to no result. All
passed away like the smoke of his artillery, and
left no trace. He left France smaller, poorer,
feebler, than he found it; and the whole contest
for freedom was to be begun again.[2] The attempt was in principle suicidal. [France served
him with life and limb and estate, as long as it
could identify its interest with him;] but when
men saw that after victory was another war;
after the destruction of armies, new conscriptions; and they who had toiled so desperately
were never nearer to the reward,— they could
not spend what they had earned, nor repose on
their down-beds, nor strut in their châteaux,—
they deserted him. Men found that his absorbing egotism was deadly to all other men. It resembled the torpedo, which inflicts a succession

of shocks on any one who takes hold of it, producing spasms which contract the muscles of the
hand, so that the man can not open his fingers ;
and the animal inflicts new and more violent
shocks, until he paralyzes and kills his victim.
So this exorbitant egotist narrowed, impover-
ished and absorbed the power and existence of
those who served him ; and the universal cry
of France and of Europe in 1814 was, "Enough
of him ;" "*Assez de Bonaparte.*"

It was not Bonaparte's fault. He did all
that in him lay to live and thrive without moral
principle. It was the nature of things, the eternal law of man and of the world which baulked
and ruined him ; and the result, in a million experiments, will be the same. Every experiment,
by multitudes or by individuals, that has a
sensual and selfish aim, will fail. The pacific
Fourier will be as inefficient as the pernicious
Napoleon. As long as our civilization is essentially one of property, of fences, of exclusive-
ness, it will be mocked by delusions. Our riches
will leave us sick ; there will be bitterness in our
laughter, and our wine will burn our mouth.
Only that good profits which we can taste with
all doors open, and which serves all men.

VII

GOETHE; OR, THE WRITER

GOETHE; OR, THE WRITER

I FIND a provision in the constitution of the world for the writer, or secretary, who is to report the doings of the miraculous spirit of life that everywhere throbs and works. His office is a reception of the facts into the mind, and then a selection of the eminent and characteristic experiences.

Nature will be reported. All things are engaged in writing their history. The planet, the pebble, goes attended by its shadow. The rolling rock leaves its scratches on the mountain; the river its channel in the soil; the animal its bones in the stratum; the fern and leaf their modest epitaph in the coal. The falling drop makes its sculpture in the sand or the stone. Not a foot steps into the snow or along the ground, but prints, in characters more or less lasting, a map of its march. Every act of the man inscribes itself in the memories of his fellows and in his own manners and face. The air is full of sounds; the sky, of tokens; the round is all memoranda and signatures, and every object covered over with hints which speak to the intelligent.

Goethe

written, first or last; and he would report the
Holy Ghost, or attempt it. Nothing so broad,
so subtle, or so dear, but comes therefore commended to his pen, and he will write. In his
eyes, a man is the faculty of reporting, and the
universe is the possibility of being reported. In
conversation, in calamity, he finds new materials; as our German poet said, "Some god
gave me the power to paint what I suffer."
He draws his rents from rage and pain. By
acting rashly, he buys the power of talking
wisely. Vexations and a tempest of passion
only fill his sail; as the good Luther writes,
"When I am angry, I can pray well and preach
well:" and, if we knew the genesis of fine
strokes of eloquence, they might recall the com-
plaisance of Sultan Amurath, who struck off
some Persian heads, that his physician, Vesalius, might see the spasms in the muscles of the
neck.¹ His failures are the preparation of his
victories. A new thought or a crisis of passion
apprises him that all that he has yet learned and
written is exoteric, — is not the fact, but some
rumor of the fact. What then? Does he throw
away the pen? No; he begins again to describe
in the new light which has shined on him, —
if, by some means, he may yet save some true

word. Nature conspires. Whatever can be thought can be spoken, and still rises for utterance, though to rude and stammering organs. If they can not compass it, it waits and works, until at last it moulds them to its perfect will and is articulated.

This striving after imitative expression, which one meets every where, is significant of the aim of nature, but is mere stenography. There are higher degrees, and nature has more splendid endowments for those whom she elects to a superior office ; for the class of scholars or writers, who see connection where the multitude see fragments, and who are impelled to exhibit the facts in order, and so to supply the axis on which the frame of things turns. Nature has dearly at heart the formation of the speculative man, or scholar. It is an end never lost sight of, and is prepared in the original casting of things. He is no permissive or accidental appearance, but an organic agent, one of the estates of the realm, provided and prepared from of old and from everlasting, in the knitting and contexture of things. Presentiments, impulses, cheer him. There is a certain heat in the breast which attends the perception of a primary truth, which is the shining of the spiritual sun down into the shaft of the mine. Every thought which dawns on the mine, in the moment of its emergence announces its own rank, — whether it is some whimsy, or whether it is a power.

If he have his incitements, there is, on the other side, invitation and need enough of his gift. Society has, at all times, the same want, namely of one sane man with adequate powers of expression to hold up each object of monomania in its right relations. The ambitious and mercenary bring their last new mumbo-jumbo, whether tariff, Texas, railroad, Romanism, mesmerism, or California; and, by detaching the object from its relations, easily succeed in making it seen in a glare; and a multitude go mad about it, and they are not to be reproved or cured by the opposite multitude who are kept from this particular insanity by an equal frenzy on another crotchet. But let one man have the comprehensive eye that can replace this isolated prodigy in its right neighborhood and bearings, — the illusion vanishes, and the returning reason of the community thanks the reason of the monitor.[1]

The scholar is the man of the ages, but he must also wish with other men to stand well with his contemporaries. But there is a certain ridicule, among superficial people, thrown on the scholars or clerisy, which is of no import unless the scholar heed it. In this country, the emphasis of conversation and of public opinion commends the practical man ; and the solid portion of the community is named with significant respect in every circle. Our people are of Bonaparte's opinion concerning ideologists. Ideas are subversive of social order and comfort, and at last make a fool of the possessor. It is believed, the ordering a cargo of goods from New York to Smyrna, or the running up and down to procure a company of subscribers to set a-going five or ten thousand spindles, or the negotiations of a caucus and the practising on the prejudices and facility of country-people to secure their votes in November, — is practical and commendable.

If I were to compare action of a much higher strain with a life of contemplation, I should not venture to pronounce with much confidence in favor of the former. Mankind have such a deep stake in inward illumination, that there is much to be said by the hermit or monk in defence of his life of thought and prayer. A certain partiality, a headiness and loss of balance, is the tax which all action must pay. Act, if you like, —

but you do it at your peril. Men's actions are too strong for them. Show me a man who has acted and who has not been the victim and slave of his action. What they have done commits and enforces them to do the same again. The first act, which was to be an experiment, becomes a sacrament. The fiery reformer embodies his aspiration in some rite or covenant, and he and his friends cleave to the form and lose the aspiration. The Quaker has established Quakerism, the Shaker has established his monastery and his dance; and although each prates of spirit, there is no spirit, but repetition, which is anti-spiritual. But where are his new things of to-day ? In actions of enthusiasm this drawback appears, but in those lower activities, which have no higher aim than to make us more comfortable and more cowardly ; in actions of cunning, actions that steal and lie, actions that divorce the speculative from the practical faculty and put a ban on reason and sentiment, there is nothing else but drawback and negation. The Hindoos write in their sacred books, " Children only, and not the learned, speak of the speculative and the practical faculties as two. They are but one, for both obtain the selfsame end, and the place which is gained by the followers of the one is gained by the followers of the other. That man seeth, who seeth that the speculative and the practical doctrines are one." For great action must draw on the spiritual nature. The measure of action is the sentiment from which it proceeds. The greatest action may easily be one of the most private circumstance.

This disparagement will not come from the leaders, but from inferior persons. The robust gentlemen who stand at the head of the practical class, share the ideas of the time, and have too much sympathy with the speculative class. It is not from men excellent in any kind that disparagement of any other is to be looked for. With such, Talleyrand's question is ever the main one; not, is he rich? is he committed? is he well-meaning? has he this or that faculty? is he of the movement? is he of the establishment? — but, *Is he anybody?* does he stand for something? He must be good of his kind. That is all that Talleyrand, all that State-street, all that the common-sense of mankind asks. Be real and admirable, not as we know, but as you know. Able men do not care in what kind a man is able, so only that he is able. A master likes a master, and does not stipulate whether it be orator, artist, craftsman, or king.[1]

Society has really no graver interest than the well-being of the literary class. And it is not to be denied that men are cordial in their recognition and welcome of intellectual accomplishments. Still the writer does not stand with us on any commanding ground. I think this to be his own fault. A pound passes for a pound. There have been times when he was a sacred person: he wrote Bibles, the first hymns, the codes, the epics, tragic songs, Sibylline verses, Chaldean oracles, Laconian sentences, inscribed on temple walls. Every word was true, and woke the nations to new life. He wrote without levity and without choice. Every word was carved before his eyes into the earth and the sky; and the sun and stars were only letters of the same purport and of no more necessity. But how can he be honored when he does not honor himself; when he loses himself in a crowd; when he is no longer the lawgiver, but the sycophant, ducking to the giddy opinion of a reckless public; when he must sustain with shameless advocacy some bad government, or must bark, all the year round, in opposition; or write conventional criticism, or profligate novels, or at any rate write without thought, and without recurrence by day and by night to the sources of inspiration?

degradation of artist.

Some reply to these questions may be furnished by looking over the list of men of literary genius in our age. Among these no more
instructive name occurs than that of Goethe to
represent the powers and duties of the scholar
or writer.[1]

I described Bonaparte as a representative of
the popular external life and aims of the nineteenth century. Its other half, its poet, is
Goethe, a man quite domesticated in the century, breathing its air, enjoying its fruits, impossible at any earlier time, and taking away,
by his colossal parts, the reproach of weakness
which but for him would lie on the intellectual
works of the period.[2] He appears at a time
when a general culture has spread itself and
has smoothed down all sharp individual traits;
when, in the absence of heroic characters, a
social comfort and coöperation have come in.
There is no poet, but scores of poetic writers;
no Columbus, but hundreds of post-captains,
with transit-telescope, barometer and concentrated soup and pemmican; no Demosthenes,
no Chatham, but any number of clever parlia-
mentary and forensic debaters; no prophet or
saint, but colleges of divinity; no learned man,
but learned societies, a cheap press, reading-

rooms and book-clubs without number. There
was never such a miscellany of facts. The world
extends itself like American trade. We conceive
Greek or Roman life, life in the Middle Ages,
to be a simple and comprehensible affair; but
modern life to respect a multitude of things,
which is distracting.

Goethe was the philosopher of this multi-
plicity; hundred-handed, Argus-eyed, able and
happy to cope with this rolling miscellany of
facts and sciences, and by his own versatility to
dispose of them with ease; a manly mind, unem-
barrassed by the variety of coats of convention
with which life had got encrusted, easily able
by his subtlety to pierce these and to draw his
strength from nature, with which he lived in
full communion.¹ What is strange too, he lived
in a small town, in a petty state, in a defeated
state, and in a time when Germany played no
such leading part in the world's affairs as to swell
the bosom of her sons with any metropolitan
pride, such as might have cheered a French,
or English, or once, a Roman or Attic genius.
Yet there is no trace of provincial limitation in
his muse. He is not a debtor to his position,
but was born with a free and controlling genius.

The Helena, or the second part of Faust, is a

philosophy of literature set in poetry; the work
of one who found himself the master of histories, mythologies, philosophies, sciences and national literatures, in the encyclopædical manner
in which modern erudition, with its international
intercourse of the whole earth's population, researches into Indian, Etruscan and all Cyclopean
arts; geology, chemistry, astronomy; and every
one of these kingdoms assuming a certain aerial
and poetic character, by reason of the multitude.
One looks at a king with reverence; but if one
should chance to be at a congress of kings, the
eye would take liberties with the peculiarities of
each. These are not wild miraculous songs, but
elaborate forms to which the poet has confided
the results of eighty years of observation.¹ This
reflective and critical wisdom makes the poem
more truly the flower of this time. It dates itself.
Still he is a poet,— poet of a prouder laurel
than any contemporary, and, under this plague
of microscopes (for he seems to see out of every
pore of his skin), strikes the harp with a hero's
strength and grace.

The wonder of the book is its superior intelligence. In the menstruum of this man's wit,
the past and the present ages, and their religions, politics and modes of thinking, are dis-

solved into archetypes and ideas. What new
mythologies sail through his head! The Greeks
said that Alexander went as far as Chaos; Goethe
went, only the other day, as far; and one step
farther he hazarded, and brought himself safe
back.

There is a heart-cheering freedom in his
speculation. The immense horizon which journeys with us lends its majesty to trifles and to
matters of convenience and necessity, as to sol-
emn and festal performances. He was the soul
of his century. If that was learned, and had
become, by population, compact organization
and drill of parts, one great Exploring Expe-
dition, accumulating a glut of facts and fruits
too fast for any hitherto-existing savans to clas-
sify, — this man's mind had ample chambers
for the distribution of all. He had a power to
unite the detached atoms again by their own
law. He has clothed our modern existence with
poetry. Amid littleness and detail, he detected
the Genius of life, the old cunning Proteus,
nestling close beside us, and showed that the
dulness and prose we ascribe to the age was
only another of his masks: —

   " His very flight is presence in disguise : " ¹
— that he had put off a gay uniform for a fa-

tigue dress, and was not a whit less vivacious
or rich in Liverpool or the Hague than once in
Rome or Antioch. He sought him in public
squares and main streets, in boulevards and
hotels; and, in the solidest kingdom of routine
and the senses, he showed the lurking dæmonic
power; that, in actions of routine, a thread of
mythology and fable spins itself: and this, by
tracing the pedigree of every usage and practice,
every institution, utensil and means, home to
its origin in the structure of man.[1] He had an
extreme impatience of conjecture and of rhetoric. " I have guesses enough of my own; if a
man write a book, let him set down only what
he knows." He writes in the plainest and lowest tone, omitting a great deal more than he
writes, and putting ever a thing for a word.
He has explained the distinction between the
antique and the modern spirit and art. He has
defined art, its scope and laws. He has said the
best things about nature that ever were said.[2]
He treats nature as the old philosophers, as the
seven wise masters did, — and, with whatever
loss of French tabulation and dissection, poetry
and humanity remain to us; and they have some
doctoral skill. Eyes are better on the whole
than telescopes or microscopes. He has con-

tributed a key to many parts of nature, through
the rare turn for unity and simplicity in his
mind. Thus Goethe suggested the leading idea
of modern botany, that a leaf or the eye of a
leaf is the unit of botany, and that every part
of a plant is only a transformed leaf to meet a
new condition; and, by varying the conditions,
a leaf may be converted into any other organ,
and any other organ into a leaf. In like manner, in osteology, he assumed that one vertebra
of the spine might be considered as the unit of
the skeleton : the head was only the uttermost
vertebræ transformed. "The plant goes from
knot to knot, closing at last with the flower and
the seed. So the tape-worm, the caterpillar, goes
from knot to knot and closes with the head.
Man and the higher animals are built up through
the vertebræ, the powers being concentrated in
the head." In optics again he rejected the artificial theory of seven colors, and considered that
every color was the mixture of light and darkness in new proportions. It is really of very
little consequence what topic he writes upon.
He sees at every pore, and has a certain gravitation towards truth. He will realize what you
say. He hates to be trifled with and to be made
to say over again some old wife's fable that has

had possession of men's faith these thousand
years. He may as well see if it is true as
another. He sees it. I am here, he would say,
to be the measure and judge of these things.
Why should I take them on trust? And therefore what he says of religion, of passion, of marriage, of manners, of property, of paper-money,
of periods of belief, of omens, of luck, or whatever else, refuses to be forgotten.

Take the most remarkable example that could
occur of this tendency to verify every term in
popular use. The Devil had played an important part in mythology in all times. Goethe would
have no word that does not cover a thing. The
same measure will still serve: "I have never
heard of any crime which I might not have committed." So he flies at the throat of this imp.
He shall be real; he shall be modern; he shall
be European; he shall dress like a gentleman,
and accept the manners, and walk in the streets,
and be well initiated in the life of Vienna and
of Heidelberg in 1820 — or he shall not exist.
Accordingly, he stripped him of mythologic
gear, of horns, cloven foot, harpoon tail, brim-
stone and blue-fire, and instead of looking in
books and pictures, looked for him in his own
mind, in every shade of coldness, selfishness

and unbelief that, in crowds or in solitude,
darkens over the human thought, — and found
that the portrait gained reality and terror by
every thing he added and by every thing he took
away. He found that the essence of this hobgoblin which had hovered in shadow about the
habitations of men ever since there were men,
was pure intellect, applied, — as always there is
a tendency, — to the service of the senses : and
he flung into literature, in his Mephistopheles,
the first organic figure that has been .added for
some ages, and which will remain as long as the
Prometheus.[1]

I have no design to enter into any analysis of
his numerous works. They consist of translations, criticism, dramas, lyric and every other
description of poems, literary journals and portraits of distinguished men. Yet I cannot omit
to specify the Wilhelm Meister.

Wilhelm Meister is a novel in every sense,
the first of its kind, called by its admirers the
only delineation of modern society, — as if other
novels, those of Scott for example, dealt with
costume and condition, this with the spirit of
life. It is a book over which some veil is still
drawn. It is read by very intelligent persons
with wonder and delight. It is preferred by some

such to Hamlet, as a work of genius. I suppose
no book of this century can compare with it in
its delicious sweetness, so new, so provoking to
the mind, gratifying it with so many and so solid
thoughts, just insights into life and manners and
characters ; so many good hints for the conduct
of life, so many unexpected glimpses into a
higher sphere, and never a trace of rhetoric or
dulness. A very provoking book to the curiosity of young men of genius, but a very un-
satisfactory one. Lovers of light reading, those
who look in it for the entertainment they find in
a romance, are disappointed. On the other hand,
those who begin it with the higher hope to read
in it a worthy history of genius, and the just
award of the laurel to its toils and denials, have
also reason to complain. We had an English
romance here, not long ago, professing to embody the hope of a new age and to unfold the
political hope of the party called ' Young England,' — in which the only reward of virtue is a
seat in Parliament and a peerage. Goethe's romance has a conclusion as lame and immoral.
George Sand, in Consuelo and its continuation,
has sketched a truer and more dignified picture.
In the progress of the story, the characters of
the hero and heroine expand at a rate that shivers

the porcelain chess-table of aristocratic convention : they quit the society and habits of their
rank, they lose their wealth, they become the
servants of great ideas and of the most generous
social ends ; until at last the hero, who is the
centre and fountain of an association for the rendering of the noblest benefits to the human race,
no longer answers to his own titled name; it
sounds foreign and remote in his ear. " I am
only man," he says ; " I breathe and work for
man ; " and this in poverty and extreme sacri-
fices.¹ Goethe's hero, on the contrary, has so
many weaknesses and impurities and keeps such
bad company, that the sober English public,
when the book was translated, were disgusted.
And yet it is so crammed with wisdom, with
knowledge of the world and with knowledge of
laws; the persons so truly and subtly drawn,
and with such few strokes, and not a word too
much, — the book remains ever so new and un-
exhausted, that we must even let it go its way
and be willing to get what good from it we can,
assured that it has only begun its office and has
millions of readers yet to serve.

The argument is the passage of a democrat to
the aristocracy, using both words in their best
sense. And this passage is not made in any mean

or creeping way, but through the hall door.
Nature and character assist, and the rank is made
real by sense and probity in the nobles. No
generous youth can escape this charm of reality
in the book, so that it is highly stimulating to
intellect and courage.'

The ardent and holy Novalis characterized
the book as " thoroughly modern and prosaic;
the romantic is completely levelled in it; so is
the poetry of nature; the wonderful. The book
treats only of the ordinary affairs of men: it is
a poeticized civic and domestic story. The wonderful in it is expressly treated as fiction and enthusiastic dreaming:" — and yet, what is also
characteristic, Novalis soon returned to this
book, and it remained his favorite reading to the
end of his life.

What distinguishes Goethe for French and
English readers is a property which he shares
with his nation, — a habitual reference to interior
truth. In England and in America there is a
respect for talent; and, if it is exerted in support of any ascertained or intelligible interest or
party, or in regular opposition to any, the public is satisfied. In France there is even a greater
delight in intellectual brilliancy for its own sake.
And in all these countries, men of talent write

from talent. It is enough if the understanding is occupied, the taste propitiated, — so many columns, so many hours, filled in a lively and creditable way. The German intellect wants the French sprightliness, the fine practical understanding of the English, and the American adventure; but it has a certain probity, which never rests in a superficial performance, but asks steadily, *To what end?* A German public asks for a controlling sincerity. Here is activity of thought; but what is it for? What does the man mean? Whence, whence all these thoughts?'

Talent alone can not make a writer. There must be a man behind the book; a personality which by birth and quality is pledged to the doctrines there set forth, and which exists to see and state things so, and not otherwise; holding things because they are things. If he can not rightly express himself to-day, the same things subsist and will open themselves to-morrow. There lies the burden on his mind, — the burden of truth to be declared, — more or less understood; and it constitutes his business and calling in the world to see those facts through, and to make them known. What signifies that he trips and stammers; that his voice is harsh or hissing; that his method or his tropes are inadequate? That message will find method and imagery, articulation and melody. Though he were dumb it would speak. If not, — if there be no such God's word in the man, — what care we how adroit, how fluent, how brilliant he is?

It makes a great difference to the force of any sentence whether there be a man behind it or no. In the learned journal, in the influential newspaper, I discern no form; only some irresponsible shadow; oftener some moneyed corporation, or some dangler who hopes, in the mask and robes of his paragraph, to pass for somebody. But through every clause and part of speech of a right book I meet the eyes of the most determined of men; his force and terror inundate every word; the commas and dashes are alive; so that the writing is athletic and nimble, — can go far and live long.

In England and America, one may be an adept in the writings of a Greek or Latin poet, without any poetic taste or fire. That a man has spent years on Plato and Proclus, does not afford a presumption that he holds heroic opinions, or undervalues the fashions of his town.¹ But the German nation have the most ridiculous good faith on these subjects: the student, out of the lecture-room, still broods on the lessons;

and the professor can not divest himself of the
fancy that the truths of philosophy have some
application to Berlin and Munich. This earnestness enables them to outsee men of much more
talent. Hence almost all the valuable distinctions which are current in higher conversation
have been derived to us from Germany. But
whilst men distinguished for wit and learning,
in England and France, adopt their study and
their side with a certain levity, and are not
understood to be very deeply engaged, from
grounds of character, to the topic or the part
they espouse, — Goethe, the head and body of
the German nation, does not speak from talent,
but the truth shines through : he is very wise,
though his talent often veils his wisdom. However excellent his sentence is, he has somewhat
better in view. It awakens my curiosity. He
has the formidable independence which converse
with truth gives : hear you, or forbear, his fact
abides; and your interest in the writer is not
confined to his story and he dismissed from
memory when he has performed his task credit-
ably, as a baker when he has left his loaf ; but
his work is the least part of him. The old Eternal Genius who built the world has confided
himself more to this man than to any other.

I dare not say that Goethe ascended to the highest grounds from which genius has spoken. He has not worshipped the highest unity; he is incapable of a self-surrender to the moral sentiment. There are nobler strains in poetry than any he has sounded. There are writers poorer in talent, whose tone is purer, and more touches the heart. Goethe can never be dear to men. His is not even the devotion to pure truth; but to truth for the sake of culture. He has no aims less large than the conquest of universal nature, of universal truth, to be his portion: a man not to be bribed, nor deceived, nor over-awed; of a stoical self-command and self-denial, and having one test for all men, — *What can you teach me?* All possessions are valued by him for that only; rank, privileges, health, time, Being itself.

He is the type of culture, the amateur of all arts and sciences and events: artistic, but not artist; spiritual, but not spiritualist. There is nothing he had not right to know: there is no weapon in the armory of universal genius he did not take into his hand, but with peremptory command that he should not be for a moment predisposed by his instruments. He lays a ray of light under every fact, and between himself and his dearest property. From him nothing was hid, nothing withholden. The lurking dæmons sat to him, and the saint who saw the dæmons; and the metaphysical elements took form. " Piety itself is no aim, but only a means whereby through purest inward peace we may attain to highest culture." And his penetration of every secret of the fine arts will make Goethe still more statuesque. His affections help him, like women employed by Cicero to worm out the secret of conspirators. Enmities he has none. Enemy of him you may be, — if so you shall teach him aught which your good-will can not, were it only what experience will accrue from your ruin. Enemy and welcome, but enemy on high terms. He can not hate anybody; his time is worth too much. Temperamental antagonisms may be suffered, but like feuds of emperors, who fight dignifiedly across kingdoms.[1]

His autobiography, under the title of Poetry and Truth out of my Life, is the expression of the idea — now familiar to the world through the German mind, but a novelty to England, Old and New, when that book appeared — that a man exists for culture; not for what he can accomplish, but for what can be

accomplished in him. The reaction of things on
the man is the only noteworthy result. An intellectual man can see himself as a third person;
therefore his faults and delusions interest him
equally with his successes. Though he wishes
to prosper in affairs, he wishes more to know
the history and destiny of man; whilst the clouds
of egotists drifting about him are only interested
in a low success.

This idea reigns in the Dichtung und Wahr-
heit and directs the selection of the incidents;
and nowise the external importance of events,
the rank of the personages, or the bulk of in-
comes. Of course the book affords slender
materials for what would be reckoned with us
a Life of Goethe; — few dates, no correspondence, no details of offices or employments, no
light on his marriage; and a period of ten years,
that should be the most active in his life,
after his settlement at Weimar, is sunk in silence. Meantime certain love affairs that came
to nothing, as people say, have the strangest
importance: he crowds us with details: — certain whimsical opinions, cosmogonies and religions of his own invention, and especially his
relations to remarkable minds and to critical
epochs of thought: — these he magnifies. His

Daily and Yearly Journal, his Italian Travels, his Campaign in France and the historical part of his Theory of Colors, have the same interest. In the last, he rapidly notices Kepler, Roger Bacon, Galileo, Newton, Voltaire, etc.; and the charm of this portion of the book consists in the simplest statement of the relation betwixt these grandees of European scientific history and himself; the mere drawing of the lines from Goethe to Kepler, from Goethe to Bacon, from Goethe to Newton. The drawing of the line is, for the time and person, a solution of the formidable problem, and gives pleasure when Iphigenia and Faust do not, without any cost of invention comparable to that of Iphigenia and Faust.

This lawgiver of art is not an artist. Was it that he knew too much, that his sight was microscopic and interfered with the just perspective, the seeing of the whole? He is fragmentary; a writer of occasional poems and of an encyclopædia of sentences. When he sits down to write a drama or a tale, he collects and sorts his observations from a hundred sides, and combines them into the body as fitly as he can. A great deal refuses to incorporate: this he adds loosely as letters of the parties, leaves

from their journals, or the like. A great deal
still is left that will not find any place. This the
bookbinder alone can give any cohesion to ; and
hence, notwithstanding the looseness of many
of his works, we have volumes of detached para-
graphs, aphorisms, *Xenien,*[1] etc.

I suppose the worldly tone of his tales grew
out of the calculations of self-culture. It was
the infirmity of an admirable scholar, who loved
the world out of gratitude; who knew where
libraries, galleries, architecture, laboratories,
savans and leisure were to be had, and who
did not quite trust the compensations of poverty
and nakedness. Socrates loved Athens ; Montaigne, Paris; and Madame de Staël said she
was only vulnerable on that side (namely, of
Paris). It has its favorable aspect. All the geniuses are usually so ill-assorted and sickly that
one is ever wishing them somewhere else. We
seldom see anybody who is not uneasy or afraid
to live. There is a slight blush of shame on the
cheek of good men and aspiring men, and a
spice of caricature. But this man was entirely
at home and happy in his century and the world.
None was so fit to live, or more heartily enjoyed
the game. In this aim of culture, which is the
genius of his works, is their power. The idea

of absolute, eternal truth, without reference to
my own enlargement by it, is higher. The surrender to the torrent of poetic inspiration is
higher; but compared with any motives on
which books are written in England and America, this is very truth, and has the power to
inspire which belongs to truth. Thus has he
brought back to a book some of its ancient
might and dignity.

Goethe, coming into an over-civilized time
and country, when original talent was oppressed
under the load of books and mechanical auxiliaries and the distracting variety of claims, taught
men how to dispose of this mountainous miscellany and make it subservient. I join Napoleon with him, as being both representatives of
the impatience and reaction of nature against
the *morgue* of conventions, — two stern realists,
who, with their scholars, have severally set the
axe at the root of the tree of cant and seeming,
for this time and for all time. This cheerful
laborer, with no external popularity or provo-
cation, drawing his motive and his plan from
his own breast, tasked himself with stints for a
giant, and without relaxation or rest, except by
alternating his pursuits, worked on for eighty
years with the steadiness of his first zeal.

IV

It is the last lesson of modern science that the highest simplicity of structure is produced, not by few elements, but by the highest complexity. Man is the most composite of all creatures: the wheel-insect, *volvox globator*, is at the other extreme. We shall learn to draw rents and revenues from the immense patrimony of the old and the recent ages. Goethe teaches courage, and the equivalence of all times; that the disadvantages of any epoch exist only to the faint-hearted. Genius hovers with his sunshine and music close by the darkest and deafest eras. No mortgage, no attainder, will hold on men or hours. The world is young: the former great men call to us affectionately. We too must write Bibles, to unite again the heavens and the earthly world. The secret of genius is to suffer no fiction to exist for us; to realize all that we know; in the high refinement of modern life, in arts, in sciences, in books, in men, to exact good faith, reality and a purpose; and first, last, midst and without end, to honor every truth by use.[1]

NOTES

NOTES

REPRESENTATIVE MEN

MR. EMERSON eagerly sought anecdote or evidence
which made good the oracles of the inspired minds.
Not only in boyhood, when such enthusiasm is natural, he
took keen pleasure in brave achievement, whether in the closet
or the field: all through life he held to his faith in the Individual rather than the Organization. It was largely from him that
the young Charles Russell Lowell learned his faith, later acted
up to on the battlefield, that "the world advances by impossibilities achieved."

The astounding passage of the Alps by the First Consul
with his army would have been among the first stories of
the great world that reached Emerson's ears as a boy, and later
the fame of the Emperor's rapid marches across Europe and
repeated overthrow of the armies of the banded monarchs of
Feudalism, compelling them to treat for peace at the very
gates of their capitals. Mr. Emerson used to say, "I like people who can do things." No wonder that Napoleon was
chosen as one type of the great man in this book. But the
moral element was lacking, and the sudden reverse of the
scale —

> "When one that sought but Duty's iron crown
> On that loud Sabbath shook the Spoiler down" —

made the lesson complete; showed the sure working of the
great Law.

There is no need of seeking when the young Emerson made
a friend of Shakspeare. In those serious New England days

daily terrors of his school for young ladies in Bóston, was seeking for some bit of spiritual refreshment in the remains of his father's library. Among the books of desiccated sermons and the commentaries on the Scriptures he came upon an odd volume of Cotton's translation of Montaigne which proved a friend indeed. In the lecture on Montaigne in this volume he relates this experience, but in the journal for 1873 he adds, "No book before or since was ever so much to me as that."

In the fourth year after leaving college, when he had left the desk of the schoolmaster for his study at Divinity Hall, Emerson read a little book newly published in Boston, *The Growth of the Mind*, by Sampson Reed, which first attracted his attention to Swedenborg. Its author, a quiet druggist in Boston, and a member of the Swedenborgian Church, had graduated at Harvard at the end of Emerson's Freshman year. Some early verses, never finished, entitled only *S. R.*, seemed to show that even then something in Sampson Reed had attracted him. They begin, —

> Demure apothecary,
> Whose early reverend genius my young eye
> With wonder followed and undoubting joy,
> Believing in that cold and modest form
> Brooded alway the everlasting mind,
> And that thou, faithful, didst obey the soul.

This book made Mr. Emerson a reader of Swedenborg, even in his days of study for the ministry.

To the writings of Goethe there can be little doubt that he was first introduced by Coleridge. In his "Blotting Book," in which he noted and copied passages which pleased him in his reading, in the autumn of 1830 are several from *Wilhelm Meister* and other writings of Goethe, as well as from the

* A Correspondence between John Sterling and Ralph Waldo Emerson. Boston, Houghton, Mifflin & Co., 1897.

* The Correspondence of Thomas Carlyle and Ralph Waldo Emerson. Supplementary Letters. Boston, Ticknor & Co., 1886.

spur to the sides of that dull horse I have charge of. But many of its advantages must be regarded at a long distance." The course of seven lectures was first given before the Boston Lyceum in the Odeon in the winter of 1845–46.

When in response to the urgent invitation of several friends, Mr. Emerson, in the late autumn of 1847, crossed the ocean to lecture in England, his first course after landing, given before the Manchester Athenæum, was that on "Representative Men." The lectures on Napoleon and on Shakspeare were later given in Exeter Hall in London.

The record of the impression made on one of his hearers by this American lecturer at his first appearance before English audiences may be interesting. It is from the Memoir by the late Mr. Alexander Ireland of Manchester.[1]

"The first impression one had in listening to him in public was that his manner was so singularly quiet and unimpassioned that you began to fear the beauty and force of his thoughts were about to be marred by what might almost be described as monotony of expression. But very soon was this apprehension dispelled. The mingled dignity, sweetness and strength of his features, the earnestness of his manner and voice, and the evident depth and sincerity of his convictions gradually extorted your deepest attention and made you feel that you were within the grip of no ordinary man, but of one 'sprung of Earth's first blood' with 'titles manifold;' and as he went on with serene self-possession and an air of conscious power reading sentence after sentence, charged with well-weighed meaning and set in words of faultless aptitude, you could no longer withstand his 'so potent spell,' but were forthwith compelled to surrender yourself to the fascination of his elo-

[1] *Ralph Waldo Emerson, his Life, Genius and Writings.* London: Simpkin, Marshall & Co. 1882.

quence. He used little or no action. . . . Perhaps no orator ever succeeded with so little exertion in entrancing his audience, stealing away each faculty, and leading the listeners captive to his will. He abjured all force and excitement — dispensing his regal sentences in all mildness, goodness and truth, but stealthily and surely he grew upon you from the smallest proportions, as it were; steadily increasing, until he became a Titan. . . . The moment he finished he took up his MS. and quietly glided away, — disappearing before his audience could give vent to their applause.''

Representative Men was published January 1, 1850. A copy was sent to Carlyle, who, '' a remorseful man,'' acknowledged it in an affectionate letter written July 19, 1850, telling, however, that his own life had been meanwhile '' black with care and toil.'' In it he said : '' Chapman, with due punctuality at the time of publication, sent me the *Representative Men ;* which I read in the becoming manner: you now get the book offered you for a shilling, at all railway stations; and indeed I perceive the word ' representative man ' (as applied to the tragic loss we have had in Sir Robert Peel) has been accepted by the Able-Editors and circulates through newspapers as an appropriate household word, which is some compensation for the piracy you suffer from the typographic Letter-of-Marque men here. I found the book a most finished, clear and perfect set of *Engravings in the line manner ;* portraitures full of *likeness,* and abounding in instruction and materials for reflection to me: thanks always for such a Book; and Heaven send us many more of them. *Plato,* I think, though it is the most admired by many, did the least for me: little save Socrates with his clogs and big ears remains alive with me from it. *Swedenborg* is excellent in *likeness ;* excellent in many respects ; yet I said to myself, on reaching your general conclusion about the man and his struggles : ' Missed the consummate flower and divine ultimate elixir of Philosophy, say you ? By Heaven, in clutching at *it*, and almost getting it, he has tumbled into Bedlam, — which is a terrible *miss*, if it were never so *near* ! A miss fully as good as a mile, I should say.' — In fact, I generally dissented a little about the *end* of all these Essays ; which was notable, and not without instructive interest to me, as I had so lustily shouted ' Hear, hear ! ' all the way from the beginning up to that stage. — On the whole let us have another book with your earliest convenience : that is the modest request one makes of you on shutting this.''

Earlier in the letter Carlyle had said, '' Though I see well, enough what a great deep cleft divides us, in our ways of practically looking at this world, — I see also (as probably you do yourself) where the rock-strata, miles deep, unite again : and the two souls are at one.''

The new book was well received on both sides of the ocean. It was naturally at that time a more popular book than the *Essays* had been. It received a most appreciative yet critical notice in the *Revue des Deux Mondes* from Emile Montégut, who was struck with Emerson's detachment from the political and religious excitements of the moment, for it appeared just after the Revolution in France of 1848. He said, '' Revolutions and reactions intimidate him not at all and do not draw him in the least from his convictions. In nothing does he offer sacrifice to the spirit of the moment. He speaks of Swedenborg and Plato at the moment when the whole universe has ears only for Proudhon and Louis Blanc. He praises the skepticism of Montaigne as if he did not live in a century which boasts of having the most absolute philosophies.''

Mr. Emerson's friend Horatio Greenough, the sculptor, in a letter written in December, 1851, said : —

" I found your *Representative Men* in the hands of a *dame du Palais* at Vienna in '48 and have learned that she has been exiled, having made herself politically obnoxious.''

This " Representative Men" may have been a newspaper report of the lectures as delivered in London, or, more probably, Mr. Greenough made a mistake either in the volume or the date.

But the book was not everywhere valued. Mr. George W. Cooke tells in his book on Mr. Emerson that a writer in the *New Englander* found it " purely ridiculous for any one to laboriously write out and gravely read to large assemblies such gratuitous absurdities," and made other severe strictures ; among other things, saying that a large part of what Mr. Emerson had then written "must be little else than a caricature of himself." The same idea in a more courteous and complimentary form was, after Emerson's death, expressed by Dr. Holmes in his *Memoir*, thus : "He shows his own affinities and repulsions, and, as everywhere, writes his own biography, no matter about whom or what he is talking. There is hardly any book of his better worth study by those who wish to understand not Plato, not Plutarch, not Napoleon, but Emerson himself. All his great men interest us for their own sake, but we know a good deal about most of them, and Emerson holds the mirror up to them at just such an angle that we see his own face as well as that of his hero unintentionally, unconsciously, no doubt, but by a necessity which he would be the first to recognize.''

There is a story of the effect of this book on a schoolboy looking for light which should here be told : —

" I remember a day when I stood idly over a counter looking at the backs of what seemed to be newly published books. I drew out one, bound in plain black muslin. Its title, *Repre-*

sentative Men, attracted me, because I had just been reading Plutarch's *Lives*, and for the first time had been aroused by the reading of any book. Those Greek and Roman men moved my horizon some distance from its customary place. The titles of the books were at least cousins, and I wondered if there had been any representative men since Epaminondas and Scipio. I opened the volume at the beginning, ' Uses of Great Men,' and read a few pages, becoming more and more agitated until I could read no more there. It was as if I had looked into a mirror for the first time. I turned around, fearful lest some one had observed what had happened to me; for a complete revelation was opened in those few pages, and I was no longer the same being that had entered the shop. These were the words for which I had been hungering and waiting. This was the education I wanted — the message that made education possible and study profitable, a foundation, and not a perpetual scaffolding. These pages opened for me a path, and opened it through solid walls of ignorance and the limiting environment of a small country academy. All that is now far, far away, and seems indeed an alien history ; yet however much one may have wandered among famous books, it would be ungrateful not to remember the one book which was the talisman to all its fellows.'' [1]

USES OF GREAT MEN

Page 3, note 1. Mr. Emerson tells in his *Poems* how, when the west wind was making music in the Æolian harp in his study windows, —

[1] *Remembrances of Emerson*, by John Albee. New York: International Book and Publishing Co. 1900.

[illegible]

[illegible]

"[illegible]"

[illegible]

[illegible]

"[illegible]"

[illegible] [illegible] the [illegible] and [illegible] were [illegible]. [illegible] the opportunities [illegible] inclined [illegible] young [illegible]. "[illegible] must be [illegible] my father's business." [illegible] more than [illegible] England village was enough for him. His [illegible] 1833, the [illegible] of which appears in the [illegible] *English Traits*, shows this. The verses, "*Written at Rome, 1833*," in the *Poems*, end with a long-ing [illegible] man, whom a few weeks later he sought [illegible] moors.

Page 4, note 2. · To the same purpose is a passage about "the masses" early in "Considerations by the Way," in *Conduct of Life,* and in a more human and sympathetic tone in the last pages of the present essay.

Page 4, note 3.

"We find in our dull road their shining track."

Lowell's *Commemoration Ode.*

Page 5, note 1. As elsewhere this idealist concedes — "Treat men and women well. Treat them as if they were real. Perhaps they are."

Page 7, note 1. It is not easy for the generation who remember only the end of the nineteenth century to believe that the persons thus described abounded in New England at the time when this book was written. When the period of unrest is again followed by one of eager aspiration, the like may occur.

Page 8, note 1. When young people brought their problems to Mr. Emerson, they may at first have experienced disappointment at not receiving the easy answers for which they hoped. His answer was a large one, more serviceable later, if they considered it. Their individualities were different from his, and scope must be left for these. He wrote in his journal, "If we could speak the direct solving words, it would solve us too." Compare the last part of the "Celestial Love" in the *Poems.*

Page 8, note 2. Jacob Behmen, or Boehme, a Silesian of humble birth in the sixteenth century, a mystic whose writings later attracted much attention. Mr. Emerson was early interested in his works and often mentions them.

Page 9, note 1. He welcomed each discovery for its use

not beauty, but more in its significance, which it was his delight to find. He said of Nature, —

Does she not lure for her darlings in her much she asked more;
In her hundred-gated Thebes every chamber was a door,
A door to something grander, — loftier walls and vaster floor.

And Nature says, —

He lives not who can refuse me;
All my force saith, Come and use me.

Page 9, note 2. Among other sentences in the original lecture which were printed but in the essay because their substance occurs later, was this strong one : " Man is a piece of the Universe made alive."

Page 10, note 1. William Gilbert, the greatest man of science of Queen Elizabeth's reign, especially noted for his discovery that the earth is a great magnet.

Hans Christian Oersted of Denmark, who in 1820 announced his discovery of the identity of electricity and magnetism.

Page 10, note 2. Journal, 1835; compare passage, varied, in *Nature*, p. 27. " Natural History by itself has no value: it is like a single sex, but marry it to human history and it is poetry. Whole floras, all Linnæus's or Buffon's volumes, contain not one line of poetry; but the meanest natural fact, the habit of a plant, the organs, or work, or noise of an insect, applied to a fact in human nature, is beauty, is poetry, is truth at once."

Page 11, note 1.

I am the doubter and the doubt.

"Brahma," *Poems.*

Page 11, note 2. Compare the motto of " Wealth " in *Conduct of Life.*

Page 13, note 1. But not forgetting, in the material gain, its main use — the spiritual.

Page 14, note 1. This idea is found in the poems "Destiny" and "Fate."

Page 15, note 1.

> Me too thy nobleness has taught
> To master my despair;
> The fountains of my hidden life
> Are through thy friendship fair.
>
> "Friendship," *Poems.*

Page 15, note 2. In his afternoon walks through the Walden woods while he was writing this book, Mr. Emerson saw with respect the unprecedented day's work of the newly imported Irishmen on the Fitchburg Railroad, then in process of construction.

Page 15, note 3. This introductory chapter to the *Representative Men* may be compared with Carlyle's *Heroes and Hero-worship,* published ten years earlier. In Mr. Emerson's essay on *Aristocracy,* called *Natural Aristocracy* when read as a lecture in England, are several passages similar to the one on this page, sympathizing with the admiration for " men who are incomparably superior to the populace in ways agreeable to the populace, showing them the way they shall go, doing for them what they wish done and cannot do ; " — " the steel hid under gauze and lace under flowers and spangles."

Page 16, note 1. This was his own rule — never to " talk down " to others. When in 1834 he made his home in Concord, and began his new life as lecturer and writer, he entered in his journal this resolve : —

" Henceforth I design not to utter any speech, poem or

IV

book that is not entirely and peculiarly my work. I will say at public lectures and the like those things which I have meditated for their own sake, and not for the first time with a view to that occasion." And again, "Do not cease to utter them and make them as pure of all dross as if thou wert to speak to sages and demigods, and be no whit ashamed if not one, yea, not one in the assembly should give sign of intelligence. Is it not pleasant to you — unexpected wisdom ? depth of sentiment in middle life, persons that in the thick of the crowd are true kings and gentlemen without the harness and envy of the throne ?"

Page 17, note 1. Mr. Emerson, in the lecture on Shakspeare in this volume, tells of such an experience while seeing *Hamlet* performed.

Page 18, note 1. He did not believe that men could be forced or pledged to reform. When the way was made beautiful to them, they could not choose but take it. He wished no disciples. "The poet," he said, "is the liberator."

Page 19, note 1. The Over-Soul doctrine.

Page 20, note 1. That is, the ideal, instead of the outward shows of things.

Page 21, note 1. From a noble poem by John Sterling, entitled "Dædalus," in honor of Greek sculpture and lamenting the lost art. This poem by his friend is included in Emerson's collection *Parnassus.*

Page 21, note 2. Out of these losses he redeemed "Days," which he once said he thought perhaps his best poem.

Page 21, note 3. Probably suggested by Balzac's *Peau de Chagrin.*

Page 23, note 1. Journal, April, 1839. "Yesterday I read Beaumont and Fletcher's tragedy 'The False One,' which, instead of taking its name from Septimius, ought to have been

'Cleopatra.' A singular fortune is that of the man Cæsar, to have given name as he has to all that is heroic ambition in the imaginations of painters and poets. Cæsar must still be the speaking-trumpet through which this large wild commanding spirit must always be poured. The Poet would be a great man. His power is intellectual. Instantly he seizes these hollow puppets of Cæsar, of Tamerlane, of Boadicea, of Belisarius, and inflates them with his own vital air. If he can verily ascend to grandeur, — if his soul is grand, behold his puppets attest his weight, they are no more puppets but instant vehicles of the wine of God: they shine and overflow with the streams of that universal energy that beamed from Cæsar's eye, poised itself in Hector's spear, purer sat with Epaminondas, with Socrates, purest with thee, thou holy child Jesus."

Page 23, note 2.

> Who bides at home, nor looks abroad,
> Carries the eagles and masters the sword.
>
> "Destiny," *Poems.*

Page 24, note 1. Mr. Emerson gives in a journal an instance of the humble compensations — a case of a poor feeble-minded girl who went about the house bragging that *she was not dead.*

Page 25, note 1. He told Mr. John Albee, who, still a boy in Andover Academy, visited him, that it was a great day in a man's life when he first read the *Symposium.*

Page 25, note 2. Mr. Emerson had great skill in lifting the conversation from a low and gossiping level, without apparent reproof or incivility.

Page 27, note 1. " *Au nom de Dieu, ne me parlez plus de cet homme là !* "

Page 27, note 2.

> If love his moment over-stay,
> Hatred's swift repulsions play.
>
> "The Visit," *Po*

Page 28, note 1. The Oriental doctrine, alluded tc
poem "Uriel": —

> Doomed to long gyration
> In the sea of generation.

Page 30, note 1.

> In vain: the stars are glowing wheels,
> Giddy with motion Nature reels,
> Sun, moon, man, undulate and stream,
> The mountains flow, the solids seem,
> Change acts, reacts; back, forward hurled,
> And pause were palsy to the world.
>
> "The Poet," *Poems*, Appendix

Page 33, note 1. Mr. Emerson's frequent use of
classical education, not pedantically, but to secure the atten
of the reader and make the expression exact and picturesc
is well shown in the choice of the word *flagrant* as if
human world were traced out in the general dimness by
blazing beacon lights. "*Federal* errors," a few pages earl
for mistakes sanctioned by custom is another example.

Page 33, note 2. Immortality in some form seems tal
for granted by this expression.

Page 34, note 1.

> The word unto the prophet spoken
> Was writ on tables still unbroken.
>
> "The Problem," *Poems.*

Page 35, note 1. The constant security of Mr. Emerson

belief in Evolution in its highest sense appears here as everywhere in his prose and verse, and also his belief in the genius of mankind, which is another word for the Universal Mind. He wrote thus of the Poet in his journal of 1838: —

" Morning and evening he blessed the world. Where he went the trees knew him, and the earth felt him to the roots of the grass. Yet a few things sufficed. One tree was to him as a grove; the eyes of one maiden taught him all charms; and by a single wise man he knew Jesus and Plato and Shakspeare and the angels.''

PLATO; OR, THE PHILOSOPHER

Dr. Richard Garnett, in his *Life of Emerson*, ends his comment on the previous chapter, the "Uses of Great Men," by saying that " we find ourselves landed at last in Emerson's favourite conclusion [the Universal Mind], with but slight idea how we have arrived at it. ‘ Genius appears as the exponent of a vaster mind and will. The opaque self becomes transparent with the light of a First Cause.’ It is the purpose of the remaining lectures to resolve this pure ray of primal intellect into the sixfold spectrum of philosopher, mystic, skeptic, poet, man of the world, and writer respectively personified by Plato, Swedenborg, Montaigne, Shakspeare, Napoleon, and Goethe.''

In Mr. Emerson's journal in the spring of 1845 is this note: " A Pantheon course of lectures should consist of heads like these. [Here follow the six names of the subjects of these chapters.] Jesus should properly be one head, but it requires great power of intellect and of sentiment to subdue the biases

of the mind of the age and render historic justice to the v
chief saint.''

As has been said in the introductory note, **Mr. En**
began in his college days to make the acquaintance of
and the readings thereafter were a frequent refresh
When he went to lonely Nantasket Beach to write his or
The Method of Nature, he read in Plato for inspiration
wrote thence to a friend: —

18 JULY, 184

I brought here *Phædrus, Meno* and the *Banquet,* v
I have diligently read. What a great uniform gentlem
Plato! Nothing is more characteristic of him than his g
breeding. Never pedantic, never wire-drawn or too
and never, O never obtuse or saturnine ; but so accomplis
so good humoured, so perceptive, so uniting wisdom
poetry, acuteness and humanity, into such a golden aver
that one understands how he shall enjoy his long Augu
empire in literature. I have also three volumes new to me
Thomas Taylor's translations, Proclus, Ocellus Lucanus,
Pythagorean Fragments.

The next year he writes to the same friend : —

CONCORD, 7 MAY, 1842.

. . . I read last week the *Protagoras* and *Theages*
Plato. The first is excellent and gave me much to thin
With what security and common sense this Plato treads t
cliffs and pinnacles of Parnassus, as if he walked in a stree
and came down again into a street as if he lived there.

My dazzling friends of Alexandria, the New Platonist
have none of this air of facts and society about them. Thi
Socrates is as good as Don Quixote all the time. What im
penetrable armor of witty courtesy covers him every moment

In his journal, under the head of "The Poppy-wreath," he says, "Plato, well guarded from those to whom he does not belong by a river of sleep."

Journal, 1845. "It requires for the reading and final disposition of Plato, all sorts of readers, Frenchmen, Germans, Italians, English, and Americans. If it were left to apprehensive, gentle, imaginative, Plato-like persons, no justice would be done to his essence and totality, through the excess or violence of affection that would be spent on his excellence of reason and imagination. But Frenchmen have no reverence, they seize the book like merchants, it is a piece of goods, and is treated without ceremony after the manner of commerce; and though its diviner merits are lost by their profanation, the coarser, namely, the texture and coherence of the whole and its larger plan, its French availableness, its fitness to French taste, by comprehending that. Too much seeing is as fatal to just seeing as blindness is. People speak easily of *Cudworth*, but I know no book so difficult to read as Cudworth proper. For, as it is a magazine of quotations, of extraordinary ethical sentences, the shining summits of ancient philosophy, and as Cudworth himself is a dull writer, the eye of the reader rests habitually on these wonderful revelations, and refuses to be withdrawn; so that after handling the book for years, the method and the propositions of Cudworth still remain a profound secret. Cudworth is sometimes read without the Platonism; which would be like reading Theobald's Shakspeare, leaving out only what Shakspeare wrote.

"I think the best reader of Plato the least able to receive the totality at first, just as a botanist will get the totality of a field of flowers better than a poet."

Page 39, note 1. The less usual use of "secular," as

applied to books, in its strict classic sense, to mean *through the ages*, is characteristic.

Omar the Caliph was Mahomet's cousin and sec cessor.

Page 39, note 2. Here came in, in the original lec sentences: " Nothing but God can give invention. thing else, one would say, the study of Plato would

Page 39, note 3. And yet Plato quotes from th men, as mentioned later in this essay and in " Quota Originality," *Letters and Social Aims.*

Page 40, note 1. This rare book is thus entit *Practical Philosophy of the Muhammadan People, e. in its professed connection with the European, so as to either an introduction to the other ; being a translatioı AKHLAK-I-JALALY, the most esteemed work of Asia, from the Persian of Fakir Jāny Muhammad (with references and notes), by W. F. Thomson, E the Bengal Civil Service.* London, 1839.

The translator says in his introduction, " The latter the fifteenth century may indeed be considered as the ⅃ tan age of Persian letters," that about that time the Ak Jalaly was produced, and that it is " the best digest important topics of which it treats." He says that tł the translations of the Greek philosophers, or, in some the transference " in extract from writer to writer,' Moslem people came to have a knowledge of the great (systems of thought. " The most successful efforts ₒ entire people" to reconcile the Greek philosophy wit social and religious systems of the Mohammedans " m said to be concentrated in the work before us ; but the tɪ from which it more particularly originates is the Kiı Jaharat, an Arabic work composed in the tenth centɪ

This work " is an amalgam of Platonic and Aristotelian philosophy, carried out, however, to the most minute practical application," etc. This Arabic work, having passed with improvements, due to the increase of knowledge in five hundred years, through the hands of two Persian writers, appears as the *Akhlak-i-Jalaly*. It treats, after an *Exordium*, in Book I. of *The Individual State ;* in Book II. of *The Domestic State ;* in Book III. of *The Political State*, and in the Conclusion gives, I. *Platonic Maxims on Ethics ;* II. *Aristotelian Maxims on Politics.*

Page 42, note 1. Dr. Holmes thus comments on this passage : " The reader will, I hope, remember this last general statement when he learns from what wide fields of authorship Emerson filled his store-houses."

Page 43, note 1. Mr. Emerson quotes Stanley as saying that Plato first used the word Poem.

Page 43, note 2. When Mr. Emerson gave this lecture in Concord, a lady walking home with her neighbor, a substantial farmer's wife, found that she did not approve of it. On pressing her to learn what she objected to, the disapproving matron said, " Well! If those old heathen did what Mr. Emerson said they did, the less said about them the better!" " Why, what do you mean ?" " He said *they ground their wives and children into paint !*"

Page 47, note 1. The majesty of planets and suns and systems, in their ordered courses, especially appealed to Emerson from his youth. He draws constantly his imagery from astronomy, and especially honored Galileo, Copernicus, Kepler, and Newton. In the years between 1835 and 1845 his journals and the scattered fragments of " The Poet " (see *Poems*, Appendix) show how constantly he sought " the sweet influence of the Pleiades " and " Arcturus and his sons."

Divine inviters, I accept
The courtesy ye have shown and kept
From ancient ages for the bard.

.   .   .   .

O birds of ether without wings!
O heavenly ships without a sail!
O fire of fire! O best of things!
O mariners who never fail!
Sail swiftly through your amber vault,
An animated law, a presence to exalt.

Page 48, note 1. These doctrines are discussed   i
Parmenides and the *Theætetus* of Plato. That of the I d e
ʿEν καὶ πᾶν, came from Xenophanes. See also Em e ɪ
" Xenophanes " in the *Poems.*

Page 49, note 1. The journal of 1845 shows th a t
Emerson was reading, not only in the Koran and Ak h l
Jalaly, but in the East Indian Scriptures, and he gives   ɪ
quotations. He writes, " The East is grand and   m
Europe appear the land of trifles." It was natural that   I
should lead him to the most ancient fountains of the re l i ɟ
of the Aryan race.

In the midsummer of 1840 Mr. Emerson told in a l e
to a near friend of his high prizing of the Vedas.[1]

" In the sleep of the great heats there was nothing for
but to read the Vedas, the bible of the tropics, which l fi
I come back upon every three or four years. It is subl i ɪ
as heat and night and a breathless ocean. It contains e v e
religious sentiment, all the grand ethics which visit in tu ɟ
each noble and poetic mind, and nothing is easier than

[1] *Letters of Emerson to a Friend,* edited by Charles Eliot Norton. B o
ton: Houghton, Mifflin & Co. 1899.

separate what must have been the primeval inspiration from the endless ceremonial nonsense which caricatures and contradicts it through every chapter. It is of no use to put away the book: if I trust myself in the woods or in a boat upon the pond, nature makes a Bramin of me presently: eternal necessity, eternal compensation, unfathomable power, unbroken silence, — this is her creed. Peace, she saith to me, and purity and absolute abandonment — these penances expiate all sin and bring you to the beatitude of the Eight Gods.''

Page 49, note 2. The thought that appears in '' Brahma,'' which is but a poetical rendering of a passage from the Bhagavat-Gita.

Page 50, note 1. This suggests Mr. Emerson's poem '' Pan,'' which has often been alluded to in these notes because it presents the doctrine of the Over-Soul.

Page 51, note 1.

> Find me, and turn thy back on Heaven.
>
> '' Brahma,'' *Poems.*

Page 54, note 1. Dr. William T. Harris said of this passage: '' What Emerson says of Plato we may easily and properly apply to himself. But he goes farther than Plato toward the Orient, and his pendulum swings farther West into the Occident. He delights in the all-absorbing unity of the Brahman, in the all-renouncing ethics of the Chinese and Persian, in the measureless images of the Arabian and Hindoo poets. But he is as practical as the extremest of his countrymen. His practical is married to his abstract tendency. It is the problem of evil that continually haunts him, and leads him to search its solution in the Oriental unity which is above all dualism of good and evil. It is his love of freedom that leads

him to seek in the same source an elevation of thougl
the trammels of finitude and complications. Finally, i
love of beauty, which is the vision of freedom manif
matter, that leads him to Oriental poetry, which spoi
the finite elements of the world as though they were
stantial dreams." [1]

Page 57, note 1. From the *Timæus.*

Page 58, note 1.

> The gods talk in the breath of the woods,
> They talk in the shaken pine,
> And fill the long reach of the old seashore
> With dialogue divine;
> And the poet who overhears
> Some random word they say
> Is the fated man of men
> Whom the ages must obey.
>
> "The Poet," *Poems,* Appendi

See also the poem "My Garden."

Page 58, note 2. Spenser's *Faerie Queene,* Book]
Canto XI.

Page 59, note 1. From the *Theætetus.*

Page 61, note 1. From the *Gorgias.*

Page 61, note 2. This suggests a passage in a letter wl
Mr. Emerson wrote to a spiritually minded Quaker frienc
1847.

"For the science of God our language is unexpressive a
merely prattle: we need simpler and universal signs, as algel
compared with arithmetic. Thus I should affirm easily *bo*

---

[1] "Emerson's Orientalism" in *The Genius and Character of Emerso*
Lectures at the Concord School of Philosophy. Boston: J. R. Osgood
Co. 1885.

those propositions, which our Mr. Griswold balances against one another; that, I mean, of Pantheism and the other *ism*.

"Personality, too, and impersonality, might each be affirmed of Absolute Being; and what may not be affirmed of it in our own mind? And when we have heaped a mountain of speeches, we have still to begin again, having nowise expressed the simple unalterable fact."

Page 62, note 1. See an early poem of Emerson's, "The Bohemian Hymn," in the Appendix to the *Poems.*

Page 63, note 1. Compare *The Republic,* Book VII.

Page 63, note 2. From the *Phædrus.*

Page 65, note 1. When, as a schoolboy, I was complaining of the difficulties of geometry, I was surprised at my father's words, for he had found mathematics so hopeless a study for himself that he always shared his children's feelings on the subject, much to their comfort. But on this occasion he said, "Geometry, yes, one must study geometry for its elegance." Plato had probably made it sacred to him — in theory. Yet there is some truth in Dr. Holmes's remark, "Lover and admirer of Plato as Emerson was, the doors of the Academy, over which was the inscription, — μηδεὶς ἀγεωμέτρητος εἰσίτω — Let no one unacquainted with Geometry enter here, — would have been closed to him."

Page 66, note 1.

> From the stores of eldest matter,
> The deep-eyed flame, obedient water,
> Transparent air, all-feeding earth,
> He took the flower of all their worth,
> And, best with best in sweet consent,
> Combinèd a new temperament.
>
> "Fragments on Life," *Poems,* Appendix.

Page 68, note 1. It was this doctrine of Symbolism w made Emerson prize Swedenborg so highly.

Page 69, note 1. See *Republic*, Book VI.

Page 69, note 2. Mr. Emerson's use of the authors to give him a spur — he "read for lustres," and in the g masters especially. Thus, writing to Carlyle in July, 1 8 he said, "I had it fully at heart to write at large leisure noble mornings, opened by prayer, or by readings of Pl or whomsoever else is dearest to the Morning Muse, a cha ter on Poetry, for which all readings, all studies, are but p paration."

Page 70, note 1. This idea appears in "Love" in t First Series of *Essays* and in the poem "Initial, Dæmoni and Celestial Love."

Page 76, note 1. This literary or philosophic coldness M Emerson satirizes in some lines which, after his death, we printed in the Appendix to the *Poems*, under the title "Ph losopher." He complained of finding this professional moo in himself at times. To pure Intellect he always assigne a lower plane than to Love. In the journal for 1845 is thi passage, headed *Buddha, or he who knows*, and also *Ic Light:* —

"Intellect puts an interval: if we converse with low things, we are not compromised, the interval saves us. But if we con verse with high things, with heroic persons, with virtues, the interval becomes a gulf, and we cannot enter into the highest good."

Page 78, note 1. What Mr. Emerson says here of Plato, and also a few pages earlier, "He cannot forgive in him self a partiality, but is resolved that the two poles of thought shall appear in his statement," cannot but recall his own method of presenting in turn different facets of the gem of truth. Churchman and Agnostic can easily find good weapons for argument in his works. Dr. Holmes says of this passage, " Some will smile at hearing him say this of another." It illustrates the felicity of the Doctor's remark that Emerson holds up the mirror to his characters at just such an angle that we see his own face as well as that of his hero.

Page 79, note 1. Dr. Richard Garnett tells a story of an occurrence which might well have happened in England : " Can you tell me," asked an auditor of his neighbor at the lecture, " what connection all this has with Plato ? " " None, my friend, save in God."

Page 81, note 1. This paragraph suggests the " Song of Nature " in the *Poems.*

Page 82, note 1. But these lines are but segments of great returning curves like the orbits of the heavenly bodies.

> In vain produced, all rays return,
> Evil will bless and ice will burn.

Page 83, note 1. The cave of Trophonius, where he delivered oracles, is more particularly told about by Plutarch in his *Lives.* The ring, strangely found by Gyges the shepherd, made him invisible and by means of it he won great temporal power (*Republic,* Book II.). The soul is figuratively represented as a pair of winged horses and a charioteer. " Now the winged horses and the charioteer of the gods are all of them noble and of noble breed, while ours are mixed, and we have a charioteer who drives them in a pair, and one of them is noble, and of noble origin, and the other is ignoble, . . . and, as might be expected, there is a great deal of trouble in managing them." (*Phædrus.*)

" God has formed you differently. Some of you have the power of command and these he has composed of gold, wherefore also they have the greatest honor; others of silver to be auxiliaries; others again who are to be husbandmen and crafts-men he has made of brass and iron; and the species will gen-erally be preserved in their children. But, as you are of the same original family, a golden parent will sometimes have a silver son or a silver parent a golden son.'' (*Republic*, Book III.)

Socrates relates that the Egyptian god Theuth, having in-vented the use of letters, showed them to Thamus the king. '' ' This,' saith Theuth, ' will make Egyptians wiser and give them better memories.' But Thamus replied, . . . ' This invention of yours will create forgetfulness in the learners' souls, because they will not use their memories.' '' (*Phædrus*.)

In the strange vision of Er, the Pamphylian, is the scheme of the planetary system whirled by the sister Fates, Lachesis singing of the Past, Clotho of the Present, and Atropos of the Future. He saw also the spirits of departed heroes choos-ing their destinies in a new life. (*Republic*, Book X.)

Page 83, note 2. Dr. Holmes says, '' These two quaint adjectives are from the mint of Cudworth.''

Page 85, note 1. These correspondences of matter and spirit Mr. Emerson celebrates everywhere.

> Subtle rhymes, with ruin rife,
> Murmur in the house of life,
> Sung by the Sisters as they spin;
> In perfect time and measure they
> Build and unbuild our echoing clay.
> As the two twilights of the day
> Fold us music-drunken in.
>
> '' Merlin,'' II., *Poems.*

Page 86, note 1.

> Vast the realm of Being is,
> In the waste one nook is his;
> Whatsoever hap befalls
> In his vision's narrow walls
> He is here to testify.
>
> "Fragments on Life," *Poems*, Appendix.

Page 87, note 1. And yet, in the winnowing of Time, Plato is not one of those who, as poet, survived " The Test " as answered in " The Solution," in the *Poems*, although, strangely, Swedenborg is. Perhaps this was because Emerson chose but one representative of a nation and Homer stood for Greece.

SWEDENBORG

As has been said in the Introduction to this volume, it is almost certain that the little book by Sampson Reed, *The Growth of the Mind*, first interested Mr. Emerson in the writings of Swedenborg. That book was published in Boston when Mr. Emerson was twenty-three years old. A few years later he wrote in his journal: —

CHARDON ST., 9TH OCTOBER, 1829.

I am glad to see that Interpretations of Scripture like those of the New Jerusalem Church can be accepted in our community. The most spiritual and sublime sense is put upon various historical passages of the New Testament. The interpretation of the passages is doubtless wholly false. The Apostle John in Patmos and our Saviour in his talking meant no

IV

such things as the commentator says he meant.   But the
timent which the commentator puts into their mouths is r
theless true and eternal.   The wider that sentiment ca
spread and the more effect it can have on men's lives
better.   And if the fool-part of man must have the lie, if
is a pill that can't go down till 't is sugared with supersti
why then I will forgive the last in (the) belief that the
will enter into the Soul natively, and so assimilantly th
will become part of the soul and so remain, when the f
hood grows dry and lifeless, and peels off.

In his first letter to Carlyle, Emerson tells him that F
sending him *The Growth of the Mind*, and the former
his answer, says, "a faithful thinker, that Swedenbor§
druggist of yours, with really deep ideas, who makes me
pause and think, were it only to consider what manner
man he must be, and what manner of thing, after all, Swed
borgianism must be. 'Through the smallest window l
well, and you can look out into the Infinite.'"

To this Emerson answered : —

NOVEMBER, 1834.

Swedenborgianism, if you should be fortunate in yo
first meetings, has many points of attraction for you: for i
stance, this article, 'The poetry of the Old Church is tl
reality of the New,' which is to be literally understood, f
they esteem, in common with all the Trismegisti, the Natur
World as strictly the symbol or exponent of the Spiritual, an
part for part. . . . It is only when they come to their de
scriptive theism, if I may say so, and then to their drolles
heaven, and to some autocratic, not moral, decrees of God
that the *mythus* loses me.   In general, too, they receive the
fable instead of the moral of their Æsop.   They are to me,

however, deeply interesting, as a sect which I think must contribute more than all other sects to the new faith which must arise out of all.

The value which Mr. Emerson set upon Swedenborg was a notable case of his taking people and things "by their best handle." His recoil from all the parson and sexton and controversial elements of Swedenborg's writing, the Hebraism and prosiness of expression and the wearisome length, is sanely expressed with a kindly humor. But the perception by Swedenborg, though no poet, of the meaning of things, the rhyme of matter and spirit, delighted the poet.

Dr. Garnett says, "Nothing can be more generous than his trampling down of prejudice in recognizing the true inspiration of Swedenborg, or more crushing than his criticism of the purely mechanical element in that seer."

As a contrast and showing the difference in the temperament and the method of the men, part of Carlyle's comment on Emerson's estimate of Swedenborg already quoted may be recalled: "*Missed* the consummate flower and divine ultimate elixir of Philosophy, say you? By Heaven, in clutching at *it*, and almost getting it, he has tumbled into Bedlam, — which is a terrible *miss*, if it were never so *near*! A miss fully as good as a mile, I should say!" — Mr. Leslie Stephen, quoting this passage, says: "Emerson would apparently reply not by denying the truth of the remark, but by declaring it to be irrelevant. Swedenborg, like other prophets, fell into absurdities when he became a system-monger, and Emerson could condemn some of the results sharply enough. He was not the less grateful for the inspiration because associated with absurdities which might qualify the prophet for Bedlam." (*Studies in Biography*.)

Page 94, note 1. In a fragment of verse on the gifts he said : —

> But over all his crowning grace,
> Wherefor thanks God his daily praise,
> Is the purging of his eye
> To see the people of the sky:
> From blue mount and headland dim
> Friendly hands stretch forth to him,
> Him they beckon, him advise
> Of heavenlier prosperities
>
> .   .   .   .   .   .
>
> Than the wine-fed feasters know.

Poems, Appendix

Page 95, note 1. This story, and the poetical quota before it, would seem, from the context in the journal, to from the *Akhlak-i-Jalaly,* referred to in the notes on " Pla or, the Philosopher."

Page 96, note 1. The quotation came from Plato's *Me* where, as also in the *Phædrus,* the doctrine of Reminiscer is brought forward, and here is reconciled with that of t Universal Mind.

Page 97, note 1. From Dryden's *Absalom and Achi phel.*

Page 97, note 2. Shakspeare, *Hamlet,* Act I., Scene iv

Page 102, note 1. John Selden (1584–1654), juris antiquarian, orientalist, author. His *Table-Talk* was publishe in 1681.

Page 104, note 1. William Gilbert (1540–1603), physi cian to Queen Elizabeth, was a man of great scientific attain ments. He wrote on the magnet and explained that th

Earth was a vast magnet. On his recumbent statue in Trinity Church, Colchester, is engraved *Magneticarum virtutum primus indagator Gilbertus.*

René des Cartes (1596–1650), born in France but passing much of his life in Germany, Holland, and Sweden. Dr. Alfred Weber in his *History of Philosophy* says of him that he should be regarded as "a geometrician with a taste for metaphysics rather than a philosopher with leanings toward mathematics," and that those who regard him as the author of the psychological method are right in so far as observation is one of the phases and the preparatory stage . . . in the Cartesian method, but err in regarding it as more than a kind of provisional scaffolding for deductive reasoning which is the soul of his philosophy. The schoolman had said *Credo ut intelligam.* Descartes said *Dubito ut intelligam.* Self-evidence alone was needed to make man certain of anything. *Cogito ergo sum* was his formula, and he held that the idea of God in the human mind implied the existence of the perfect Being. The *Vortex* in his philosophy was a collection of material particles forming a fluid or ether endowed with a rapid, rotatory motion about an axis and filling all space, by which Descartes accounted for the motions of the Universe.

Page 104, note 2. Marcello Malpighi of Bologna (1628–1694) is considered a founder of microscopic anatomy. At the age of seventeen he studied Aristotle and the use of the microscope. Having studied medicine, he held chairs in the universities of Pisa, Messina, and for twenty-five years at Bologna. He was physician to Innocent XII. His investigations of anatomical structure and physiological processes were crowned with great success. He discovered the capillary circulation and the minute secreting structure of the various glands.

Leucippus in the fifth century b. c. held an atomic theory, later expounded by Lucretius in his poem *De Rerum Natura*.

Page 104, note 3. This statement, which, seen with after-lights, seems so rash, did not seem very startling half a century ago before the improvement of the microscope, and the general use resulting therefrom.

Swammerdam, a brilliant Dutch naturalist of the seventeenth century, especially noted for his minute studies of the viscera, and system of injection of vessels. Leuwenhoek, his countryman and contemporary, made notable discoveries with regard to capillary circulation and the blood corpuscles of man and animals; also in botany and entomology.

Winslow, a Dane, but worked in Paris, and wrote on purely descriptive anatomy. Eustachius of Salerno, a brilliant investigator of human structure, especially of the ear and the viscera, though less reputed than the great Flemish anatomist Andreas Vesalius, who was persecuted for daring to teach the real facts of human anatomy in face of the mistaken authority of Galen. Heister was also an anatomist.

Herman Boerhaave (1668–1738), born in Holland and educated at the University of Leyden, to which his name and teachings later gave great fame. He studied philosophy and medicine and became a distinguished practitioner and writer mainly on medical subjects. His character and great abilities won him great and lasting honors throughout Europe.

Page 105, note 1. *Natura semper sibi similis* is an expression of Malpighi's, though here given as the faith of the great Swedish botanist and scholar who gave his name to and took for his device the delicate little twin-flowered Linnæa of northern forests of the Old and New Worlds. Mr. Emerson delighted to find this rare flower among the older woods near Walden.

The maxim of the broad and high-minded Leibnitz (1646–1715), *Everything is for the best in the best of possible worlds,* would have recommended him: and his theory of monads, each a mirror of the universe; their effort; the continuity of unorganized and organized creation, and "preestablished harmony," seemed to lead the way to the Evolution doctrines of the nineteenth century.

Page 108, note 1. Oken and Goethe saw in the skull a few modified vertebræ. To Oken the whole trunk with all its systems was repeated in the head with due modifications.

Page 109, note 1. Mr. Emerson wrote in his journal while crossing the Atlantic on his return from Europe in 1833: —

"I believe in this life. I believe it continues. As long as I am here I plainly read my duties as with a pencil of fire. They speak not of death. They are woven of immortal thread."

The notion of the plane of dæmonic life, between those of mortal and celestial, is told of in the *Symposium* of Plato, and the image is used in the poem "Initial, Dæmonic, and Celestial Love."

Page 111, note 1. Dr. James J. Garth Wilkinson, "the editor of Swedenborg, the annotator of Fourier, and the champion of Hahnemann, has brought to physics and to physiology a native vigor with a catholic perception of relations equal to the highest attempts, and a rhetoric like the armory of the invincible knights of old. There is in the action of his mind a long Atlantic roll not known except in deepest waters, and only lacking what ought to accompany such powers, a manifest centrality." (*English Traits.*)

Page 112, note 1. Among some notes for a lecture on

Swedenborg is the following: "His brilliant treatis natural philosophy, Miltonic, sensuous."

Page 112, note 2. The "flowing of nature" is t] doctrine of Heracleitus. The answer of Amasis, Ki Egypt, is related in "The Banquet" in Plutarch's *Mɛ*

Page 113, note 1. Lucretius, *De Rerum Natura*, Li 835.

Page 118, note 1. This paragraph suggests some lin Samuel Daniel which are copied in Mr. Emerson's jc of 1830: —

> "The recluse hermit oft-times more doth know
> Of the world's inmost wheels than worldlings can.
> As man is of the world, the heart of man
> Is an epitome of God's great book
> Of creatures, and men need no farther look."

Also the last verse in Emerson's "Sphinx": —

> Thorough a thousand voices
> Spoke the universal dame :
> "Who telleth one of my meanings
> Is master of all I am."

Page 120, note 1. In the *Timæus* it is told that So heard from Egyptian priests this account of the great At] nians of the first State, which was destroyed by an earthqu thousands of years earlier.

Page 121, note 1. In the journal of 1845 Mr. Emers made these notes, headed *Symbolism,* the first paragra] referring to a lady visiting occasionally in Concord, who singing always pleased him. He had little ear for music notes, but much for expressive rendering.

"B. R.'s music taught us what song should be; how sligh

and thin its particular meaning; you would not be hard and emphatic on the burden of a song, as *tira-lira*, etc., *Lilli-bulero*, etc.

" The world is enigmatical, everything said and everything known and done, and must not be taken literally, but genially. We must be at the top of our condition to understand anything rightly."

Page 122, note 1. Before the passage which follows in the text, I find in some stray leaves about Swedenborg these sentences : —

" The fascination which his mind has for those bred in the old churches, in woeful Calvinism, in sentimental Christianism, is this, that they come to a mind which believes the world has a meaning, a meaning that can be known, and which the good only can know. Swedenborg is to furnish a key to the eternal and universal engine, an explanation of the sky, of the sea, of their tenants, of our doing and suffering, of our weapons and means. What ! and no longer to receive certain cold results from catechism and priest, but I am to be a party to every result by seeing its reason and these results are no longer remote at arm's length, at life's length."

Page 124, note 1. Among fragmentary notes for a lecture are these with reference to the Swedenborgian sect : —

" What I mean by popular religion the Swedenborgians have not conceived, but it is true that who would see truly must forsake a great as well as a little conventionalism; that of Christendom as well as that of his parish."

" *Fascination* of Swedenborg.

" I cannot flatter the Swedenborgian by finding in him any resemblance to the genius and tendency of the great man whose name he bears."

" Very dangerous study to any but a mind of great elasticity

and power. Like Napoleon as military leader, a m:
such extraordinary extent of Nature and not to be a
by any other, that he must needs be a god to the you
enthusiastic.''

'' Exceeding good behavior of the Sect a few year
he was pilloried in a pamphlet of garbled extracts :
Swedenborgians circulated his book.''

'' Their excellent spirit of superior tactics — nothing
in their propagandism ; they treated men respectfully an
the manners of people holding valuable truth.''

Page 127, note 1. Casella, Dante's friend, the be:
singer, whom meeting, in Purgatory, he besought to
Casella began *Amor che nella mente mi ragiona,* and a
souls flocked to hear.

Page 129, note 1. The poems '' Give All to Love ''
'' To Rhea '' are in this strain, and also the verses ''
shall not love me for what daily spends,'' etc., among
'' Fragments on Life '' in the Appendix to the *Poems.*

Page 132, note 1.

MANUSCRIPT NOTES FOR LECTURE ON SWEDENBORG.

'' Beware of interference. Direct service the God rese:
to himself. The condition of greatness, that is of health
poise ; and reception only from the Soul ; illustration fr
men, but reception only from God through Self. Every str(
individual is tyrannical — Swedenborg, Luther, Mahom
Moses ; and the Mahomets of our own acquaintance. Appe
them whilst they are with you, bow and assent, if you canr
answer ; but when they have taken their hats, as thou live
recover thy erectness. No matter what they say about the
credentials from God — tell them it is all gammon, self-delusi(
and a lie ; that God never speaks by a third person, for he

nearer than the nearest. You exist from him. It is as if some one came from the other side of the planet to tell me what I thought. We inhabit a thousand and a thousand planes. Go home now to thy closet, to thy heart, to Being, and Swedenborgize. Go, that is, and sit and ascertain what truth of you this man fantastically said, but yet said, and subtract what vast amounts of individualism have mixed with that pure universalism that is yours as well as his, neither yours nor his, but Being's."

Page 133, note 1. Journal, 1838. "Swedenborgianism is one of the many forms of Manichæism. It denies the omnipresence of God or pure Spirit."

Journal, 1839. "The Swedenborgian violates the old law of rhetoric and philosophy *Nec deus intersit dignus nisi vindici nodus* in its forcible interposing of a squadron of angels for the transmission of thought from God to man. I say I think or I receive, in proportion to my obedience, truth from God; I put myself aside, and let him be. The New Churchman says, — No, that would kill you, if God should directly shine into you : there is an immense continuity of mediation. As if that bridged the gulf from the infinite to the finite by so much as one flank. Would He not kill the highest angel into whom he shone just as quick ? "

Page 134, note 1. The manuscript notes above quoted furnish the following : "It was impossible also for this gifted man to say one word of God."

And of the dulness and repetition Mr. Emerson goes on to say, "I hold him responsible for every yawn of mine," and "The civilest reader at the tenth page says, ' I conceive that I read something like this once before.' "

Page 135, note 1. There is an entry in the journal for 1841 : "It seems as if the Jewsharp had sounded long enough."

Page 136, note 1. One of the examples of Laconic given by Plutarch in the *Life of Lycurgus.*

Page 138, note 1.

      εἰ θεοί τι δρῶσι φαῦλον, οὐκ εἰσὶν θεοί.

More literally rendered : —

    If gods do wrong, surely no gods they are.

                Quoted in Plutarch's *Mora*

Page 138, note 2. The verses in the " Fragments on Poet " in the Appendix to the *Poems* are suggested : —

        Let me go where'er I will
        I hear a sky-born music still, etc.;

and also the lines in the poem " Beauty " : —

        In dens of passion and pits of woe,
        He saw strong Eros struggling through,
        To sun the dark and solve the curse,
        And beam to the bounds of the universe.

The quoted line below is from Burns's poem, " Addres the Deil."

Page 140, note 1. Here follows in his manuscript no the sentence: " Or, without going to eminent exampl the most eminent, the soul itself, is near enough to testify we will hold the ear close and listen."

And again a fragmentary sheet: " Into the urn I pu *The Spirit never Gossips.* What we receive from any man ever indirect truth: we learn him: we learn Swedenbor and have huge deductions and corrections to make in order get pure truth. I admire it as poetry; you wish I should fe it as fact. But who is Swedenborg ? A man who saw Go and nature as he could for a fluid moment. You cannot mak an universal self of him. My concern is with the universal truth of Plato's or Swedenborg's or Behmen's sentences, not at all with their circumstance or vocabulary. To seek too much of that were low and gossiping. He may and must speak to his circumstance and the way of events and belief around him, to Christendom or Islamism as his birth befel: he may speak of angels or Jews or gods or Lutherans or gypsies, or whatever figures come next to hand; I can readily enough translate his rhetoric into mine."

Page 141, note 1. This healthy feeling of Emerson's about the petty or besmirching quality of alleged results of prying behind the great curtain is fully expressed in his early paper on "Demonology" which was posthumously published in *Lectures and Biographical Sketches.*

It may not be uninteresting to present here the letter received by Mr. Emerson from Mr. Wilkinson, the translator of Swedenborg, acknowledging his gift of *Representative Men.*

25 CHURCH ROW, HAMPSTEAD [ENGLAND],
FEB. 5, 1850.

MY DEAR SIR, —

I have to thank you . . . for your *Representative Men,* read with delight a month ago. It is for me full of vistas and views, a regular exhibition of the optics of the soul. You show your men and things by new properties of light, hinting at all kinds of polarizations of these through which we see. . . . I am especially grateful to your *Swedenborg, the Mystic,* which to reverse will require some tough work at long arts and sciences. It seems to me, however, that there is yet to be a consideration of some things that you have dismissed. The spiritual world in the old ghostly and mythological sense, is deep in man's heart, and not easily to be shelved. There

are facts about it which, whether pleasant or unpleasai
come gravely on the carpet during the experimental a;
the presence of these, all backs feel cold streams, and
stands on end as of yore. . . . Swedenborg's allegai
his intercourse will, I believe, be found to be a genuin
tion to knowledge, in no way created by those curio
which saw into another life. But as to any finality in S\
borg, I give up the point at once, and concede that the
ual world is not absolute, but fluxional or historical, ai
be found changed and changing by each fresh traveller
I can by no means disallow it altogether. . . .

I need not say what I feel at your mention of me ii
book. I feel now thoroughly hopeless and divided; th
the little man which is myself, and the Brocken shadc
which people are walking up. They will soon find oi
truth, and say that in one instance at least you have too k
believed in a shadow.

Yours most truly,
J. J. G. Wilkinso.

Page 143, note 1. As an instance of the sweet and wh
some way in which Behmen looks at man and nature Mr. Ei
son says in the journal, speaking of " this era of triviality
verbiage:" " Once ' the rose of Sharon perfumed our grav
as Behmen said: but now, if a man dies, it is like a grave
in the snow; it is a ghastly fact abhorrent to nature, and
never mention it. Death is as natural as life and should bi
sweet and graceful."

Page 145, note 1. From a poem by Nathaniel P. Wi
called " Lines on Leaving Europe," in which he thus (
presses his assurance of his safe return across the ocean becai
of his waiting mother's love and faith.

Page 145, note 2. It is worth while to note Mr. Emerson's steady allegiance to the supremacy of right in contrasting this final weighing of Swedenborg in the balance and not finding him wanting in what was greatest, while of Goethe he says: " He has not worshipped the highest Unity. He is incapable of a self-surrender to the moral sentiment. . . . Goethe can never be dear to men. His is . . . devotion to truth for the sake of culture." And of Napoleon he said: " He did all that in him lay to live and thrive without the moral principle. . . . It was the nature of things, the eternal law of man and the world which baulked and ruined him, and the result in a million experiments will be the same."

MONTAIGNE; OR, THE SKEPTIC

As he tells in the *Essays*, Mr. Emerson made a friend of Montaigne in his youth, — felt that Montaigne, three centuries earlier, had, with wit and frank courage, written of things as he himself would have liked to, in boyish protest at timid observance and decorum. There was obvious contrast between their conditions. The French lord, baptized into the communion of the Church of Rome, bred to the usual military accomplishments, with something of a courtier's experience, and a student of law, heir of a castle and full feudal rights, and living in troublous times, stirred the imagination of a delicate and studious youth, growing up well-bred but poor in the very heart of Puritan simplicity and democracy in New England. Yet there were bonds stronger than their differences, — a greater Catholicism, a brave love of truth, and disgust at cant, and desire to make their protest freely; a human way

of looking at men and things and the teaching of each
a love of wild nature and the independence and retirement
country householder, — these, and their common love of F
and of Plutarch. As to writing, Emerson's word in his jo
nal about Montaigne was true of himself: " Montaigne
Socrates would quote Paul of Tarsus and Goody Two-sh
with equal willingness.''

During the time of his Boston ministry, on Christmas d
1831, he wrote to his Aunt Mary, who eagerly followed
nephews' reading and discussed it with them: —

" No effeminate parlor workman is he on an idea got at
evening lecture or a young men's debate, but roundly to
what he saw or what he thought of when he was riding
horseback or entertaining a troop at his château. A gro:
semi-savage indecency debases his book, and ought doubtle
to turn it out of doors, but the robustness of his sentiment
the generosity of his judgment, the downright truth witho
fear or favor, I do embracé with both arms. It is wild an
savory as sweet-fern. Henry the Eighth loved to see a man
and it is exhilarating once in a while to come across a genuin
Saxon stump, a wild, virtuous man, who knows books, bu
gives them their right place, lower than his reason. Books an
apt to turn reason out of doors. You find men talking every
where from their memories instead of from their understand
ing. If I stole this thought from Montaigne, as is very likely,
I don't care. I should have said the same myself.''

Later, in his journal, appreciating the brave, out-of-door,
half-military aspect of the man, he notes, "We can't afford to
take the horse out of Montaigne's Essays.'' Again, valuing
Montaigne's solid basis, he writes: "Montaigne has the *de
quoi* which the French cherubs had not when the courteous
archbishop implored them to sit down.'' In the story the

kind prelate said, *Asseyez vous, mes enfans,* and the fluttering cherubs answered, *Monseigneur, nous n'avons pas de quoi.*

In his first summer in Concord after he made it his home, at the age of thirty-two, Mr. Emerson made this entry in his journal: —

8th AUGUST [1835].

Yesterday I delighted myself with Michel de Montaigne. With all my heart I embrace the grand old sloven. He pricks and stings the sense of virtue in me, the wild gentile stock, I mean, for he has no Grace. But his panegyric of Cato and of Socrates in his essay On Cruelty (vol. ii.) do wind up again for us the spent springs, and make virtue possible without the discipline of Christianity; or rather do shame her of her eye-service and put her upon her honor. I read the Essays in Defence of Seneca and Plutarch; On Books; On Drunkenness; and On Cruelty. And at some fortunate line, which I cannot now recall, the spirit of some Plutarch hero or sage touched mine with such thrill as the war-trump makes in Talbot's ear and blood.

Eight years later he writes: —

"I once took so much delight in Montaigne, that I thought I should not need any other book; then in Plotinus, in Synesius, in Goethe, — even in Bettini; but to-day I turn the pages of either of them languidly enough, whilst I still cherish their genius. . . . It is too strong for us, this onward trick of Nature. *Pero si muove.*"

Two months after the above entry, Mr. Emerson said in a letter written to his young friend Henry Thoreau, then teaching in his brother William Emerson's family in Staten Island: —

"We have had the new Hazlitt's Montaigne which con-

IV

tained the ' Journey to Italy,' new to me, and the narr:
of the death of the renowned friend Étienne de la Boéce.

Page 149, note 1. This image of the two-facedness
things is used to a different purpose in Emerson's poem " '
Chartist's Complaint," originally entitled "Janus." Bu:
almost every essay, though sometimes in separate essays,
own habit is to contemplate one facet of a truth at a time, :
then, often abruptly, go to another point of view.

Page 150, note 1. "Aristotle, founding on the quali:
of matter, is the European skeptic, Plato the believer." (*Jo:
nal,* 1845.)

Page 150, note 2. Strangely in contrast with this attitu
of the timid or intolerant man of the gown was Mr. Eme
son's own interested, respectful, and often admiring attitue
towards the man of deeds, whether laborer, mechanic, me
chant, or statesman.

Page 151, note 1. This recalls the first lines of Micha
Angelo's sonnet to Vittoria Colonna translated by Emerson: —

> Never did sculptor's dream unfold
> A form which marble doth not hold
> In its white block; yet it therein shall find
> Only the hand secure and bold
> Which still obeys the mind.

Poems, Translations.

Page 152, note 1. Mr. Emerson, on his way to town
meeting, saw his honest neighbor George Minot, a farmer
and pot-hunter, at work, and asked him if he were not going
to cast his vote for Freedom, in the sad days of the Fugitive
Slave Law. "No," said Minot, "I ain't a-goin'. It's no
use a-ballotin', for it won't stay so. What you do with a
gun 'll stay."

Page 154, note 1. This was the remark of his next neighbor on the other side, a laborer.

Page 155, note 1. Here come in favorite images: that the planet is bearing its solidest materialists, helpless, whither they know not, at frightful speed through stellar space, drugged and cheated by the illusions of the senses which they cannot interpret, the Maia of the Oriental philosophers.

Page 155, note 2. These lines are borrowed from George Herbert's poem entitled "Affliction." When a youth he longed to leave Cambridge University, but his mother would not permit him to do so.

> " Whereas my birth and spirit rather took
>   The way that takes to town:
> Thou didst betray me to a lingering book,
>   And wrapt me in a gown:
> I was entangled in a world of strife;
> Before I had the power to change my life."

Page 156, note 1. Here is a momentary indulgence at the expense of Mr. Emerson's long-sitting reformer visitors, from the journal of 1842, yet showing a magnanimity to the borers which he was fighting on his peach-trees in those days.

" The borer on our peach-trees bores that she may deposit an egg; but the borer into theories and institutions and books, bores that he may bore."

Page 157, note 1. Mr. Emerson recognized Nature's secret of Identity through all fugitive forms in the fable of the sea-god Proteus, who, when caught sleeping by a mortal, took shapes of beasts, of serpents, of fire, to disconcert his captor, yet, if held fast in spite of all, must answer his questions.

Page 158, note 1. It will be remembered that this book was written at the end of a decade which had witnessed an

extraordinary awakening in the minds and consciences of
England people and their neighbors. Mr. Emerson's p.
on "The Times," "The Transcendentalist," "New :
land Reformers" in *Nature, Addresses and Lectures,* an<
"Historical Notes of Life and Letters in New Englar
in *Lectures and Biographical Sketches* bear witness to
ferments that were at work on the questions of Emancipat
Temperance, Non-Resistance, Communities, Labor, as '
as in Religion, Education, and Literature.

Page 162, note 1. The following passage is copied fi
some stray leaves of the lecture on Montaigne: —

"Talent without character is friskiness. The charm
Montaigne's egotism, and of his anecdotes, is, that there i
stout cavalier, a seigneur of France, at home in his châtei
responsible for all this chatting.

"Now suppose it should be shown and proved that t
famous 'Essays' were a *jeu d'esprit* of Scaliger, or oth
scribacious person, written for the booksellers, and not resti
on a real status picturesque in the eyes of all men. Wou.
not the book instantly lose almost all its value?"

Page 163, note 1. The brilliant John Sterling, with whor
Emerson formed a strong friendship through correspondenc
due at first to their common affection for Carlyle. The}
never met, for Sterling died in 1844. In his journal for 184;
Mr. Emerson records, almost in the same words as here, his
pleasure, when a boy, in Cotton's *Montaigne* and his visit to
Père Lachaise and of reading Sterling's "loving criticism on
Montaigne in the *Westminster Review,*" adding, "and soon
after, Carlyle writes me word that this same lover of Montaigne is a lover of me. Now I have been introducing to his
genius two of my friends, James and Tappan, who warm to

him as to a brother. So true is S. G. W.'s saying that all whom he knew met." Sterling's biography was written both by Archdeacon Hare, who edited his works, and by Carlyle. His Correspondence with Emerson was published in 1897.

Page 165, note 1. Mr. Emerson drew this contrast between Montaigne and Plutarch in his essay on the latter, printed in *Lectures and Biographical Sketches :* —

"Plutarch had a religion, which Montaigne wanted, and which defends him from wantonness ; and, though Plutarch is as plain-spoken, his moral sentiment is always pure."

Page 166, note 1. Had Montaigne been a living, instead of a dead friend, Mr. Emerson's tolerance would have been sorely strained by this habit, and he would have wished to counsel him that "there is one topic peremptorily forbidden to all well-bred, to all rational mortals, namely, their distempers," as he tells at large as a final word of advice in the essay on "Behavior" in *Conduct of Life.*

Page 166, note 2. Miss Edgeworth's stories for children are so little read in this generation that it may be well to say that Old Poz was a character who bore this nickname because he was positive of his knowledge on all topics.

Page 168, note 1. In the journal for 1840 are the following sentences continuous with the foregoing passage : —

"I know nobody among my contemporaries except Carlyle who writes with any sinew and vivacity comparable to Plutarch and Montaigne. Yet always the profane swearing and bar-room wit has salt and fire in it. I cannot now read Webster's speeches. Fuller and Browne and Milton are quick, but the list is soon ended. Goethe seems to be well alive, no pedant: Luther too."

Page 172, note 1. In the journal he tells of "a walk to

the river with [a friend] and saw the moon interrogat
interrogating." The skeptic considered as a man in "
vestibule of the temple," suggests what has been said by 1
fessor Weber of Strasburg on the doubts of Descartes as
provisional skepticism, a means which he hastens to aban
as soon as he has discovered a certain primary truth." *Du.*
ut intelligam.

Page 174, note 1. The valued friend here alluded
Mr. Charles K. Newcomb, was of a sensitive and beaut
character, a mystic, but with the Hamlet temperament
such an extent that he was paralyzed for all action by
tenderness of his conscience and the power with which
sides of a question presented themselves to him in turn. I
was a member of the Brook Farm Community, a welcome b
rare visitor at Mr. Emerson's house, and when he came
brought his writings, which interested his host greatly.
think they never came to publication, except a few papers
the *Dial.* His sense of duty sent him to the war for th
Union in the ranks. He remained a bachelor all his life an
in his last years lived much abroad.

Page 174, note 2. The last passage appears in the journa
for 1845 thus: —

"Skepticism and gulfs of skepticism; strongest of all, tha
of the Saints. They come to the mount, and in the larges
and most blissful communication to them, somewhat is lef
unsaid, which begets in them doubt and horrible doubt. So
then, say they, before they have yet risen from their knees,
Even this does not justify: we must still feel that this our
homage and beatitude is partial and deformed. We must fly
for relief and sanity to that other suspected and reviled part
of nature, the kingdom of the understanding, the gymnastics
of talent, the play of fancy."

Page 175, note 1. Here appears the cause which all his life he stood for, — The Church against the churches.

Page 177, note 1. Compare in the poem " Voluntaries "

> Fate's grass grows rank in valley clods,
> And rankly on the castled steep.

Page 177, note 2. His method of dealing with these formidable doubts in the following pages is characteristic of the man; no attempt at dogmatically solving the question for all, but throwing of side-lights here and there, suggestive perhaps to other minds both of the magnitude of the problem, and how to approach it in their own way. Among many of his sayings on the subject of Indirection these may serve as specimens: " In good society — say among the angels in Heaven — is not everything spoken by indirection." " If we could speak the direct solving speech it would solve us too."

Page 180, note 1. Journal, 1845. " There are many skepticisms. The universe is like an infinite series of planes, each of which is a false bottom, and when we think our feet are planted now at last on the adamant, the slide is drawn out from under us.

" Value of the skeptic is the resistance to premature conclusions. If he prematurely conclude, his conclusion will be shattered, and he will become malignant. But he must limit himself with the anticipation of law in the mutations, — flowing law."

Page 182, note 1. This paragraph is exactly a case of Mr. Emerson's holding the mirror to his characters at just such an angle that you see something of his own face too, as Dr. Holmes said. His ecclesiastical sin had been, in Dr. Bartol's words, his excess of spirituality, and all sorts of well-meaning men were wishing him to spend himself on details and partial

reforms while he was trying to hear and transmit the un
laws. He has honestly endeavored in this essay to sta
difficult problems fully and clearly, not "Sunday obje
made up on purpose to be put down." But, after all, I
longs to the minds that are made "incapable of skeptici
"a man of thought who must feel the thought which is
ent to the Universe."

Page 183, note 1. About the time when Mr. Em
was parting from his church he was reading with great
sure the life of George Fox, the founder of the Societ
Friends, and making many extracts from it in his jou
The simple worship of the Quakers and their obedience to
moving Spirit always recommended them to him.

Page 183, note 2. In an early journal is this entry: —

"Fools and clowns and sots make the fringe of every or
tapestry of life and give a certain reality to the picture. W
could we do in Concord without Bigelow's and Wesso
bar-rooms and their dependencies? What without such
tures as Uncle Sol and old Moore, who sleeps in Dr. Hur
barn, and the red Charity-house over the brook? Trage
and Comedy go ever hand in hand."

And again in "The Poet": —

He, foolish child,
A facile, reckless, wandering will,
Eager for good, not hating ill,
Thanked Nature for each stroke she dealt;
On his tense chords all strokes were felt,
The good, the bad with equal zeal,
He asked, he only asked, to feel.
Timid, self-pleasing, sensitive,
With Gods, with fools, content to live.

Poems, Appendix.

Page 184, note 1. This thought appears in his poem
" The Day's Ration."

Page 186, note 1. In the " Woodnotes," II., the pine-
tree sings —

Of *tendency* through endless ages.

Page 186, note 2. A line that he valued most of those of
the poet Channing, his friend, from " A Poet's Hope."

There is a summary, not appearing in the essay in the
journal of 1845, perhaps obscure in its ending, but interesting. The " cowage " of the first sentence was an herb which
used to be prescribed for intestinal worms, and acted, not as
a poison, but by piercing them with its sharp fibres.

" Montaigne good against bigots as cowage against worms,
acts mechanically.

" But there is a higher Muse there, sitting where he durst
not soar, a muse that follows the flowing power, a Dialectic
that respects results: and it requires a muse, as Hafiz expresses himself only in musical phrases, the hyphens are small
unities, not parts."

SHAKSPEARE ; OR, THE POET

This essay was read as a lecture in Exeter Hall, in London,
in June, 1848.

Perhaps it is well to bear in mind that Mr. Emerson was
reared for the ministry and ordained a clergyman, and that his
ancestors for several generations had exercised that office, and
moreover that, •in New England, up to his day, theatrical
representations had been looked at with disfavor by serious
and God-fearing people, and the witnessing of such by a min-

ister would, like dancing, have been considered unbe
indulgence. Although Mr. Emerson emancipated I
from bonds that were merely professional or artificial,
an inbred distaste for the common amusements of s‹
feeling that they were unbecoming to a scholar, and t.
was not adapted for them, though he was tolerant of th
other people. There was a natural earnestness, and a :
and cheerful asceticism in his early and later life. Yet
in his later life, when he had been induced to go to see
and Mrs. Barney Williams in some bright comedy, he p:
their acting and admitted to his daughter that he really :
enjoyed theatrical performances, in spite of the feeling
they were not for him. Dancing, for instance, which he
sidered a proper part of youths' education, would have see
unbecoming for himself. He says, " It shall be writ in
memoirs . . . as it was writ of St. Pachonius, *Pes eju.
saltandum non est commotus omni vita sua.*" His staying a
from theatrical entertainments was instinctive, but he was
eral in the matter and would go to see a real artist. He e
went to see the performance of the beautiful dancer Fa:
Elssler, although a story which has been too often repea
of his remarks to Margaret Fuller on the subject is as false
it is silly.

In Paris he saw Rachel during the Revolution of 184
and often told his children of her fierce and splendid declam
tion of the *Marseillaise* in the theatre, holding the tricol
aloft. On London in that same year he wrote of seeii
Macready in *Lear*, with Mrs. Butler as Cordelia. It was us
ally to see one of Shakspeare's heroes rendered by some mast‹
that he went, and probably he never was inside a theat1
twenty times in his life, and, so sensitive was he to bad tas1
or ranting, that he was usually sorry that he had gone.

The rendering of *Richard II.* (I cannot remember by whom) more than satisfied him, and he liked to recall the actor's tones in reading this play, an especial favorite of his, to his children. *Coriolanus* and *Julius Cæsar* too he enjoyed reading to them, and he selected passages from Shakspeare for them and trained them very carefully for their recitation in school.

He saw Edwin Booth in Boston, and met him later at the house of a friend and had some talk with him. Booth later mentioned with pleasure to their host the fact that Mr. Emerson had not once alluded to his profession or performance in their conversation.

Mr. Emerson once defined the cultivated man as "one who can tell you something new and true about Shakspeare." And he read a good omen for our age in Shakspeare's acceptance: "The book only characterizes the reader. Is Shakspeare the delight of the nineteenth century? That fact only shows whereabouts we are in the ecliptic of the soul."

In writing of Great Men in 1838 in his journal, he says: —

"Swedenborg is scarce yet appreciable. Shakspeare has, for the first time, in our time found adequate criticism, if indeed he have yet found it: — Coleridge, Lamb, Schlegel, Goethe, Very, Herder.

"The great facts of history are four or five names, Homer — Phidias — Jesus — Shakspeàre. One or two names more I will not add, but see what these names stand for. All civil history and all philosophy consists of endeavours more or less vain to explain these persons."

In the journal for 1843 he writes: "Plato is weak inasmuch as he is literary. Shakspeare is not literary, but the strong earth itself." Yet from another point of view he writes, "Shakspeare and Plato each sufficed for the culture of a nation."

That Shakspeare and Milton should have been born much to him and to mankind. "Who saw Milton, wl Shakspeare, saw them do their best, and utter their heart manlike among their contemporaries."

And again, "No man can be named whose mind sti on the cultivated intellect of England and America wi energy comparable to that of Milton. As a poet, Shaks undoubtedly transcends and far surpasses him in his popu with foreign nations: but Shakspeare is a voice merely: and what he was that sang, that sings, we know not."

Page 189, note 1. Mr. Emerson said of Nature: —

> No ray is dimmed, no atom worn,
> My oldest force is good as new,
> And the fresh rose on yonder thorn
> Gives back the bending heavens in dew; —

and her cheerful lesson for the artist or poet was that he could forever re-combine the old material into fresh and spl did pictures. He rejoiced that "the poet is permitted to his brush into the old paint-pot with which birds, flowe the human cheek, the living rock, the broad landscape, ocean and the eternal sky were painted," and turning fr the reading of the plays he says: "'T is Shakspeare's fa that the world appears so empty. He has educated you w: his painted world, and this real one seems a huckster's-shop. Again as to his true rendering of men's characters, "I val Shakspeare as a metaphysician and admire the unspoken log which upholds the structure of Iago, Macbeth, Antony ar the rest."

Page 190, note 1. Again the ancient doctrine of the Flow ing, and the modern onward and upward stream of Evolu tion.

Page 191, note 1.

> The passive Master lent his hand
> To the vast soul that o'er him planned.
>> " The Problem," *Poems.*

Page 192, note 1. The stage was to Shakspeare his opportunity, as the Lyceum was to Emerson.

Page 196, note 1. *Henry VIII.*, Act V., Scene iv.

Page 196, note 2. This estimate of the value of memory to the poet, typified by the Greeks in their making the Muses the daughters of Mnemosyne, is enlarged upon in the Essay on " Memory " in *Natural History of Intellect.* Mr. Emerson said once, " Of the most romantic fact the memory is more romantic," and he quotes Quintilian as saying, *Quantum ingenii, tantum memoriæ.*

Page 197, note 1. In a fragment of verse written in Mr. Emerson's journal of 1831 on the yearning of the poet to enrich himself from the Treasury of the Universe, he says: —

> And if to me it is not given
> To fetch one ingot thence
> Of that unfading gold of Heaven
> His merchants may dispense,
> Yet well I know the royal mine,
>> And know the sparkle of its ore,
> Know Heaven's truth from lies that shine, —
>> Explored, they teach us to explore.
>> " Fragments on the Poet," *Poems,* Appendix.

Page 197, note 2. Milton, " Il Penseroso."

Page 198, note 1. Taine, in his *History of English Literature,* thus justifies Chaucer's borrowing or rendering: —

" Chaucer was capable of seeking out, in the old common

forest of the middle ages, stories and legends, to replant
in his own soil and make them send out new shoots.
He has the right and power of copying and translating be
by dint of retouching he impresses . . . his original r
He re-creates what he imitates. . . . At the distance
century and a half he has affinity with the poets of Eliza
by his gallery of pictures.''

The dates of Lydgate and Caxton show a mistake as to
use of them. Caxton, following Chaucer, when he introdu
the printing-press to England, printed his poems and those
,Lydgate, who was younger than Chaucer. In his *House*
Fame, Chaucer places, in his vision, '' on a pillar hig
than the rest, Homer and Livy, Dares the Phrygian, Gu
Colonna, Geoffrey of Monmouth and the other historians
the war of Troy,'' [1] a due recognition of his debt for *Tro:*
and Cryseyde. As for Gower, he was Chaucer's exact c
temporary and friend, and Chaucer dedicated this poem
him.

Page 199, note 1. Kipling irreverently tells of Home
borrowings thus: —

    '' When 'Omer smote 'is bloomin' lyre,
       He 'd 'eard men sing by land an' sea ;
       An' what he thought 'e might require,
         'E went an' took — the same as me!''

And says of his humble audience : —

    '' They knew 'e stole ; 'e knew they knowed.
       They did n't tell, nor make a fuss,
       But winked at 'Omer down the road,
         An' 'e winked back — the same as us!''

     [1] Taine's *History of English Literature.*

Page 199, note 2. Dr. Holmes's remark with regard to the preceding page is : "The reason why Emerson has so much to say on this subject of borrowing, especially when treating of Plato and Shakspeare, is obvious enough. He was arguing his own cause — not defending himself," etc. In *Letters and Social Aims*, Mr. Emerson discusses Quotation and Originality.

Page 200, note 1. Mr. Emerson had tender associations with the Book of Common Prayer. His mother had been brought up in the Episcopal communion, and the prayer-book of her youth was always by her,[1] though after her marriage she attended her husband's church.

Page 201, note 1. Landor says of these borrowings of Shakspeare, "He breathed upon dead bodies and brought them to life."

Page 201, note 2. The princes Ferrex and Porrex, brothers and rivals for the ancient British throne, are characters in the tragedy *Gorboduc* by Norton and Sackville, to which the date 1561 is assigned. *Gammer Gurton's Needle* is a comedy of the same period.

Page, 202, note 1. Journal, 1864. "Shakspeare puts us all out. No theory will account for him. He neglected his works, perchance he did not know their value? Ay, but he did; witness the sonnets. He went into company as a listener, hiding himself, ὁ δ᾽ ἥϊε νυκτὶ ἐοικώς ; was only remembered by all as a delightful companion."

Page 203, note 1.

> England's genius filled all measure
> Of heart and soul, of strength and pleasure,

---

[1] In Mr. Cabot's *Memoir*, vol. ii. p. 572, see Mr. Emerson's letter on his mother's death.

Gave to the mind its emperor,
And life was larger than before :
Nor sequent centuries could hit
Orbit and sum of Shakspeare's wit.
The men who lived with him became
Poets, for the air was fame.

" The Solution," Poe

Page 204, note 1. While writing this, Mr. Emersoi surrounded by persons paralyzed for active life in the con world by the doubts of conscience or entangled in over- spun webs of their intellect.

Page 205, note 1. Journal, 1837. " I either read o: ferred to-day in the *Westminster Review* that Shakspeare not a popular man in his day. How true and wise. He alone and walked alone, a visionary poet, and came with piece, modest but discerning, to the players, and was too ; to get it received, whilst he was too superior not to see transcendent claims."

Page 206, note 1. The following is the " Exordium o: lecture on Poetry and Eloquence," given in London in 184

" Shakspeare is nothing but a large utterance. We canr find that anything in his age was more worth telling th anything in ours; nor give any account of his existence, b only the fact that there was a wonderful symbolizer and e: presser, who has no rival in the ages, and who has throw an accidental lustre over his time and subject."

In the lecture on " Works and Days " he wrote, "Shak speare made his *Hamlet* as a bird weaves its nest." An(in that on " Inspiration " in *Letters and Social Aims:* "Shak speare seems to you miraculous, but the wonderful juxtaposi- tions, parallelisms, transfers, which his genius effected, were all to him locked together as links of a chain, and the mode precisely as conceivable and familiar to higher intelligence as the index-making of the literary hack.''

Journal, 1838. '' Read *Lear* yesterday and *Hamlet* to-day with new wonder and mused much on the great Soul in the broad continuous daylight of these poems. Especially I wonder at the perfect reception this wit and immense knowledge of life and intellectual superiority find in us all in connection with our utter incapacity to produce anything like it. The superior tone of Hamlet in all the conversations how perfectly preserved, without any mediocrity, much less any dulness in the other speakers.

'' How real the loftiness! an inborn gentleman; and above that, an exalted intellect. What incessant growth and plenitude of thought, — pausing on itself never an instant, and each sally of wit sufficient to save the play. How true then and unerring the *earnest* of the dialogue, as when Hamlet talks with the Queen. How terrible his discourse! What less can be said of the perfect mastery, as by a superior being, of the conduct of the drama, as the free introduction of this capital advice to the players; the commanding good sense which never retreats except before the Godhead which inspires certain passages — the more I think of it, the more I wonder. I will think nothing impossible to man. No Parthenon, no sculpture, no picture, no architecture can be named beside this. All this is perfectly visible to me and to many, — the wonderful truth and mastery of this work, of these works, — yet for our lives could not I, or any man, or all men, produce anything comparable to one scene in *Hamlet* or *Lear*. With all my admiration of this life-like picture, set me to producing a match for it, and I should instantly depart into mouthing rhetoric. . . . One other fact Shakspeare presents us; that not by books are great poets made. Somewhat —

IV

and much, he unquestionably owes to his books; but you

not find in his circumstances the history of his poems.

made without hands in his invisible world. A mightier

than any learning, the deep logic of cause and effect he st

its roots were cast so deep, therefore it flung out its br

so high.''

Page 207, note 1. Mr. Edwin P. Whipple, writi

Harper's Monthly in 1882, relates how in a long drive

Mr. Emerson, after a lecture, '' The conversation a

drifted to contemporary actors who assumed to personate

ing characters in Shakspeare's greatest plays. Had I ever

an actor who satisfied me when he pretended to be Haml

Othello, Lear or Macbeth? Yes, I had seen the elder B

in these characters. Though not perfect, he approached n

to perfection than any other actor I knew. . . .

'' ' Ah,' said Emerson, [after] the three minutes I

sumed in eulogizing Booth, . . . ' I see you are one of

happy mortals who are capable of being carried away by

actor of Shakspeare. Now, whenever I visit the theatre to

ness the performance of one of his dramas, I am carried av

by the poet. I went last Tuesday to see Macready in *Ham*

I got along very well until he came to the passage: —

> '' thou, dead corse, again, in cómplete steel,
> Revisit'st thus the glimpses of the moon:'' —

and then actor, theatre, all vanished in view of that solvi

and dissolving imagination, which could reduce this big glc

and all it inherits into mere '' glimpses of the moon.'' T

play went on, but, absorbed in this one thought of the migh

master, I paid no heed to it.'

'' What specially impressed me, as Emerson was speakin

was his glance at our surroundings as he slowly uttere

' glimpses of the moon,' for here above us was the same moon
which must have given birth to Shakspeare's thought. . . .
Afterward, in his lecture on Shakspeare, Emerson made use
of the thought suggested in our ride by moonlight. He said,
' That imagination which dilates the closet he writes in to the
world's dimensions, crowds it with agents in rank and order,
as quickly reduces the big reality to be the " glimpses of the
moon." ' . . . In the printed lecture, there is one sentence
declaring the absolute insufficiency of any actor, in any theatre,
to fix attention on himself while uttering Shakspeare's words,
which seems to me the most exquisite statement ever made of
the magical suggestiveness of Shakspeare's expression. I have
often quoted it, but it will bear quotation again and again,
as the best prose sentence ever written on this · side of the
Atlantic: ' The recitation begins; one golden word leaps out
immortal from all this painted pedantry, *and sweetly torments
us with invitations to its own inaccessible homes.*' "

Page 208, note 1.

> The little Shakspeare in the maiden's heart
> Makes Romeo of a ploughboy on his cart;
> Opens the eye to Virtue's starlike meed
> And gives persuasion to a gentle deed.
>> "The Enchanter," *Poems*, Appendix.

Page 210, note 1. And yet perhaps there is some truth in
Dr. Richard Garnett's word in his *Life of Emerson:* "Emerson is incapable of contemplating Shakspeare with the eye of
a dramatic critic."

Just after Mr. Emerson settled in Concord he read with
great pleasure Henry Taylor's play *Philip van Artevelde,*
then recently published. He wrote in his journal for 1835: —

"I think Taylor's poem is the best light we have ever had

upon the genius of Shakspeare. We have made a mira
Shakspeare, a haze of light instead of a guiding torc
accepting unquestioned all the tavern stories about his
of education, and total unconsciousness. The internal evi
all the time is irresistible that he was no such person. H
a man, like this Taylor, of strong sense and of great cu
tion; an excellent Latin scholar, and of extensive and ɛ
reading, so as to have formed his theories of many histc
characters with as much clearness as Gibbon or Niebuh
Goethe. He wrote for intelligent persons, and wrote ʋ
intention. He had Taylor's strong good sense, and adde
it his own wonderful facility of execution which aerates
sublimes all language the moment he uses it, or more trʋ
animates every word.''

Page 211, note 1. Lowell, in one of his essays, calls atte
tion to the survival in New England of the type of face of ɩ
English in Queen Elizabeth's day even more than in the motl
country, and also to the old English expressions, obsolete
England, but still current on New England farms.

Page 212, note 1. Journal, 1838. ''Shakspeare fills ɩ
with wonder the first time we approach him. We go away
and work and think, for years, and come again, — he astonishe
us anew. Then, having drank deeply and saturated us wit
his genius, we lose sight of him for another period of years
By and by we return, and there he stands immeasurable as a
first. We have grown wiser, but only that we should see him
wiser than ever. He resembles a high mountain which the
traveller sees in the morning, and thinks he shall quickly near
it and pass it, and leave it behind. But he journeys all day
till noon, till night. There still is the dim mountain close
by him, having scarce altered its bearings since the morning
light.''

Page 216, note 1.

> And yet it seemeth not to me
> That the high gods love tragedy;
> For Saadi sat in the sun,
> And thanks was his contrition;
>
> .   .   .   .
>
> And yet his runes he rightly read,
> And to his folk his message sped.
>
> <div align="right">"Saadi," <i>Poems.</i></div>

Page 217, note 1. This image appears in "The Apology" in the *Poems.*

Page 218, note 1. The Puritan shrinking from the form in which the great poet embodied his thought or oracles or dreams still appears in the journal of 1852, yet, contrasted to the dismal seers, Shakspeare is well-nigh pardoned his levity.

"There was never anything more excellent came from a human brain than the plays of Shakspeare, bating only that they were plays. The Greek has a real advantage of them in the degree in which his dramas had a religious office. Could the priest look him in the face without blenching?"

In 1839 Mr. Emerson had written : —

"It is in the nature of things that the highest originality must be moral. The only person who can be entirely independent of this fountain of literature and equal to it, must be a prophet in his own proper person. Shakspeare, the first literary genius of the world, leans on the Bible : his poetry supposes it. If we examine this brilliant influence, Shakspeare, as it lies in our minds, we shall find it reverent, deeply indebted to the traditional morality, in short, compared with the tone of the prophets, *Secondary.* On the other hand, the

Prophets do not imply the existence of Shakspeare or]
— to no books or arts, — only to dread Ideas and emo

Page 219, note 1. All through his life Mr. Emer
increasing thankfulness for "the Spirit of joy which
speare had shed over the Universe." In 1864 he wro

"When I read Shakspeare, as lately, I think the cr
and study of him to be in their infancy. The wonder
of his long obscurity : — how could you hide the only
that ever wrote from all men who delight in reading ?"

And again he wrote : "Your criticism is profane. :
speare by Shakspeare. The poet in his interlunation
critic," — that is, his worst is criticised by his best perf
ance.

Journal, 1864. "How to say it I know not, but I k
that the point of praise of Shakspeare is the pure p(
power : he is the chosen closet companion, who can, at
moment, by incessant surprises, work the miracle of my
logizing every fact of the common life; as snow, or moonlig
or the level rays of sunrise lend a momentary glow to ev
pump and wood-pile."

And again : 1836. "It is easy to solve the problem
individual existence. Why Milton, Shakspeare, or Canc
should be there is reason enough. But why the million shou
exist drunk with the opium of Time and Custom does n
appear."

But even Shakspeare must not be idolized. The soul mu
rely on itself, that is, on the universal fountain of beaut)
wisdom and goodness to which it is open. So thus he draw
the moral: —

1838. "The indisposition of men to go back to the sourc
and mix with Deity is the reason of degradation and decay
Education is expended in the measurement and imitation of

effects in the study of Shakspeare, for example, as itself a perfect being — instead of using Shakspeare merely as an effect of which the cause is with every scholar. Thus the college becomes idolatrous — a temple full of idols. Shakspeare will never be made by the study of Shakspeare. I know not how directions for greatness can be given, yet greatness may be inspired."

Feb. 1838. "Consider too how Shakspeare and Milton are formed. They are just such men as we all are to their contemporaries, and none suspected their superiority, — but after all were dead, and a generation or two besides, it is discovered that they surpass all. Each of us then take the same moral to himself."

NAPOLEON; OR, THE MAN OF THE WORLD

The man of action, made on the largest pattern, with intellect to match his will, and yet a believer in his star, to which, though it turned out to be but a lurid planet, not a sun, he "hitched his wagon," could not fail to interest Emerson.

"That world's earthquake, Waterloo," occurred when he was twelve years old.

He supplemented his Plutarch's *Lives* by all the memoirs of Napoleon then written, and especially enjoyed his letters to his brother, the King of Spain.

Courage, address and disbelief in the impossible were virtues as much needed by the scholar as the soldier, but executive ability, knowledge how to deal directly with men and things, was admired by the man of the gown. He said, "I

like people who can do things." In his journal of 1
thus contrasted temperaments: —

"The advantage of the Napoleon temperament, imp
unimpressible by others, is a signal convenience ove
other tender one, which every aunt and every gossipir
can daunt and tether. This weakness, be sure, is r
cutaneous, and the sufferer gets his revenge by the shar
observation that belongs to such sympathetic fibre. As
in college I was already content to be 'screwed' ii
recitation room, if on my return, I could accurately pair
fact in my youthful journal."

And in 1856 his interest in "other people's facts," tc
in them the law applicable to his own or every man's
thus appears: —

"'Whatever they may tell you, believe that one fi
with cannon as with fists,' said Napoleon; 'when once the
is begun, the least want of ammunition renders what you h
already done useless.' I find it easy to translate all his te
nics into all of mine, and his official advices are to me m
literary and philosophical than the *mémoires* of the Academy

And again in 1844: —

"I myself can easily translate, not without some terr
the maxim, 'that an army should never have more than c
line of operation' and the principle of 'never joining yc
columns before your enemy or near him.'"

This lecture on Napoleon, like that on Shakspeare, w
read in Exeter Hall, London, in 1848.

Page 223, note 1. Malpighi's dictum of *tota in minim
existit Natura.*

Page 225, note 1. Anecdotes of this kind, which Mr
Emerson used as parables, always interested him, and in hi

lectures he found their sure value, though when he pruned these with a classic severity for his essays, many were omitted. Mrs. Emerson objected to this, but he said that when the lectures were published "they must have on their Greek jackets." On coming home from church in 1835 he wrote in his journal: —

"I cannot hear a sermon without being struck by the fact that amid drowsy series of sentences what a sensation a historical fact, a biographical name, a sharply objective illustration makes! Why will not the preacher heed the admonition of the silence momentary of his congregation and (what is often shown him) that this particular sentence is all they carry away ? Is he not taught hereby that the synthesis is to all grateful, and to most indispensable, of abstract thought and a concrete body ? Principles should be verified by the adducing of facts and sentiments incorporated by their appropriate imagery. Only in a purely scientific composition, which by its text and structure addresses itself to philosophers, is a writer at liberty to use mere abstractions."

Page 228, note 1. Dr. Richard Garnett in his *Life of Emerson* says in connection with this paragraph: "The discussion on Napoleon shows Emerson at his best as a connoisseur of men, and would alone prove that he did not addict himself to speculation out of incapacity or contempt for the affairs of the world. The ideologist judges the man of action more shrewdly and justly than the man of action would have judged the ideologist; and after having most brilliantly painted Napoleon's perfect sufficiency in all things for which virtue is not needful, puts him on his right footing with ' Bonaparte is the idol of common men,' " etc.

In the following extract from the journal the scholar owns his debt to the great soldier : —

May 1, 1838. "I sat in sunshine this afternoon
my little pond in the woods, and thought how wide
works and my plays from those of the great men I read
think of. And yet the solution of Napoleon, whose life
been reading, lies in my feelings and fancies as I loit
this rippling water. I am curious concerning his da
what filled it, — the crowded orders, the stern determina
the manifold etiquette. The soul answers, Behold his
In the sighing of these woods, in the quiet of these gray f
in the cool breeze that sings out of those Northwestern m
tains, in the workmen, the boys, the girls you meet, in
hopes of the morning, the ennui of noon, and saunte
of afternoon, in the disquieting comparisons, in the regre
want of vigor, in the great idea and the puny execution, bel
Napoleon's day; another, yet the same ; behold Byro
Webster's, Canning's, Milton's, Scipio's, Pericles's day
Day of all that are born of woman."

Page 229, note 1. Mr. Emerson was alive to the faili
of his class. The one fault that he finds with Plato is that
dealing with the questions of life and passion and sin and he
"he is always literary and never otherwise."

Page 230, note 1. There is in one of Mr. Emerson
note-books a newspaper cutting containing a translation of
remarkable characterization of Napoleon by Fichte in a lectu
given at Berlin in 1813. The following is quoted from it: –

"Let us now look at the man who has placed himself
the head of that people. First of all, he is no Frenchman
If he were, those social fundamental views and that regar
for the opinions of others, or, in short, for something outside
of himself, as well as that benevolent weakness and inconse
quence which manifested themselves, for instance, in Louis
XIV., — in my opinion the worst outgrowth of French na-

tional character, — would also have been exhibited in him. But he came from a people which, even among the ancients, were notorious as savages; which at the time of his birth had relapsed into still greater barbarism, through bitter slavery; which had fought a hard struggle to break its chains, and . . . been cheated out of its freedom. . . . He received his education among the French people, whom he thus became acquainted with; the character of that nation exhibiting itself at that time in a revolution whereof he had opportunity to observe the most secret motives. He could not fail soon to comprehend with convincing clearness this people to be a very excitable body, capable of taking any direction given to it from without, but utterly incapable of giving to itself a self-determined and permanent direction. . . . This complete clearness concerning the true character of the nation over which he assumed supreme rule was reinforced by a powerful and inflexible will, grounded in his descent from a strong people, and hardened through his continual but secret conflict with the surroundings of his youth. Armed with these two components of human greatness, calm clearness and firm will, he would have become the benefactor and savior of mankind, if but the slightest presentiment of the moral nature of man had fallen upon his soul. But it did not. And thus he became an example for all time as to what these two components, purely by themselves and without any contemplation of the spiritual, can achieve."

Page 231, note 1. In the journal the quotation from Las Casas, which follows in the text, is preceded by this sentence: " It was observed that the Emperor was not fond of setting forward his own merits: ' That is,' said he, ' because with me morality and generosity are not in my mouth, but in my nerves.' "

Page 231, note 2. There is a remarkable passage i:
oration called "Literary Ethics" (*Nature, Addresses ana
tures,* p. 179) on Napoleon's utter "faithfulness to fa
in his campaigns, but also his reserve belief "in the free
and quite incalculable force of the soul."

Page 235, note 1. "As I quote at second hand, and
not procure Seruzier, I dare not adopt the high figure I fin
Note to First Edition.

Page 240, note 1. This, and the story of Cæsar's ci\
eating the asparagus which his poor host had dressed wii
salve, and his reproving his officers for their grimaces of
gust, always strongly appealed to Mr. Emerson's natural f(
ings of consideration and courtesy to the humblest pers(
He was drawn more to Napoleon by this speech, "Resp
the burden, Madam," than by any other story told of hi
and he frequently used it as a lesson to his children and othe:
of honor and consideration for laborers and servants.

Page 242, note 1. Journal, 1836. "I like the man
O'Meara's picture. He is good-natured, as greatness always i
and not pompous."

Page 246, note 1. Mr. Emerson delights in a liberator c
man. He defines the poet as such in one way, and the hei
of this chapter in another way.

Napoleon's sharing the hardships of his soldiers, and per
sonal knowledge of them, his power of labor, his faith i:
means, his breaking down the bars of feudalism and throwin;
open the door, closed for centuries to native power anc
merit in the humblest, went far with Emerson.

> Laurel crowns cleave to deserts,
> And power to him who power exerts.

In the essay on "Aristocracy," in *Lectures and Biographica(
Sketches,* is much to this purpose.

But the touch of softness and of imagination in this Man of
Destiny found in the following anecdote gave especial pleasure:

Journal, 1844. "Bonaparte was sensible to the music of
bells. Hearing the bell of a parish church, he would pause
and his voice faltered as he said, 'Ah ! that reminds me of
the first years I spent at Brienne. I was then happy.'"

> The sexton, tolling his bell at noon,
> Deems not that great Napoleon
> Stops his horse and lists with delight
> Whilst his files sweep round yon Alpine height.
> "Each and All," Poems.

Page 247, note 1. Journal. "History is zoölogy and not
a chapter of accidents."

Page 251, note 1. A curious prophecy of the natural
antitoxins.

Page 251, note 2. Journal, 1838. "Napoleon like all
men of genius, is greatly impersonal in his habit of thought.
He sees the sublime laws and not the individual men. Men
are to him but illustrations, and hence a magnanimous tolerance. . . . The Admiral Cockburn admits that 'Napoleon
is the most good-natured and reasonable of the whole set.'
Able men generally have this vast fund of justice and good
dispositions, because an able man is nothing else than a good
free vascular organization whereinto the Universal Spirit freely
flows, so that his fund of justice is not only vast, but infinite."

Page 251, note 3. Journal, 1845. "Napoleon stands at
the confluence of the two streams of thought and of matter,
and derives thence his power."

Page 256, note 1. "Jupiter Scapin" is a title which
appears to have been applied to Napoleon by Abbé de Pradt.

Page 257, note 1. Journal. "Napoleon was called by

his men *Cent Mille*. Add honesty to him, and they
have called him Hundred Millions.''

Page 257, note 2. Journal, 1838. "The only fa
Napoleon's Biography is that he was beaten at Wat
What can Genius avail against Facts, which are the C
of God ?''

"Bonaparte by force of intellect is raised out of all
parison with the strong men around him. His mar:
though able men, are as horses and oxen. He alone is a
tragic figure related to the dæmons, and to all time. Ac
much force of intellect again, to repair the immense defec
this *morale*, and he would have been in harmony with the i
world.''

> Boded Merlin wise,
> Proved Napoleon great, —
> Nor kind nor coinage buys
> Aught above its rate.
> Fear, Craft and Avarice
> Cannot rear a State.
> Out of dust to build
> What is more than dust, —
> Walls Amphion piled
> Phœbus stablish must.

Motto to "Politics," *Essays, Second Series.*

GOETHE, OR, THE WRITER

In the third decade of the nineteenth century New Eng
land was introduced to German thought and literature b
Everett, Frothingham, Norton, Ticknor and others of her bril
tiant or ambitious scholars, returning from foreign travel, anc

from courses at continental universities to which they had
been incited by the study of Coleridge.   In his "Historic
Notes of Life and Letters in New England," in the volume
Lectures and Biographical Sketches, Mr. Emerson tells of the
awakening influence of this breeze from Germany when he
was an undergraduate and a divinity student.   His older
brother William, destined, like his ancestry for several generations, for the ministry, graduating from Harvard at the age
of seventeen, had after four years of school-teaching gone
to Göttingen to study, as soon as the earnings of Ralph and
Edward left him free to leave the family, of which since his
father's death he had shared with his mother the heavy respon-
sibility.   William's mind was exact and judicial and his conscience active.   The German philosophy and the Biblical
criticism shook his belief in the forms and teachings of the religion in which he had been brought up.   There is a letter,
still preserved in the family, to his honored step-grandfather,
the Rev. Ezra Ripley of Concord, in which he respectfully but
with great clearness states his reasons for thinking that the rite
of the Lord's Supper was not authoritatively established by
Jesus for perpetual observance as a sacrament by Christians.
His brother Waldo several years later parted with his church
on this issue, and, in his sermon explaining his reasons, does
not urge primarily his own feeling that, as a form, it is a
hindrance rather than a help to true devotion and unsuited
to our race and our day, but enters, in a way unusual and
remarkable for him, into a critical and systematic consideration of the scriptural authorities for the rite.   There is hardly
room for doubt that this argument was supplied by the elder
brother.   To William, beset by distressing doubt at Göttingen,
it occurred that, but eighty miles away at Weimar, lived the
wisest man of the age.   He forthwith sought him out, was

kindly received, and laid his doubts before him. He ↑
no doubt, that Goethe could clear these up, and show
way in which he could honorably and sincerely exerci
priestly office. The counsel which he received was in
— for unhappily there is no written record and the story
on family tradition — to persevere in his profession, co
with the usual forms, preach as best he could, and not tr
his family and his hearers with his doubts. Happily the y
at this parting of the ways where the great mind of the
acted the part of the Tempter, turned his back, and a
listened to the inward voice. He left the ancestral path,
up at the age of twenty-four his plan of life for which he
been with diligence and sacrifice preparing himself, and stu
law. He was an honorable and successful practitioner,
his standard of work, and the sacrifices and heroic ascetic
of his early life made him a sufferer all his days.

This counsel of Goethe's to William to do the expedient,
the heroic, must have made a lasting impression on the youn
brother's mind, and, soon after, *Wilhelm Meister*, translat
by Carlyle in 1824, must, in spite of its breadth and its fascir
tion, have shocked the young New England minister with its
continental morals. After his visit to Carlyle at Ecclefech
in 1834, his love for and faith in his friend led Emerson
comply with his urgency that he study Goethe. For Carlyle
sake immediately on his return he procured Goethe's Collecte
Works in the original and, hitherto unacquainted with German
set himself to read them in the original.

"NOVEMBER 20, 1834.

"Far, far better seems to me the unpopularity of this Philosophical Poem (shall I call it?), *Sartor Resartus*, than the
adulation that followed your eminent friend Goethe. With him

I am becoming better acquainted, but mine must be a qualified admiration. It is a singular piece of good-nature in you to apotheosize him. I cannot but regard it as his misfortune, with conspicuous bad influence on his genius, — that velvet life he led. . . . Then the Puritan in me accepts no apology for bad morals in such as *he*. We can tolerate vice in a splendid nature whilst that nature is battling with the brute majority in defence of some human principle. The sympathy his manhood and his misfortunes call out adopts even his faults; but genius pampered, acknowledged, crowned, can only retain our sympathy by turning the same force once expended against outward enemies now against inward, and carrying forward and planting the standard of Oromasdes so many leagues farther on into the envious Dark.''

In his answer Carlyle said: —

'' I will tell you in a word why I like Goethe: his is the only *healthy* mind, of any extent, that I have discovered in Europe for long generations; it was he that first convincingly proclaimed to me (convincingly, for I saw it *done*): Behold, even in this scandalous Sceptico-Epicurean generation, when all is gone but hunger and cant, it is still possible that Man be a Man! For which last Evangel, the confirmation and rehabilitation of all other Evangels whatsoever, how can I be too grateful? On the whole, I suspect you yet know only Goethe the Heathen (Ethnic); but you will know Goethe the Christian by and by, and like that one far better.''

In the journal of 1836 Mr. Emerson records that he has been reading '' our wise, but sensual, loved and hated Goethe,'' on the open secret of life : '' There sits he at the centre of all visibles and knowables, blowing bubble after bubble, so transparent, so round, so coloured, that he thinks and you think they are pretty good miniatures of the all.

IV

Such attempts are all his minor poems, proverbs, *Xenien*
ables. Have you read the *Welt Seele?* The danger of
attempts as this striving to write universal poetry is, —
nothing is so shabby as to fail.

"Yes, you may write an ill romance or play, and 't
great matter. Better men have done so; but when
should be greatest truths flat out into shallow truisms,
are we all sick. But much I fear that Time, the s
Judge, will not be able to make out so good a verdic
Goethe as did and doth Carlyle. I am afraid that unde
faith is no-faith, — that under his love is love-of-ease. H
ever his mind is Catholic as ever any was."

Affection for Carlyle gave at first a great impulse tow
the work of tunnelling through this mountain of universal le
ing in hard German, which never became easy for Mr. En
son to read, but as he read, real interest grew in this mig
mind and the eye which

> . . . bounded to the horizon's edge
> And searched with the sun's privilege.

In writing to his friend in April, 1840, Mr. Emers
said: "You asked me if I read German, and I forget if
have answered. I have contrived to read almost every volur
of Goethe, and I have fifty-five, but I have read nothing el
[*i. e.* in German]: but I have not now looked even in
Goethe for a long time. There is no great need that I shoul
discourse to you on books, least of all on his books; but in
lecture on Literature, in my course last winter, I blurted all m
nonsense on that subject, and who knows but Margaret Fulle
may be glad to print it and send it to you?" This paper ap
peared in the *Dial* in "Thoughts on Modern Literature,'
now included in the volume *Natural History of Intellect.*

Though Goethe opened vistas of knowledge and thought, the gods were speaking in the breath of the wood a purer word, and the new day shed fresher light on things and men. So he wrote in one of the pocket volumes: —

> Six thankful weeks, — and let it be
> A meter of prosperity, —
> In my coat I bore this book,
> And seldom therein could I look,
> For I had too much to think,
> Heaven and earth to eat and drink.
> Is he hapless who can spare
> In his plenty things so rare?

Always in his praise of Goethe there was a reserve, a protest spoken or unspoken, but, with all abatements, he acknowledged the debt of mankind to him. In the essay in this volume it is noticeable how he refrains from the obvious criticisms of Goethe's morals, of which he thought enough had been said in Old and New England. He wrote, in 1844, of strictures by a clergyman on Goethe's religious speculations: —

"—— pleased the people of Boston by railing at Goethe in his Phi Beta Kappa oration because Goethe was not a New England Calvinist. If our lovers of greatness and goodness after a local type and standard could expand their scope a little, they would see that a worshipper of truth, and a most subtle perceiver of truth like Goethe, with his impatience of all falsehood and scorn of hypocrisy, was a far more useful man and incomparably more helpful ally to religion than ten thousand lukewarm church members who keep all the traditions and leave a tithe of their estates to establish them. But this clergyman should have known that the movement which in America created these Unitarian dissenters of which he is one, began in the mind of this great man he traduces; he is precisely the individual in whom the new ideas appe: and opened to their greatest extent and with universal appl tion, which more recently the active scholars in the diffei departments of Science, of State, and of the Church have (ried in parcels and thimblefuls to their petty occasions.''

In the *Poems* he bids the severe critic of the dead Goeth shortcomings consider, instead, his great debt to him for vast achievement.

> Set not thy foot on graves ;
> Nor seek to unwind the shroud
> Which charitable Time
> And Nature have allowed
> To wrap the errors of a sage sublime.
>
> "To J. W."

Page 262, note 1. The old doctrine of " the Flowing ' again in the *living* record of the living, changing fact, — flowing Nature as the apparition of the living God. Goin₁ down to the river, whether of Memory or Experience, w(find the river the same, but the waters not those of yesterday. The motto of " Spiritual Laws " is suggested here.

Page 263, note 1. As a further instance of his doctrine of Compensation, Mr. Emerson might have mentioned that when the great anatomist Vesalius had the luck to have this vivi-secting experiment performed for him by the amiable Sultan, he was on an enforced pilgrimage to the Holy Land at the edict of the Inquisition in *expiation* of his heresy in saying that Galen's descriptions, being founded on dissections of ani-mals, were incorrect concerning men.

Page 265, note 1. " Let the scholar not quit his belief that a pop-gun is a pop-gun, though the ancient and honourable of the earth affirm it to be the crack of doom." — "The American Scholar," *Nature, Addresses and Lectures.*

Page 268, note 1. The thoughts of this paragraph are strongly presented in "Aristocracy," and those in the next, on the importance and duty of the Writer, in "The Scholar" and "The Man of Letters," all in *Lectures and Biographical Sketches.*

Page 270, note 1. Having all respect, and more, — wonder, — at Goethe's vast mental range and insight, and at his enormous work and achievement, Mr. Emerson chooses " instructive," and no stronger word; for, as to duties, he felt that the lesson was in what was done, and what left undone.

Page 270, note 2. Journal, 1851. "Goethe is the pivotal man of the old and new times with us. He shuts up the old, he opens the new. No matter that you were born since Goethe died, — if you have not read Goethe, or the Goethans, you are an old fogy, and belong with the antediluvians."

Page 271, note 1. Journal, 1836. "Goethe the observer. What sagacity! what industry of observation! what impatience of words ! To read Goethe is an economy of time; for you shall find no word that does not stand for a thing, and he is of that comprehension as to see the value of truth. But I am provoked with his Olympian self-complacency."

Journal, 1837. "A characteristic of Goethe is his choice of topics. What an eye for the measure of things ! Perhaps he is out in regard to Byron, but not of Shakspeare; and in Byron he has grasped all the peculiarities. Paper money; periods of belief; cheerfulness of the poet; French Revolution; how just are his views of these trite things! What a multitude of opinions and how few blunders ! The estimate of Sterne I suppose to be one."

Page 272, note 1. Journal, 1851. "One listens to the

magnifying of Goethe's poem by his critic, and replies, ' '
it is good, if you all agree to come in, and be pleased; '
you fall into another company and mood, and like it 1
It is so with Wordsworth. But to Shakspeare alone (
granted the power to dispense with the humours of his cc
pany. They must needs all take *his*. He is always go
and Goethe knew it, and said, ' It is as idle to compare Ti
to me as me to Shakspeare.'

"I looked through the first part of *Faust* to-day and fou
it a little too modern and intelligible. We can make sucl
fabric at several mills, though a little inferior [referring
Bailey's *Festus* and Browning's *Paracelsus*]. The mirac
lous, the beauty which we can manufacture at no mill, c
give no account of, it wants. The cheerful, radiant, profu
beauty of which Shakspeare, of which Chaucer, had tl
secret.'' Some of the above extracts and more concernii
Faust are printed in "Papers from the Dial ; Thoughts c
Modern Literature," in the volume *Natural History of I*
tellect.

Again of the second part of *Faust* he wrote in the journ:
of 1843 : —

"In Helena, Faust is sincere and represents actual culti
vated, strong-natured man. The book would be farrago with
out the sincerity of Faust. I think the second part of *Faus*
the grandest enterprise of literature that has been attemptec
since the *Paradise Lost*."

Journal, Aug. 18, 1832. "To be genuine. Goethe, the)
say, was wholly so. The difficulty increases with the gift:
of the individual. A ploughboy can be, but a minister, an
orator, an ingenious thinker, how hardly ! George Fox was.
' What I am in words,' he said, ' I am the same in life.'
Swedenborg was. ' My writings will be found,' he said, ' an-

other self.' George Washington was, — ' the irreproachable Washington.' ''

Page 273, note 1. This line is probably a translation from some Arabic or Persian source, from the connection in which it appears in the note-book.

Page 274, note 1. Journal, 1831. " As History's best use is to enhance our estimate of the present hour, so the value of such an observer as Goethe, who draws out of our consciousness some familiar fact, and makes it glorious by showing it in the light of this [hour], is this, that he makes us prize all our being by suggesting its inexhaustible wealth; for we feel that all our experience is thus convertible into jewels. He moves our wonder at the mystery of our life."

Page 274, note 2. Journal, 1839. " Goethe unlocks the faculties of the artist more than any writer. He teaches us to treat all subjects with greater freedom, and to skip over all obstruction, time, place, name, usage, and come full and strong on the emphasis of the fact."

Journal, 1856. " When Goethe says, Nature, love, truth, insight, it is quite another thing than if some one else used those words."

Page 277, note 1. In the essay called " Historic Notes of Life and Letters in New England," Mr. Emerson thus spoke of the first part of *Faust*, always distasteful to him: —

" The age of arithmetic and of criticism has set in . . . the age of analysis and detachment. . . . In literature the effect appeared in the decided tendency of criticism. The most remarkable literary work of the age has for its hero and subject precisely this introversion: I mean the poem of *Faust*."

And again in " The Man of Letters " in the same volume he says: —

" Our profoundest philosophy (if it were not contradiction

in terms) is skepticism. The great poem of the age is 1
agreeable poem of *Faust*, of which the *Festus* of Bail
the *Paracelsus* of Browning are English variations.''

" Goethe, the surpassing intellect of modern times,
hends the spiritual but is not spiritual."

Page 279, note 1. Among the few novels that Mr
erson read he always praised *Consuelo*.

Page 280, note 1. One merit noted in *Wilhelm M*
is this, from the journal: —

"Goethe certainly had good thoughts on the subje
female culture. How respectful to woman and hopeful a:
portraits in *Wilhelm Meister*."

The book is considered at some length in the "Tho
on Modern Literature." In its realism Mr. Emerson
thus much to his liking, — an eventual good coming out of
takes and failures, a Power

Forging, through swart arms of offence,
The silver seat of Innocence.

But he regrets that a mind like Goethe's chooses to paint
Actual. He sets him down as the poet of this, and not of
Ideal, " the poet of limitation, not of possibility; of this wo:
and not of religion and hope; in short, if we may say so,
poet of prose, and not of poetry. He accepts the base d:
trine of Fate, and gleans what straggling joys may yet rem
out of its ban." Lacking "a moral sense proportionate to :
powers, . . . the cardinal fact of health or disease . . .
failed in the high sense to be a creator, and, with divi
endowments, drops by irreversible decree into the comm(
history of genius.''

Page 281, note 1. Journal, 1844. " Goethe with his e:
traordinary breadth of experience and culture, the security wit

which, like a great continental gentleman, he looks impartially over all literatures of the mountains, the provinces and the sea, and avails himself of the best in all, contrasts with the vigour of the English, and superciliousness and flippancy of the French. His perfect taste, the austere felicity of his style.

" It is delightful to find our own thought in so great a man:"

Page 282, note 1. But a few years after this passage was written Mr. Emerson had occasion to write the like with more vigor and feeling concerning American statesmen; as thus : —

" Very little reliance must be put on the common stories that circulate of this great senator's or that great barrister's learning, their Greek, their varied literature. That ice won't bear. Reading! do you mean that this senator or that lawyer who stood by and allowed the passage of infamous laws was a reader of Greek books ? That is not the question, but to what purpose did they read. . . . They read that they might know, did they not ? Well, these men did not know. . . . They were utterly ignorant of that which every boy or girl of fifteen knows perfectly, — the rights of men and women." "The Man of Letters," *Lectures and Biographical Sketches.*

Page 285, note 1. Yet Mr. Emerson felt that Goethe fell short of the highest culture thus elsewhere defined by him: —

" The foundation of culture, as of character, is at last the moral sentiment. This is the fountain of power, preserves its eternal newness, draws its own rent out of every novelty of science. Science corrects the old creeds. . . . Yet it does not surprise the moral sentiment. That was older, and awaited expectant these larger insights." — " Progress of Culture," *Letters and Social Aims.*

Page 288, note 1. Xenien, from the Greek, was used by Goethe and Schiller to denote epigrams.

NOTE

www.ingramcontent.com/pod-product-compliance
Lightning Source LLC
LaVergne TN
LVHW012206040326
832903LV00003B/157